PLACE IN RETURN BOX to remove this checkout from your record.
TO AVOID FINES return on or before date due.

DATE DUE	DATE DUE	DATE DUE

2/17 #20 White   FORMS/DateDueForms_2017.indd - pg.1

TANZANIA:
YOUNG NATION
IN
A HURRY

TANZANIA:

General Editor
EDWARD WAKIN

YOUNG NATION
IN
A HURRY

ALEXANDER MacDONALD

Hawthorn Books, Inc.   Publishers   New York

First Edition, April, 1966

9030

To Marion, the Lady Chesham,
who has contributed so much to Tanzania,
the country of her adoption

FOREWORD

On maps which distinguish one country from another by a separate color, the belt of twenty-nine countries across the middle of Africa looks like a cartographical patchwork quilt. The effect suggests the bustle and ferment taking place on the scene itself. Newly freed of the political bonds of colonialism, the countries across Africa are now discarding the repugnant and retaining the desirable from cultural and economic forms established under the colonial system. It is a pragmatic process of selection, and not always an orderly one.

Although the process began less than a decade ago, the results are already impressive. In that time, stable new governments have emerged, joining forces in the Organization for African Unity. Black Africans have taken leading roles in the United Nations and in a wide range of allied international activities. Like their Negro brothers in America, Africans are on the march; by 1970 historians very likely will have agreed that the sixties were the Decade of the Black Man.

White Americans need to be reminded of this revolution and the opportunity to join forces with it. Freed of the old colonialism, the African states need new foreign friends. They are turning to both East

7

and West for aid, without strings attached. The emergent nations have added this concept to international diplomacy, and called it non-alignment. They are not merely neutral, which suggests passivity. Rather, their nonalignment is more venturesome. Nonaligned, a country can traffic with both sides. It can solicit and accept aid from all quarters but give allegiance to none. It is a daring, possibly dangerous game.

Of all the new African nations, the most unabashed exponent of nonalignment is Tanzania, the young republic on the continent's east coast, created in 1964 by the union of Zanzibar and Tanganyika. If nonalignment succeeds anywhere in Africa, it should in Tanzania. For all its poverty (its ten million inhabitants have an average income of less than $60 per year), and for all its history of exploitation, the country is obsessed with a determination to succeed. Its people come from 120 tribes, from the humble Sagara to the proud Masai, but they are united by a truly inspired sense of national purpose.

This national spirit in Tanzania was generated almost singlehand-edly by a remarkable man with a remarkable plan. Julius Kambarage Nyerere, a mild schoolteacher turned politician, led his people first to political independence, then to mobilization for one of the most challenging socio-economic campaigns undertaken by a state in modern history: Tanzania's national self-help program, in which every inhabitant of the country has a part. The campaign, launched as the republic's Five-Year Plan, was the first phase in a fifteen-year program to revolutionize the social and economic structure of Tanzania. For a young nation, described not many years ago as "a colonial slum," the plan's challenges have been breath-taking. Yet within a year of its execution many of its primary goals were being achieved. If the early momentum can be maintained, a vital Tanzania will emerge.

There are hazards to complete success, of course. At home, the army (which mutinied early in 1964) might upset political stability; and labor, which was somewhat reluctantly recruited into the national campaign, is perennially restive. One problem concerns a minority: the affluent Asians. Internationally, there are cold-war pressures. Both East and West had declared a stake in the Five-Year Plan and none of the millions invested from overseas was without some share of self-interest. Any one of these various domestic and foreign forces could endanger the plan.

These factors, plus Tanzania's sensitive place near the heart of the continent, argue for a close inspection of the country: its plans, problems and national experience. Involved are Tanzania's history, people, culture, economy, and rival political and tribal factions; taken together, they indicate the republic's chances for dynamic independence and political survival. This book undertakes the task of inspection, not as a scholar's treatise but as a journalist's report on the forces currently active on the scene and how the people, and the events, impressed him during a critical year in the area. The report has been written in the sincerest hope that the aspirations of these long-suppressed people of Africa will soon be fully attained.

A. M.

Marblehead, Mass.
February 1, 1966

CONTENTS

11

CHAPTER ONE

THE DISCOVERERS

One day in October 1964, Mr. Saidi S. Chamshama, representing the northeastern constituency of Lushoto, rose in Tanzania's
National Assembly at Dar es Salaam and declaimed:

"Tanzania has proved to the world that we black Africans are no
second-class race. If anything, it is the white man who is inferior for
he stems from man born right here in Africa. It is Africa, Tanzania
itself, that is the cradle of mankind."

Mr. Chamshama had brought the claim into debate only paren-
thetically (as part of a routine appropriation bill), and when he took
his seat some sentences later, there was merely a patter of applause.
If the statement had been made months earlier, the reaction would
have been more enthusiastic. But at this point the educated public
was well enough aware of the exciting anthropological events taking
place up north in Serengeti, at the fossil sites in Olduvai Gorge.

Olduvai is part of the Great Rift Valley which splits the continent
of Africa, stretching through to Asia Minor and up toward Russia.
In the gorge, two hundred miles west of Mount Kilimanjaro, Tan-

zania's crowning glory, Professor Louis Leakey and his wife had in 1959 discovered the skull of Zinjanthropus, the Man of Zinj (the Arabic word for black). The discovery rocked the scientific world, for radiation tests proved the skull a million years older than the oldest remains of human fossils, such as the Java Man and the Peking Man, found in other parts of the world. The Man of Zinj, along with sheep seven feet tall and pigs as large as rhinoceroses, had roamed the plain of Serengeti in northern Tanganyika 1,750,000 years ago.

In early 1964 Dr. Leakey topped the news of Zinjanthropus by announcing discovery of the remains of a race of upright, small-brained pygmies who lived in Olduvai Gorge 1,820,000 years ago. More important, these Homo Habilis (Man of Ability) seemed directly connected with the genus Homo Sapiens (Thinking Man) and therefore should be the ancestors of modern man.

Even geologically, Tanzania seems fitting as the birthplace of man. Few countries are so topographically spectacular. Its land mass of 362,000 square miles boasts the extremes of deep depressions and awesome heights. Along its 500-mile front on the Indian Ocean runs a low coastal belt, 10 to 40 miles wide, where humid tropical conditions (including a climate averaging 80 degrees Fahrenheit) prevail. Behind this coastal strip the country rises to a great central plateau more than 4,000 feet high where the climate is moderate and dry. To the north Kilimanjaro (only five degrees of latitude from the equator but permanently capped in ice and snow) rises 19,340 feet above sea level. On the northwest border lies Lake Victoria, second in size only to America's Lake Superior. To the west the plateau falls off into the deep, trough-like depression making up the Great Rift Valley. Partially filling the valley on the country's west border are Lake Tanganyika, second deepest lake in the world, and Lake Nyasa. Running eastward into the ocean, a succession of rivers drain the central plateau: the Pangani, the Wami, the Ruvu, Rufiji and the Ruvuma. The violence and grandeur of Tanzania's varied landscape indeed provided dramatic surroundings for early man.

So Mr. Chamshama had a valid point. Tanzania, more than any other country in the world, could claim to be the birthplace of man. It was a possibility more and more Africans were pointing to with pride. And pride was just the right ingredient to spur the new supranationalism.

The Leakeys having traced "Africans" back nearly two million years into what science previously had thought to be the Ice Age, Tanzanians might now claim that the Bushmen of the Stone Age were their own link with Leakey's prehistoric people. The Bushmen were short, yellow-skinned primitives who hunted the plains over much of sub-Sahara Africa. When the more powerful Negroes arrived from the direction of India about 3000 B.C., they either pushed the Bushmen south out of East Africa or intermarried with them. And when the blade-nosed Hamitic invaders came across the Arabian peninsula into East Africa, most of the Negroes departed in the great exodus to West Africa. The Hamites intermarried with those who remained, and there grew from this Negro-Bushman-Hamite mixture the great Bantu tribe which today peoples the greater part of peninsular Africa.

Most of Tanzania's 120 tribes are branches of the Bantu. Largest is the Sukuma, with more than a million members spread in the land south of Lake Victoria. West of them are the Ha, now, as always, ruled by a chieftainess. Close by are the Nyamwezi, excellent soldiers who fought for the Germans in World War I and for the British in World War II. Another warlike people are the Hehe who, more than any tribe, resisted colonial occupation. In the south are the Ngoni (descendants of Zulus who came up from South Africa), and on the coast the Zaramo, long the target of Arab exploitation. On the slopes of Kilimanjaro in the north are clustered the Meru, the Arusha and the Chagga. The remainder of the Bantu make up the scores of tribal fragments, each prizing its own kinship and culture. This accounts for the widespread but thin settlement of Tanzania, a land area larger than that of France and Germany combined.

Greatly outnumbered by the Bantu but by no means outshone by them are Tanzania's seventy thousand Masai. They are the "glamorous" tribesmen, favorites of tourist photographers and lady novelists. Tall, handsome and haughty, the Masai cling to the customs and dress of the traditional warrior. A Nilo-Hamitic people, they moved south from the Upper Nile as late as the eighteenth and nineteenth centuries, taking over any lands suitable for their cattle. The only other creatures the Masai openly respects are his cattle. He will do no work save that pertaining to them: the Chagga digs the Masai's well, the Kikuyu grows his honey and tobacco, the Dorobo makes his spears and tools and his own women build his hut. But the Masai meticulously tends his own herd, each head of which he calls by a given name. Says the Masai in greeting relative or friend: "I hope your cattle are well."

The Masai measures his wealth in cattle, but he will not sell them. They literally sustain him, for he eats only their flesh and drinks their milk and blood. A dietary staple is an urn of blood drawn from the jugular vein of a bullock. Often the milk and blood are drunk as a mixture.

Although neighboring Bantu are held in contempt by the Masai because they cultivate the soil, other tribes in the area owed a debt to the warlike newcomers for defending them from slavery. So menacing did the giant Masai appear even to hardened Arab slavers that raiding caravans carefully skirted the tribal ground in northern Tanganyika. The tribe still ranges over fourteen million acres both in Kenya and Tanganyika, including the area around Olduvai Gorge where Homo Habilis was discovered. It is typical of the Masai that they have for 80 years ignored the Kenya-Tanganyika boundary line, which in 1885 Britain and Germany agreed would cut through the middle of Masailand.

Then, though hardly a tribe, there are the Swahili. Living along the Indian Ocean coast, the Swahili (who give the country's language its common name) are a mixture of mixtures. They can be of any Bantu tribes and even incorporate blood of the European or Indian, but the common denominator is some part Arab. Whatever his genealogy, the Swahili dresses in the flowing *kanzu* robe and the fez of the Arab.

This stamp of the Arab is all over Tanzania. Despite two modern periods of European colonialism the culture, particularly along the ocean coast, is indelibly Arabic. This is not surprising, for the Arab's influence here goes back more than two thousand years. Its beginnings were partly meteorological. Over the warm 2,000-mile expanse of ocean that separates East Africa from Arabia, India and Persia, there blow two seasonal monsoons: in December southwest from Asia to the African coast, in March from Africa back to Asia. As early as 700 B.C. dark-skinned mariners from the East made this a regular Indian Ocean run, speeding down in their gull-sailed dhows late in the year with jewels, coffee and cloth, and sailing back in the spring with ivory and slaves.

An almost casual trade for centuries, this Arab contact with Africa took on purpose by the tenth century when, after Mohammed's death, the Moslem world exploded with the zeal to convert not only the infidels of Christian Europe but also the pagans of Africa. Thus began the period of the Zenj Empire in East Africa, from 975 A.D. until 1498, when the Portuguese explorers came. The empire, with its base at Kilwa (an ancient port south of today's Dar es Salaam), was held together by fortified coastal settlements from Mozambique in the south to Mogadishu in what is now Somaliland in the north. The Arabic word *Zenj* gave the name Zanzibar (Land of the Blacks) to the island which was to become the center of the booming coastal slave trade.

In their five centuries of East African rule, the Arabs contributed their religion, "urbanized" the coastal settlements with stone forts and buildings (usually in the Persian motif), and introduced banking and marketing, navigation and the arts of writing and mathematics. They also brought in new plants—bananas, rice, wheat, sugar cane —to supplement the native diet of millet, roots, herbs and fruits. But many other Arab innovations were on the debit side. They did almost nothing in cultivating fine arts, and they left few written records of their long occupation. And they organized and brought to frightful volume the trade in African slaves.

Christian slavers were later to deal in the traffic, but it was the Arabs who conceived of the millions of blacks in the African interior as an exportable product and cold-bloodedly set up the trade systems. At the same time, they prodded the pagan African to worship their one God, whose prophet was Mohammed. In their own minds there was no anomaly in this, for the Koran tolerated slavery so long as none of "the faithful" was enchained, and for the Arab the black African had always been an object of contempt. An Arab quotation noted: "Was not Bilal the only Negro mentioned in Islam? And was not he the Prophet's slave?" It is one of the perplexities of history that the black African has responded by embracing Islam. Of Africa's 240 million, today more than 100 million are Moslem, and it is predicted that by 1980 half of all Africa will follow the Prophet.

But the Moslem thrust into East Africa was to suffer a two-century setback before marching triumphantly onward. Ironically, this happened because they were doing so well elsewhere. In 1453 the Mos-

lem Turks entered Constantinople and there began the sweep west-
ward that ended on the threshold of Central Europe. The gangrenous
war of the Crescent versus the Cross blocked overland trade routes
to India and the Far East. The result was the unparalleled series of
Spanish and Portuguese explorations. Columbus went west to search
new routes to India, but Portugal's Vasco da Gama came sailing
south and east around the Cape of Good Hope and straight into the
middle of the lucrative empire that the Arabs were building up and
down the East African coast.

Da Gama tried to be friendly but the Arabs judged him, and
rightly, as a rival for their trade with the East; besides, he was an
infidel Christian. Their stone forts opened fire on the Portuguese visitor. Driven off, da Gama pushed on across the Indian Ocean to India's southwest coast, then returned to Lisbon to describe, no doubt,
the wondrous potential of the Africa-Asia trade. The result was the
dispatch of further Portuguese ships around the Cape, with tough
capitanos and helmeted troops aboard. This time the Arab forts went
down like tenpins, and by 1509 the Portuguese took charge of the
entire East African coast. Their unwieldy galleons took over the rich
trade of the dhows in ivory and slaves, in jewels and spices. For two
centuries they hung on, running what now amounted to a Portuguese
empire around the Indian Ocean. But overall they were disappointed.
They found none of the gold or copper in which the interior reportedly abounded, because they could not win over the inland tribes.
Subject to both Arab and African raids, they were forced to remain
close to their fortified trading colonies. Also, British, French and
Dutch ships were moving in on their Indian Ocean monopoly.

By the end of the seventeenth century Arab retaliation was having
its effect. After Oman won its independence in 1650, one after the
other the coastal towns began to fall back into Moslem hands. By
1740 all that remained to the Portuguese on the coast was Mozambique—in the twentieth century still their disputed possession.

At this time, the New World's demand for plantation labor was
becoming insatiable. The Arab slavers, as if to recoup the losses of
two centuries, returned mercilessly to their trade. New caravan routes
were opened into the interior, sweeping from the coast to Lake Nyasa
in the south, west to Lake Tanganyika and beyond, and around the
shores of Lake Victoria up into Uganda. Like a military host, Arab

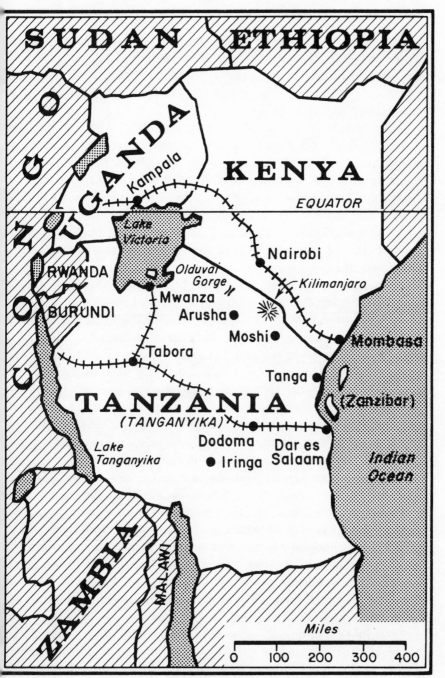

SUDAN ETHIOPIA

CONGO

UGANDA

Kampala

KENYA

EQUATOR

Lake Victoria

RWANDA

BURUNDI

Olduvai Gorge

Mwanza

Arusha

Nairobi

Kilimanjaro

Moshi

Mombasa

Tabora

Tanga

(Zanzibar)

TANZANIA

(TANGANYIKA)

Lake Tanganyika

Dodoma

Iringa

Dar es Salaam

Indian Ocean

ZAMBIA

MALAWI

Miles

0   100   200   300   400

Present Boundaries

raiders moved about the interior, attacking villages and killing all those not worth capturing for the slave market. This savagery and the firing of dwellings was done to avoid organized ambush on the return trip. Whole regions, particularly around Lake Nyasa, were depopulated and destroyed.

At key points such as Kisaki, Tabora and Ujiji in Tanganyika, the slavers established fortified posts as collection centers. It must be added that these posts often were supplied by African chiefs and headmen attracted by the profits of the trade. Encouraged by the Arabs, they too conducted raids on enemy tribes and turned captives over to the slavers. The Kabakas of Buganda, hereditary rulers in Uganda, maintained organized raiding forces for the purpose.

When enough captives had been rounded up at these inland collection points, the cruel march to the coast began. Chained in long single files, the slaves were given great loads of ivory or other products to carry. Arab overseers with whips and knouts kept the lines going. Usually less than half of the captives survived the hundreds of miles to the coast. Arriving at Kilwa, Pangani or Bagamoyo, the slaves were taken in dhows to the island of Zanzibar, hardly 30 miles across the water, from Dar es Salaam. Zanzibar, only 640 square miles of coral soil, by the nineteenth century had become not only the clearinghouse of the slave trade but the capital of the resurgent Moslem rule. Sultan Seyyed Said of Oman, who now claimed sovereignty over all the Arab lands regained from the Portuguese, had moved his capital down from the Arabian peninsula to this verdant island.

Through Sultan Seyyed Said, an unexpected affinity between tiny Zanzibar and the infant United States was nurtured. American ships had for some time been venturing into the Indian Ocean. In 1674, Yankee skippers were at Madagascar negotiating with pirates for captured merchandise and arms to smuggle home into the colonies; in 1719 a ship from Boston carried slaves from Natal to Virginia; whalers from New Bedford occasionally put in, and in 1825 the brig *Laurel* of Salem, Captain Bryant commanding, took on a cargo of tusks, cowhide and tortoise shell at Zanzibar.

Then in 1827 Edmund Roberts of Portsmouth, New Hampshire, called at Zanzibar, aboard the *Mary Ann* of New Bedford, and induced the Sultan to agree to a secret trade treaty giving U.S. goods virtually free access to Arab ports in the area. In return, the U.S.

would recognize the Sultan's tiny empire and open a consulate at Zanzibar.

An American trader on the island, Richard P. Waters of Salem, was appointed first U.S. Consul and proceeded to make a fortune for himself under the treaty arrangement. This was made largely from New England cotton, which to this day is a byword in much of East Africa. Soon Zanzibar was annually importing 7,000 bales of *Merikani*, as it has ever since been called in Swahili. Waters, in return, was exporting coffee and gum from Aden, dates from Muscat and ivory from Mozambique. At one time Zanzibar was taking $500,000 worth of goods annually from America, while $1 million was being exported from the island to the United States.

Seyyed Said rejoiced in these flourishing relations. In 1840 he dispatched his private brig, the *Sultani,* to the United States with gifts of two Arabian stallions and Persian rugs for President Van Buren. The U.S. responded by fitting out the *Sultani* with fourteen bright brass guns during her call at New York harbor.

But the U.S. Civil War and the building of the Suez Canal in 1869 sharply curtailed the Arab-American trade. Also, the trade in slaves, denounced finally even by the nations involved, was being stamped out. Sultan Barghash, son of Said, agreed in 1873 to close all the slave markets in his domain. Today, the high altar of the elegant Anglican Cathedral in Zanzibar stands on the site of the old market's whipping post.

If any single man deserves credit for ending the slave trade, it must be the indomitable little Scottish missionary who literally walked his brave heart out in opening up Africa's dark interior. Dr. David Livingstone, in Bechuanaland for the London Missionary Society, had made his first exploratory trip in 1851 when he went north and discovered the great Zambezi River. This first penetration to the very center of the continent inspired the Livingstone dream: to abolish slavery by bringing Christianity to the defense of the black man in the African interior. Thus began the series of incredible travels which took Livingstone, afoot, across the continent to the west coast in 1853, then, following the Zambezi seaward, to the Portuguese East African coast in 1856, and finally deep into the Congo to die, a wasted remnant of the young missionary of twenty years before. Death came in a village in north Tanganyika in 1872.

Livingstone's spellbinding accounts of his travels accomplished what he intended. They aroused world interest in what was going on inside Africa and jolted the world's conscience about what was happening to the black man in particular. Most of Europe had anticipated America in legally abolishing slavery, but as the last half of the nineteenth century began, it still persisted. Mainly through the efforts of Great Britain, the last remnants of the trade were being wiped out. During the remainder of the century, British patrol boats roamed the Indian Ocean, running down illegal slave ships and imprisoning their crews. Britain even paid compensation to states declaring damages because of elimination of the trade. (Portugal, on closing down its slave centers on Africa's east coast, was paid $2,000,000.) Finally, when Zanzibar itself abolished the legal status of slavery in 1897, the Scottish missionary doctor's battle could be said to be completely won.

Besides a humanitarian purpose, Livingstone's epic trips into the interior, his journals admit, sought to run literally to the ground the centuries-old legend of the "Mountains of the Moon." He longed to be the first man, knowingly at least, to gaze on the waters which were the source of the River Nile. Seventeen centuries before, Ptolemy, the Alexandrian astronomer and geographer, had drawn a remarkable map of Africa, one that remained unaltered for more than a thousand years. He described the Nile as rising between two great lakes in the middle of Africa, among the "Mountains of the Moon." His description was based on a story by one Diogenes, a Greek merchant said to have traveled twenty-five days inland from the East African coast and to have seen these mountains. Ever since, the description had excited the minds of explorers. Livingstone's search for the mountains and the Nile's source ended, of course, when he fell ill on his Congo trip. This great disappointment must have had much to do with the lethargy into which he lapsed in his final years.

Others, however, had been caught up by the dream. Two of the first were Richard Burton and John Hanning Speke, former Indian Army officers, who left London in 1857 and sailed to Zanzibar to organize an expedition. Until that time, Africa had earned its name of "Dark Continent" because of its inhospitable topography. Most of the continent was ringed by a narrow coastal belt beyond which rose the great central plateau. In East Africa the plateau rose abruptly to five thousand feet, with unnavigable rivers broken by waterfalls and rapids. Except for the Arab slavers, who for business reasons kept their knowledge to themselves, little was known by the mid-nineteenth century of Africa's heartland.

Burton and Speke wanted to find those great lakes described by Ptolemy. They had heard that due west from Zanzibar, across seven or eight hundred miles of trackless jungle and veldt, there was a great body of water called Lake Tanganyika. This was their first objective. On June 28, 1857, they set out in force with a safari caravan such as Africa had never seen. There were 132 heavily laden porters, a camel, sixteen asses, cattle, cages of fowl and a herd of goats. The group seemed prepared for a very long journey, and, indeed, it was nearly two years before they saw the coast again.

After 125 days in the bush, during part of which both Burton and Speke became ill and had to be borne in hammocks, they reached the slave station five hundred miles to the west at Kazeh (now Tabora). The Arabs, however distrustful they were of these infidel encroachers, treated the pair hospitably and even described a route to the waters that lay to the west. The ponderous train moved forward again and on February 13, 1858, they reached the shores of the great lake. The place was Ujiji and the lake stretched like a limitless sea from there in every direction. As best the explorers could gather, the Ha tribesmen in the area had ventured neither north nor south to the lake's extremity. Might the north, then, have an outlet that would be the beginning of the Nile?

Both explorers were ill again, Speke so blinded by ophthalmia that he could hardly see the lake, but impatiently they made ready two of the tribe's dugout canoes. They pushed north and scoured the coves and creeks of the shore, hoping to find the one outlet that would go coursing off on the long route through desert and ancient valleys to flow finally into the blue Mediterranean. But Lake Tanganyika did not hold the Nile's secret. They found only one river, flowing *into* the lake. Speke and Burton rounded the north shore, then fruitlessly paddled many miles down on the west. They returned dejectedly to Ujiji and then made the long march back to Kazeh, reaching the station in June.

While Burton decided to rest at the trading post, Speke set out to learn of other waters in the area, particularly those reported two hundred miles or so north of the station. Elated no doubt by the opportunity to go it alone, Speke marched with a much reduced porterage. Burton still believed that Lake Tanganyika should not be ruled out as the Nile's source, while Speke felt it lay farther to the north, and as he pushed in that direction he must have been seized by the thought that now, by himself, he would make the discovery.

And make it he did. In the early morning of August 3, 1858, he pushed through the elephant grass that choked the surrounding plain, and became the first white man to gaze upon the ruffled blue waters which he named Lake Victoria. This was at Mwanza and though he had little proof acceptable to science that he had indeed discovered the source of the Nile, Speke was convinced beyond doubt that he had.

He returned to Kazeh to announce his discovery. Burton, as might be expected, scoffed at his presumption. So it was with rather strained feelings that the expedition headed back east and finally reached Zanzibar in March 1859. The two explorers continued together as far as Aden where Burton stopped again to recuperate while Speke sailed on to London. He laid his claims at once before the Royal Geographical Society. Impressed, they agreed to finance a new expedition to explore Lake Victoria. Joining with James Grant, Speke set out in 1862 to explore the lake's western shore. On July 28 of that year they came to Ripon Falls, the northern outlet of the lake that unquestionably was the source of the Nile.

Other explorers followed: Samuel Baker and General Charles G. Gordon pushing down the Nile from the north and Joseph Thomson, Count Paul Teleki and Dr. Fischer pressing inland from the east coast to throw more light on the long-dark interior. But it was an intrepid, brash Welsh-American newspaperman whose exploits in Africa were to surpass them all.

Henry Morton Stanley won world renown on November 10, 1871, when, as a correspondent for the *New York Herald,* he went marching into Ujiji and greeted the "lost" Livingstone with his celebrated phrase. That famous meeting had more than the effect of making Stanley's name a household word. It infected him with the same restless drive that nagged all explorers. As one of the breed, Stanley was a man to set his sights high. In 1874 he announced that in a three-phase expedition he would settle the whole pattern of Central Africa's mysterious lakes and rivers. He would circumnavigate Lake Victoria to check Speke's Nile discovery, do the same on Lake Tanganyika to

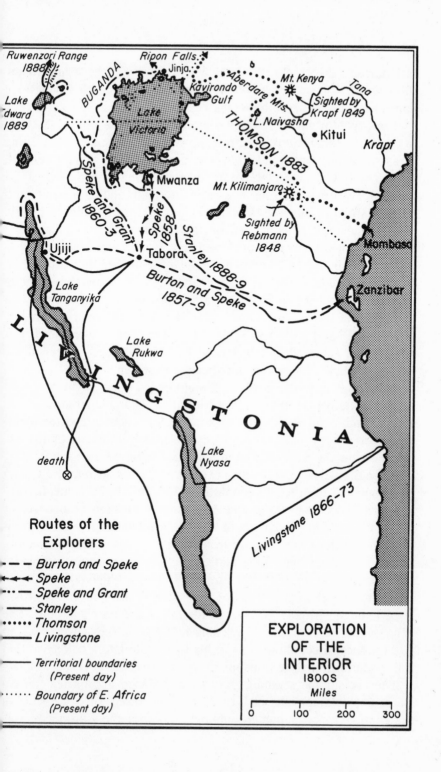

Ruwenzori Range
1888

BUGANDA

Ripon Falls
Jinja

Kavirondo
Gulf

Aberdare Mts

Mt. Kenya

Tana

Sighted by
Krapf 1849

Lake
Edward
1889

Lake
Victoria

THOMSON 1883

L. Naivasha

Kitui

Krapf

Speke and Grant
1860-3

Mwanza

Mt. Kilimanjaro

Speke 1858

Stanley 1888-9

Sighted by
Rebmann
1848

Mombasa

Ujiji

Tabora

Burton and Speke
1857-9

Zanzibar

Lake
Tanganyika

L I V I N G S T O N I A

Lake
Rukwa

death

Lake
Nyasa

Livingstone 1866-73

Routes of the
Explorers

– – – Burton and Speke
←•←• Speke
••••• Speke and Grant
——— Stanley
•••••• Thomson
——— Livingstone

——— Territorial boundaries
(Present day)

••••• Boundary of E. Africa
(Present day)

EXPLORATION
OF THE
INTERIOR
1800S
Miles

0   100   200   300

test Burton's theory that the river began there, and he would follow the entire unknown course of the Lualaba River which Livingstone had mistakenly believed to be the beginning of the Nile.

Thus, in November 1874, the most incredible exploration of all began from Zanzibar. With 356 men, women and children, including three white assistants, and a 40-foot portable boat, Stanley set out. In a 57-day sail around Lake Victoria he confirmed Speke's 1858 findings. By June 1876, he reached Ujiji again and in a two-month journey around Lake Tanganyika collapsed Burton's stubborn theory.

In late August he embarked on the Lualaba, with no idea where the wide, sluggish stream would take him. It took him across the continent. In August 1877, 999 days out of Zanzibar and after shipwreck, disease and constant tribal attack, Stanley and his starving survivors stumbled into Emboma, a tiny European trading colony on the mouth of the Congo, on the Atlantic Ocean. Barely a hundred of the original band of 356 still lived. The three whites were dead. But Stanley had achieved his objectives. The biggest blank places in the map of Central Africa had now been roughed in.

Stanley's epic conquest of the Congo ended what might be called the romantic period of African exploration. Thus far an aura of adventure and idealism—the search for the Nile's source and the elimination of slavery—had surrounded the accomplishments of the explorers. Now the hard edge of imperial ambition began to show.

When Stanley set out on his next journey, he went into the Congo on assignment from King Leopold II of Belgium. In his name, Stanley approached local chieftains and, in a manner that set the pattern for imperial agents in other parts of Africa, negotiated "protective" treaties. The result of this venture, from 1879 to 1884, was the creation, in 1885, of the Congo Free State, a ruthless commercial enterprise with Leopold sitting both as its monarch and as chief stockholder in the managing company. Tens of thousands of tribesmen were cashiered to labor virtually as slaves in the mines and on plantations. The exploitation became so embarrassing that the Belgian government in 1908 induced Leopold to convert his Free State into a colony so that a few administrative reforms might be introduced.

Thus began the scramble for Africa. France approached Sultan Barghash, nominal ruler of East Africa, and asked for concession on the coast, but the Sultan, beginning to suspect the Europeans, was wary. He refused to negotiate, and the French contented themselves with taking Madagascar and great portions of West Africa. Portugal tightened her hold on the east and west coasts of the sub-Sahara peninsula where she had for four centuries claimed Mozambique and Angola. From South Africa the agents of Cecil Rhodes, empire builder extraordinary, moved up in 1888 and negotiated with ailing Chief Lobengula for rights to all the Central African lands which were to make up the Rhodesias and Nyasaland, to be ruled in the name of the British South Africa Company.

British influence had also moved inland from Mombasa, on the coast north of Zanzibar. Joseph Thomson, young Scottish explorer, had in 1884 braved the Masai threat and crossed their tribal lands to the northern shores of Lake Victoria, then continued deep into Buganda. Three years later he again crossed Masailand and explored Mount Kenya. Largely because of his journeys, Britain would soon claim the areas to make up Kenya and Uganda.

It was the Germans who took Tanganyika. Judged in the light of the crude land-grabbing going on amongst the Europeans, Germany could claim at least a prior interest in this chunk of East Africa. In 1848 the German missionary Johann Rebmann, armed only with an umbrella, had borne the Gospel inland from Mombasa, finally to preach in Swahili to the Chagga and Taita tribes of Mount Kilimanjaro. He was the first European to sight the awesome snow-capped peak lying almost on the equator. Another German explorer was Theobald Roscher who left coastal Bagamoyo in 1859 and followed the Arab slave route to Lake Nyasa, the first European to venture south beyond Kilwa. Near the lake he was killed by Nyasa tribesmen.

But it was energetic Carl Peters who sealed the take-over in writing. Representing the German Colonisation Society, Peters arrived at Dar es Salaam in 1884 and went inland to deal secretly with the tribal chiefs who nominally paid some allegiance to Sultan Barghash. Within three weeks, twelve of them, all illiterate, had signed their lands over to the protection of the new society. Peters hurried back to Berlin with his treaties. Bismarck, ruling the newly unified Germany, decided that tropical colonies were what he needed to give prestige to William of Prussia whom he had set up as Emperor. He dispatched five German warships to Zanzibar with the message to the Sultan that within twenty-four hours the Peters treaties were to be acknowledged. Barghash appealed to Britain's agent on Zanzibar, but Gladstone had already expressed his disinterest in "that mountain country behind Zanzibar with the unrememberable name." Besides, England had just lost Khartoum in the Sudan and for the present had enough African troubles.

So England protested little as the Berlin Conference in 1885 catalogued Germany's new colonies in Africa. Rather, Gladstone agreed that a commission, including French, German and British representation, should the next year make some colonial decisions in East Africa. In 1886 the commission sat in Zanzibar and, as they talked, the Sultan saw his empire fade away like ice in the equatorial sun. When the negotiations were over, Barghash was left only his three islands—Zanzibar, Mafia and Pemba—and a narrow strip of Tanganyika coast, ten miles wide and 600 miles long.

Tanganyika, out to the lakes and the Belgian Congo, was now Germany's. For its upper boundary the Anglo-German commission members agreed on a line running from the coast below Mombasa northwest to Lake Victoria. The line barely included Mount Kilimanjaro, and the legend was that Emperor William entreated his grandmother, Queen Victoria, to allow him this highest mountain in Africa as a birthday present. At any rate, Germany got it and Britain got the area above it, which became the colony of Kenya. The southern border of the new Tanganyika abutted Portugal's Mozambique. Another result of the "pen stroke" diplomacy creating Tanganyika was that it cut in two the tribal grounds, not only of the Masai, but the Waluwo, Sigeji, Wayao, Wamakua, and the Wamakonde.

For a generation the explorers had dominated the stage in Tanganyika and the rest of East Africa. Now these discoverers were giving way to the colonizers. The blacks of Tanganyika were to know yet another two generations of domination. Some say the colonial tutelage provided first by the Germans, then the British, was not all that bad. Some say it might have been, in fact, just the right transitional formula for a people ending so long a history of subjugation.

CHAPTER TWO

THE COLONIZERS

Other European nations in the scramble for Africa were old hands at colonizing. England, France, the Netherlands and Spain had long had colonies in the Far East and the Americas. The Germans, so keen about extending their new empire, were novices. So there might be some excuse for their initial bungling in Tanganyika.

German East Africa Company officials arrived in 1887 to administer the new colony, called by them *Deutsch Ostafrika,* and immediately alienated the Arabs. One of the few privileges salvaged by the Arabs from the Anglo-German agreement in East Africa had been the right to collect customs along the narrow coastal strip left to them. The Germans began at once to importune the new Sultan to give up his last mainland holding. Seyyed Khalifa, who had only just succeeded his late brother Barghash, eventually yielded. He accepted £100 per square mile for the 6,000-mile strip.

Coastal Arabs quickly rebelled. Joined by the Swahili and led by a dashing ex-slaver named Bushiri bin Salem el Harthi, they attacked company officials at Pangani in September 1888. The revolt swept down the coast and even Dar es Salaam (Haven of Peace) was raided.

29

Several Germans, including missionaries, were killed. The German East Africa Company faced serious trouble.

The Imperial Government dispatched a competent soldier to take charge as Military Commissioner. Major Hermann von Wissman, who had earlier explored Central Africa, led a troop of 60 Germans and 800 Sudanese and Zulu *askaris* against the rebels. Bushiri survived a number of skirmishes as he retreated up the coast to Pangani. But there, in December 1889, he was captured and hanged.

Inland, some of the larger tribes challenged German rule. They had aided Bushiri by attacking German caravans going to Tabora in the northwest interior. At Tabora itself, tribesmen had forced missionaries to flee north to Mwanza. Instead of marching against Tabora, however, Wissman moved first on the Chagga around Kilimanjaro and induced some of the chiefs there to accept the idea of central government.

Wissman was still enforcing order in the interior when the German government formally took over the colony from the German East Africa Company in April 1891. The next year Major von Wissman was recalled and another military man was appointed first governor. General von Soden ran up the Imperial Eagle flag to replace the company banner and sent out a force of 1,000 men to attack Chief Mkwawa and his Hehe warriors. The tribe had continued to attack official caravans.

When the column of German officers and African *askaris* were reported approaching Iringa, stronghold of the Hehe, Mkwawa sent five emissaries with gifts of cattle to meet the force, hoping to negotiate with them. But his delegation was fired upon; only one of the five survived. The Hehe war trumpets blew and that night Mkwawa himself led 1,500 warriors to Rugaro, where the advancing column had to pass through a narrow defile. Next morning the German force was ambushed and nearly wiped out. The Hehe carried three small cannon and 500 rifles from the scene, and, with instruction from some of the captured *askaris,* prepared to make good use of the arms.

In 1894 another expedition was sent out against Mkwawa who was at Kalenga, in a fortified position, but could not hold the place against the Germans. The fort fell but even then Mkwawa tried to snatch victory from defeat by staging a surprise attack on the retiring column. Again, the Germans were too strong. With an enlarged colonial garrison now stationed at Iringa, Mkwawa and his reduced force had to keep on the move. For nearly five years he lived as a fugitive, hidden by his people. But one day in July 1899, he found himself surrounded. Rather than be taken prisoner, he shot himself. His captors cut off his head and, as if in proof that their tormentor was at last vanquished, they shipped it to Germany.

A fitting sequel to this rude gesture came in 1919 when a defeated Germany sat down to sign the Treaty of Versailles and stopped to read Article 246. It called for "the return of the skull of Sultan Mkwawa which was removed from the Protectorate of German East Africa and taken to Germany." It was many years before the demand was fulfilled. Finally the long search of German museums was rewarded in 1954 when the British Governor of Tanganyika, Sir Edward Twining, went himself to Germany and brought back a skull which the Hehe accepted as that of their brave leader.

Meanwhile, the Protectorate was putting down other tribal resistance. This was done with *Schrecklichkeit* (frightfulness), a deliberate rule of fear carried out by the young German military commanders. In 1892 Chief Siki of Unyanyembe was still attacking caravans around Tabora. A campaign against him ended in January 1893, when the Germans captured his stronghold. Rather than surrender, Siki blew up his family and himself with gunpowder.

The last of the Chagga rebels died the same year. Chief Meli of Moshi, at the foot of Kilimanjaro, had defeated a German force and killed its commander. The area administrator there was none other than Germany's Carl Peters who in 1884 had persuaded the tribes to turn over their land. Peters, known in Swahili as *Mkonowa-damu* (the man with the bloodstained hands), vowed to exterminate the Chagga chief and his followers. First winning the assurance of other Kilimanjaro tribes that they would not interfere, he sent a great troop to Moshi. They captured Meli, wiped out his followers, and hanged the chief from a tree that still stands outside his residence. The Chagga resigned then to German rule. There were outbreaks from other tribes, including the Gogo and the Yao to the south, but by 1895 real resistance had been broken.

So many tribal chiefs had revolted that, unlike other colonialists, the Germans did not turn to them to help administer the country. Instead they appointed, as assistants to their own district officers, various Arabs and Swahili called *Akidas,* each in charge of twenty or thirty thousand people. Most of these were strangers from the coast and so poorly paid that they did not hesitate to accept bribes. Under them were village administrators called *Jumbes,* who usually were local people.

The Germans made two other colonial errors. One was their failure to establish any sort of native courts. There was no protective law for the African. Almost anyone could order him flogged, without trial. The German attitude was that of parents punishing errant children. Probably worse was the second error (which existed for more than twenty years): the practice of forced labor. African work gangs could be recruited at any time, not only for public works but for private labor. Not until 1907 was a law passed forbidding this.

Such practices undoubtedly accounted for the smoldering resentment which erupted suddenly into violence in August 1905, when the whole south of the country exploded. The fuse was touched off in a village at Kibata, near ancient Kilwa on the coast. The Arab *Akida* reported that workers on the government cotton plantation were grumbling. They were visiting a Ngindo witch doctor on the nearby Rufiji River and getting magic water, which they believed would protect them from evil and even turn bullets to water. The Swahili word for water is *maji.* The workers' discontent was the beginning of the murderous Maji Maji Rebellion.

On August 25 at Samanga, near the cotton plantation, workers attacked and burned the village, killing Arab and Sudanese tradesmen there and a German cotton planter at Madaba. There were no soldiers in the area and the rebels were encouraged to further violence. Chanting tribal war songs and bearing magic water with them, they marched to Liwale, farther south, and attacked a government office, massacring the garrison of Zulu troops and two German clerks. The rebels used bows and arrows and old muzzle-loaders from which they shot scraps of telegraph wire and glass stoppers of soda bottles. Freakishly, the very first bullet fired by a Zulu defender killed two rebels. Medicine men hastily explained that the two were not protected by the magic water because they were adulterers.

A group of Roman Catholic missionaries, newly arrived from Europe and led by Bishop Cassian Speiss, came by on their way to Songea. All were murdered. The attack continued. Where there were no government offices, the rebel mobs set upon the missions. Missionaries at Nyangao and Masasi escaped. At Songea the warlike Ngoni joined the fight and a force of government troops was routed. Further north at Njombe a mission was attacked by Sangu and Bena tribesmen.

The government did not effectively act until October when 1,000 fresh soldiers arrived from Germany and were joined by Papuan and Melanesian *askaris* from the Pacific. For more than a year the troops moved methodically through the south. The rebels, having found their magic water useless, offered little resistance as the German and mercenary soldiers wreaked vengeance. The military imprisoned hundreds, hanged rebel leaders, burned houses and destroyed crops. The government was determined there should be no more rebellions. By 1907 it was estimated that 120,000 had died in this one. To maintain control, the government effectively used Sudanese and Zulu troops in still-troublesome villages, with orders that they must be fed and provided with beer and women.

But there was a positive side to the German colonial adventure. Previously, Tanganyika had been producing almost nothing beyond the bare needs of sustenance: the maize for their mealie-meal or *posho,* bananas, beans, groundnuts, dried fish, poultry and goats. The Germans introduced cotton and sisal (which were to become the country's principal exports), and encouraged more growing of coffee, which had been produced only for the chiefs. Too, the Germans built—and built to last. As headquarters for each of the nineteen administrative districts they constructed fortlike *bomas,* most of them still in use today. Dar es Salaam, the capital, began to look like a bit of Bavaria. Chunky stone buildings to house the customs and secretariat offices, cathedrals and a luxury hotel lined the waterfront, where lateen-sailed dhows and foreign steamers vied for mooring space. The churches were built by the Roman Catholics and the Lutherans, the hotel by the government and appropriately called the Kaiserhof.

More important, the Germans built railways. The first line was from Tanga (on the northern coast), inland to Moshi and Arusha. Products grown on Kilimanjaro's rich slopes could thus be shipped out. Another line, built between 1905 and 1914, followed the old slave route across the country from Dar es Salaam to Tabora and on to Kigoma on Lake Tanganyika. The railways were a start in solving the great problem of communications in the sprawling territory.

And the Germans brought education to children who might otherwise have learned only tribal legends and customs. By 1911 there were 66,000 pupils in 1,000 schools. Although all but 83 were run by missionaries, the government policy was to promote them and offer what educational means were possible. Thirty schools at the time were above the primary level, thirty others were technical schools where carpentry and practical crafts were taught. A few young Africans were sent on to Germany for study. In most of the primary schools Swahili was used; in some, German.

How far Tanganyika might have developed under German rule was not to be discovered, for World War I put an end to her colonial expansion. In Tanganyika, the 2,000 German settlers dropped their ploughs for guns. They were joined by 10,000 African *askaris,* most of them from the Nyamwezi tribe. From this unlikely recruitment General Paul von Lettow, the able German commandant, fashioned a tough, mobile unit that was to demonstrate some of the first lessons in organized guerrilla warfare.

Unless Germany won a quick victory in Europe, Von Lettow knew he hadn't a chance. He was surrounded: by British forces in Kenya to the north, by Congo Belgians to the west, and British Rhodesians and South Africans to the southwest. On the sea eastward, British warships cut him off. Even Mozambique on the southern border became enemy territory when Portugal joined the Allies.

South Africa's famed General Jan Smuts led the Allied campaign against Von Lettow. He moved deliberately, building up forces on all the borders. Not till early 1916 did they begin to close in. Smuts was with the first units which marched through the lowlands between Mounts Meru and Kilimanjaro and took Moshi. Another British force crossed Lake Victoria and took Mwanza. Another moved up from Nyasaland in the southwest toward Mbeya and Iringa. The Belgians advanced through Ruanda-Urundi toward Tabora.

Von Lettow made a lightning thrust at the British near Moshi scoring heavily, then pulled southward. From all directions Allied forces followed. Occasionally Von Lettow would turn, make his strike, then move quickly away. Across a thousand miles he scored with these hit-and-run tactics, but for both sides the chase was costly one. The British took Kondoa, Tanga and Handeni, the Belgians took Tabora. Soldiers came ashore from British ships off Dar es Salaam and took the capital with little trouble. The German government there had fled and was replaced in September 1916 by a British military government.

In 1917 Von Lettow's tattered army crossed the border into Mozambique. His African soldiers might now justifiably have deserted him, but a firm bond of loyalty had grown in two years of hardship and fighting. There were no desertions, even in 1918 when the German commander ordered a typically bold stroke. Breaking into small groups and moving mostly at night, what was left of his army made their way northward. They skirted through enemy-held Tanganyika and made the five hundred miles past Lake Nyasa to cross the border into Northern Rhodesia. There they were camped in the great Luangwa Valley when the November 11 Armistice was announced. Only then did Von Lettow surrender. Left in his gallant force were sixty Germans and one thousand *askaris*. Here, Von Lettow might have said, was an exemplary multiracial effort for succeeding British colonialists to follow.

The British had in effect been ruling Tanganyika since taking Dar es Salaam in 1916, but its ruling power was not official until the Treaty of Versailles turned administration of the territory over to Britain under League of Nations mandate. Formal confirmation by the League did not come until July 20, 1922.

Britain might well have looked askance at her inheritance. Tanganyika was in ruinous shape. Disease and famine had followed the troops fighting up and down the territory. Soldiers and civilians had died by the thousands as malaria and dysentery spread. The worldwide influenza epidemic wiped out whole villages. Among the Gogo tribe alone, thirty thousand died of hunger. At the tribal capital of Dodoma, Gogo herders offered cattle at one rupee a head. Their children were pawned for food. Retreating Germans had smashed railway installations, torn down bridges and roads. German farmers had, understandably, deserted. Trade and revenue were a fraction of prewar levels. Administratively, there was chaos. What records could be salvaged were in German. African civil servants, who might have been utilized, spoke only German.

It must have seemed a discouraging prospect to Sir Horace Byatt, the first British Governor. But with officials recruited from other parts of Africa, he began the reconstruction. He appointed an Executive Council and new district officers, but resorted to old *Akidas* and *Jumbes* used by the Germans, to run village affairs. Also, unless they conflicted with British law, he kept German regulations and ordinances on the books. Farms run by the Germans were auctioned to British, Greek and Indian settlers. New farms were opened in the south, and Africans were encouraged to grow more than subsistence crops. Gradually, production was restored.

In 1925 a new Governor was appointed, and immediately he began laying the foundations upon which Tanganyika was to stand as a free state. It was done punctiliously, for that was the nature of Sir Donald Cameron, who no doubt had given much thought to this matter while posted earlier in Nigeria. First of all, he insisted on a Legislative Council. He wanted to share responsibility with men "appointed from the unofficial side of the community." So a Legco, as Britains liked to call them, was created in March 1926, with thirteen official and ten unofficial members. Although all members were Europeans, it was intended that seats would later go to Africans who learned enough English to allow them to participate in Council proceedings. In the ensuing years this limited type of legislature was transformed, step by step, into a body of fully elected members, increasingly more of them Africans until they were wholly in control. The transition was slow and often painful, but there was no going back after this first deliberate step by Donald Cameron.

Just as important, Sir Donald turned much of the administration of the country back to the tribal chiefs. The local officials, most of them Arabs appointed by the Germans, were ousted and replaced by native chiefs and headmen. Cameron saw to it that these men were actually recognized by the tribes as their leaders. They were given power to make local laws, to hold court and to dispense funds allotted from the new Native Treasury.

This became known as government by Native Authority. Cameron preferred to call it Local Administration. It was a form of indirect rule, and his purpose was to turn over to the African as much as possible of the management of his own affairs. Cameron saw traditional tribal organization as something rooted in the hearts and minds of the people, something upon which the institutions of Western culture, especially political administration, could be based. Speaking to his staff in July 1925, the Governor explained his policy. "We must not destroy the African atmosphere, the African mind, the whole foundations of his race, and we shall certainly do this if we sweep away all his tribal organizations, and in doing so tear up all the roots that bind him to the people from whom he has sprung."

More pointedly, Sir Donald reminded his administrators: "The Mandate assumed by Great Britain is not a permanent and absolute one and is to be exercised only until the people 'can stand by themselves.' That being so, it is clearly, I submit, the duty of the Mandatory Power to train the people and make its dispositions in such a manner that, when the time arrives, a full place in the political structure shall be found for the native population."

Sir Donald was to be reminded that in encouraging tribal authority he indulged in a dangerous flirtation with the past. What if the tribes, so encouraged, became power-conscious and challenged the central authority or the strength of sister tribes? Lord Hailey in his voluminous survey of Africa mentioned the danger of tribal authority obstructing self-government for the great majority of the population. Fortunately, there was enough diversification of tribes in Tanganyika (compared, say, to Kenya or the Congo), so that by the time any of them might have consolidated their power, the momentum of the nationalist movement had, with their assent, generally encompassed them.

The political and economic progress enjoyed by the territory under Cameron's sure direction was jarred nearly to a halt with the worldwide depression of the early 1930s. Soon Tanganyika found there was no market abroad for her sisal, coffee and cotton. Government revenues fell so low that 150 senior officials had to be dismissed. The railways ran heavy losses. Crops could not be sold.

To compound the grievous economic state, Tanganyika found that foreign investment sources were drying up. Adolf Hitler could be blamed for this. Nazi leaders, preparing for conquest in Europe, let it be known that Germany would also be bidding for her lost colonies. More and more Germans began to arrive in Tanganyika as settlers. It was hinted in the press that England might return the territory in an attempt to pacify Hitler. In 1938 the British government spiked the rumor. Speaking as Secretary of State for the Colonies, Mr. Mal-

PASSING OF THE OLD GUARD: At ceremonies marking the turn-over of British administration of Tanganyika to the new Republic of Tanganyika on December 9, 1962, the departing Governor, Sir Richard Turnbull, held a final review of the King's African Rifles at Government House in Dar es Salaam. Here Sir Richard, in all the panoply of the colonial order, reviews the troops. He is followed by the KAR's commanding officer and the Governor's aide-de-camp.

INDEPENDENCE ASSURED: Following the dramatic announcement by British Colonial Secretary Iain MacLeod, in March, 1961, that Tanganyika would be granted full independence in December of that year, Julius Nyerere was borne triumphantly from Karimjee Hall, where the historic two-day discussions were held, to lead a victory procession through downtown Dar es Salaam.

colm MacDonald announced that the United Kingdom had no intention of turning over to anybody any of the territories under its administration.

At any rate, the question was decisively settled by World War II. At its outbreak, the 3,000 Germans in Tanganyika were arrested and it was found that some had indeed planned to take over the government. German district commissioners and other officials had already been selected. Nazi flags and pictures of Hitler were on hand for the anticipated take-over. Instead of joining Hitler, Tanganyika went effectively to war against Germany and her allies, Japan and Italy. The King's African Rifles went to Ethiopia and Somaliland to fight the Italians. Other units went to North Africa and the Mediterranean, still others to Burma. In all, 92,000 Africans of Tanganyika served in World War II.

Returning after the war, these *askaris* undoubtedly brought back some awareness of nationhood. Men of the K.A.R. while abroad must have felt drawn together as representatives of a country, of something greater than their own tribe. And they must have come back with some sophistication. If so, it definitely was not politically expressed in the postwar years. Out of Tanganyika's wartime experience there did not spring, as had been the case in many other African countries, the flame of nationalism. The K.A.R. veterans apparently were politically passive. It was another decade before the nationalist movement burgeoned in Tanganyika.

This might be interpreted as political backwardness, for at the time Tanganyika was virtually being prodded toward self-government. After World War II, guardianship of the territory continued under Great Britain, this time as part of the trusteeship system of the United Nations. Commenting on this, the then British Secretary of State for Foreign Affairs, Mr. Ernest Bevin, said: "The people of the territory hemselves and the world at large should be left in no doubt that the continuity of British administration will be maintained until the ultimate objective of the trusteeship system, self-government or independence, as the case may be, is attained."

Stoutest champion of Tanganyikan independence in the immediate postwar years was the United Nations itself. Britain was now obliged, as Administering Authority of the territory, to submit an annual progress report to the Trusteeship Council. These naturally told, year after year, how nicely things were going, but the Council checked further by sending an occasional UN Visiting Mission. Here was the rub.

The first Mission in 1948 came back to New York with a report that varied widely from the British accounting. Where the Administering Authority reported "the interests of the great majority of the indigenous population are largely confined to purely local and domestic matters," the Mission reported it was "greatly impressed by the quality of African minds, their general and reasonable understanding of local affairs and requirements, and their appreciation of territorial problems."

The Mission recommended measures "to accelerate the development" toward self-government. It suggested that additional seats be added in Legco so that each of the eight territorial provinces could be represented by an African, that an electoral system be set up for Legco membership, which was still being appointed, and that Africans be named to the Executive Council.

The British press stormed that this was "interference" in the administration of the trust territory. The British government somewhat snidely submitted that the Mission could not have become very familiar with the country in a six-week visit. There should be no Legco elections, it was officially stated, "because they would almost certainly result in the appointment of representatives of sectional interests, much less in touch with and responsive to the needs and wishes of the mass of people than the present carefully chosen members."

But every three years a fresh Visiting Mission arrived at Dar es Salaam to ask why constitutional reform was not moving faster. By June 1952, the incumbent Governor, Sir Edward Twining, was moved to complain: "Of all the problems with which I am faced in Tanganyika, this one of increasing the speed of progress is the most intractable." Dar es Salaam's daily newspaper, the British-owned *Tanganyika Standard,* called the report of the 1954 UN Mission "irresponsible and mischievous." The same report was described in a British government statement as "entirely unrealistic." What was particularly galling in the report was the recommendation that Tanganyika become independent by 1975 or by 1985 at the latest.

Concession by concession, however, the African population was each year granted a larger stake in territorial affairs, and by the time of the 1954 UN report, a body existed that could appropriately take over the nationalist cause. This was the Tanganyika African National Union, vitalized that year by the leadership of Julius Nyerere and destined to lead the way to freedom a full decade ahead of the "unrealistic" target set by the UN team.

Meanwhile, the greatest domestic problem faced by the colonial administration was to raise the economy above the subsistence level. Of the nine million African population only one half of one per cent were in paid employment. The rest lived, just barely, off the land. Their agricultural and livestock products made up 80 per cent of the export income, and exports made up 40 per cent of the national income. Yet most of these farmers looked upon cash crops merely as supplementary to the production of food for their own consumption.

In the first decade after World War II, the United Kingdom poured $30 million into Tanganyika through its Colonial Development Fund, but the impact of these funds on the territory's total economy was hardly perceptible. It was obvious that something rather revolutionary had to be set in motion.

In 1946 something revolutionary was indeed attempted—the Groundnut Scheme—and it turned out to be a most frantic, inefficient and calamitous agricultural project. A partly politically-inspired plan that had as its goal the production of three million tons of peanuts, it became a hundred-million-dollar fiasco. Down the drain with the hundred million went a few political and diplomatic careers, the hope that heavy-duty mechanized agriculture was the key to Tanganyika's economy, and the jobs of 27,000 Africans and 1,200 European engineers, artisans and ex-servicemen who had been induced to settle on the blistering plains of the sub-Sahara for the purpose of planting peanuts.

An industrialist started it all. Mr. Frank Samuel of Unilever was on a tour in Tanganyika, brooding presumably on the critical worldwide vegetable oil shortage and the inability of his company (the largest vegetable oil producer in the business) to take some advantage of the situation. Someone told him that only 3 per cent of Tanganyika's arable six million acres were under cultivation and Frank Samuel had his idea.

Returning to London, he took it up with the Minister of Food. The Minister listened avidly, for the shortage of fats was becoming a hot political issue. Grow groundnuts on a couple of million of those un-used acres, suggested Samuel, and you've got your oil problem licked. Within weeks the Ministry of Food had a team in Tanganyika, headed by a reputable agriculturist, making a survey for peanut sites. The experts chose three areas: 1,650,000 acres inland from Mikindani on the coast; 300,000 acres at Tabora, and 450,000 at Kongwa. An engineer who had been ridding bush areas of the tsetse fly told them that with tractors it would cost about ten dollars an acre to clear the land.

The Overseas Food Corporation was formed for the groundnut project, and its supply staff began to round up tractors from war dis-posal dumps in the Philippines, Egypt, Iraq, Palestine and Belgium. To get them the OFC had to take surplus stocks by lot, whatever might be included. So to the docks of Dar es Salaam there came not only tractors and Sherman tanks but endless crates of miscellaneous stores. One shipment contained 50 bales of duffle coats, thirteen tons of office files and a 90-year supply of angostura bitters. The 303 trac-tors and 580 tanks that arrived were in various stages of disrepair and no arrangements had been made for workshops or the needed army of mechanics.

The first planting of groundnuts was at Kongwa, with a season's target of 150,000 acres. By the end of the year only 10 per cent of the target was under cultivation. Planting was done in the wet winter months and harvesting four or five months later. Among several drawbacks at Kongwa, the most serious was the lack of rainfall. In the language of the resident Gogo tribe, Kongwa meant "to be de-ceived." This could very well have been a reference to the weather.

Mechanical diggers, used on tractors to bore a few inches and root out the nuts, were to have arrived by harvesting time in April but they were delayed at Zanzibar. By May, when they finally had arrived, the soil was dry and hard and they clanged in the ground as though on concrete. (In fact, it was found that the Gogo used this Kongwa subsoil to make tile roofs for their huts.) So the first season yielded 1,500 rather than the target of 600,000 tons. No report was made to account for 4,000 tons of seed nuts ordered for the first plantings. Back in London the new Minister of Food, Mr. John Strachey, gamely wrote the first year off as a trial period and set the 1948 target again at 600,000 tons. But by March of that year Mr. Strachey migh

have been wishing he'd never heard the word groundnut. Thus far
the scheme had cost $23 million and each month was costing three
million more.

The Minister's qualms could not have been transmitted to Kongwa.
There the bustling tent city was ruled by a new resident manager
determined to give a military air to the whole project. His own tent
stood beside two marquees outside of which hung a sign: "Resident
Member, Major Gen. Desmond Harrison, CB., D.S.O." Lesser officials summoned by the general waited in an anteroom tent until noti-
fied by an orderly to enter his presence. The military climate was
all-pervading. Office in- and out-baskets often contained sealed documents marked SECRET. Most of the target and production figures
were considered classified material.

Personnel had arrived by the hundreds from Europe: carpenters,
storekeepers, mechanics, plumbers, accountants and cooks. African
laborers were recruited by the thousands, for camps were also started
at Urambo, three hundred miles west of Kongwa, and in Nachingwea
in the southern province. At Dar es Salaam's few hotels, the new ar-
rivals were sleeping five and six to the room. At all the sites, camp
followers had gathered. In a shack town that sprang up outside
Kongwa, 147 prostitutes were counted. To help with the housing shortage at Nachingwea, the OFC approved of a sawmill designed to turn
out five prefabricated houses a day. It was built at Noli, thirty miles
from the groundnut area, at a cost of $600,000. It was then discovered
that there were no sources of timber near enough to make the mill
economically feasible.

Another $1.5 million was spent on a pipe line to carry tractor fuel
in from the coast. It got bogged down and was never completed. A war
surplus landing craft bringing in more equipment sank in Dar es
Salaam harbor, taking a cargo of sixty tractors to the bottom. Thiev-
ing and thuggery became so common in the camps that the OFC had
to organize its own police force. General Harrison and other top
officials took to the air to try to straighten things out. Planes were
chartered by the OFC to shuttle between London, Dar es Salaam and
the three main camps. "The OFC staff became compulsive about
flight," said one observer. "The air of Tanganyika was thick with
flying groundnut executives."

In early 1949 General Harrison was replaced by Mr. Richard

Plummer, a London newspaperman. In earlier days, Plummer and Minister of Food Strachey had been fellow staff members on a labor publication, *The Miner*. At Kongwa, Mr. Plummer ordered the planting of 19,249 acres of sunflower, ignoring advice that it was too late in the season for planting. The half-matured crop perished in the suns of late spring. There were other misfortunes. The cost of clearing land was running $150 an acre, rather than the ten dollars estimated. White ants began to attack the crops. One camp was plagued by baboons who found groundnuts much to their liking. For the total working force of 28,000, food stocks were running low. Many of the more competent executives were quitting.

In mid-1949, possibly as a token of home support, Mr. Plummer was knighted. This did not restrain *The Times* of London, in November, from calling for the resignations of both Sir Richard and Mr. John Strachey. Both stayed on until 1950, when defeat was finally admitted in a government white paper. Overseas Food Corporation allotments were cut and the Groundnut Scheme converted largely to a cattle ranching program operated by the Tanganyika Agricultural Corporation which replaced the OFC in 1955.

The $100 million which the groundnut dream cost was more than the total Tanganyika government expenditures during the years the scheme was in operation. The experience was well worth noting in the light of the present-day plan to revolutionize Tanganyika's economy. This time the country's whole future was at stake. But this time Tanganyika's own leaders had drawn up the plan.

At about the time the Groundnut Scheme was grinding to a halt, these Tanganyikans, led by Julius Nyerere, were beginning to mobilize into the political force that would take over from the colonizers. How that came about, and how plans for the young republic were formulated, is the story of the birth and growth of the Tanganyika African National Union.

CHAPTER THREE

THE PARTY

Political movements usually are begun by men protesting social wrongs, and the protesters usually choose as their leader a strong-jawed orator with a dramatic flair. Not so the Tanganyika African National Union. TANU began with tribal farmers having only the barest interest in politics, and it was led by a mild-mannered school-teacher whose only concession to drama was a penchant for translating Shakespeare.

Yet within a decade of its founding, TANU had taken complete political control of the country, organized the government of a modern republic and named its leader President of that republic. It might be accurately stated that in no other part of the contemporary world had a political party achieved its aims so effectively and with such voluntary participation of virtually all the people.

The farmers unwittingly started it. To the African farmer of the 1930s and 1940s it seemed that Tanganyika's colonial administrators were interfering too much with his traditional life. Eager to bring about rural reform, the local officials were pressing "Specific Orders" calling for every sort of restriction and control. There were orders

45

"to improve beeswax and honey production," "to control and eradi-
cate the banana weevil," "to enforce the stall feeding of cattle."
Farmers were told to terrace their crops, to mulch their coffee, to dip
their cattle. These all undoubtedly were laudable proposals and in
many cases would, if adopted, have effected rural improvement, but
for the African the pace was too fast. Sometimes projects were en-
forced without experimentation and failed, such as the terracing of
rice crops in the Uluguru area. Reform came hard where farming
methods had been handed down through the generations, particularly
since mistakes could mean famine.

To air their grievances, the farmers turned not to politicians but
to their tribal organizations. Bahaya coffeegrowers of Lake Victoria,
irked by new inspection regulations, protested at meetings of the
Bukoba Bahaya Union. Sukuma cattle breeders, who in 1949 lost
600,000 beasts through drought, were understandably uncooperative
with government attempts to cut down their herds. They spoke out at
Sukuma Union meetings. In the mountain region of Upare, the tribal
union resisted anti-erosion plans.

The greatest protest, and the one which first thrust African interests into the political area, was made by the Meru. The tribe protested a government decision in 1951 to evict 3,000 of their people
from a fertile valley between Mounts Meru and Kilimanjaro so that
the land might be assigned to European dairymen. When pleas to the
government at Dar es Salaam were ignored, the Meru Citizens Union
sent one of its members, Kirila Japhet, to New York to appeal to
the United Nations.

The first Tanganyikan to appear before the UN, Kirila did not
induce the Trusteeship Council to force restoration of the tribal lands.
But this uneducated coffeegrower's mission did bring to the surface
the basic question of non-African intentions in the territory. The land
and its use was the one issue over which the African looked at the
government with suspicion. What was to stop the government from
turning more and more of the country over to white settlers? This
question of alienation of land was the issue which finally brought
political consciousness to the tribes of Tanganyika.

It was as if the Tanganyika African Association had been waiting
for just such an issue. The TAA had been organized in 1927 (with
the blessing of Sir Donald Cameron, then the Governor), among the

government servants, particularly the junior officials and teachers. It functioned principally as a social club for urban Africans and by 1948 had branches in thirty-nine communities and a membership of 1,780. Yet the TAA attracted little interest from either the general African public or the European community. Its lack of program even led to some ridicule.

When the association applied for registration as a cooperative society, the Provincial Commissioner at Dar es Salaam was moved to remark: "The African Association is in the unhappy position of not knowing what it wants and will not be happy until it gets it." In 1953 the TAA saw what it wanted. It welcomed Kirila Japhet back from his trip to New York and then sent him on a tour of the territory to report on the case of the evicted Meru. He was urged also to suggest the need for national independence. The TAA suddenly had become political. And the champion of that independence was to be Julius Nyerere.

There was little about Julius Nyerere, physically, to suggest that here was a man who was to become one of Africa's greatest leaders. Slim, of less than average height, Julius Nyerere was dwarfed by the bulky figures of other Africans usually clustered about him. But his face shone with the intelligence and lively humor that drew people to him like a magnet. He came from a village in the north near Musoma on Lake Victoria, one of the 26 children born to Chief Nyerere Burito of the small Zanaki tribe. He did not begin school at Musoma until he was twelve, but he continued on to the government school at Tabora and then to Makerere College in Uganda. In 1949 he entered the University of Edinburgh, where he helped pay his way by working as a mail sorter in the Edinburgh post office. Returning home in 1952, Nyerere went to St. Francis School at Pugu, just outside Dar es Salaam, to teach biology and to become active in the TAA.

In 1953 Nyerere was elected president of the TAA and, aware of the role it must now have to play, he decided on a complete reorganization. First, there would have to be a merging of the educated urban groups and the protesting tribal farmers. He called some of the association leaders to a meeting at Dodoma where they drafted a new constitution which emphasized political objectives.

Along with this constitution, Julius Nyerere undoubtedly was con-

EVEN MINISTERS PITCH IN: In support of the national self-help movement in Tanzania, everyone from peasant to president takes part in community projects. This group includes Mr. Oscar Kambona (in print shirt), former Foreign Minister and now Minister for Regional Administration, lending a hand to a housing project at Magomeni, on the outskirts of Dar es Salaam. To spur community participation, officials of all ranks often participate in building projects in all parts of the republic. The soil this group is moving will go into making the mud and cement bricks widely used for house construction.

PALM-SHADED HARBOR OF DAR ES SALAAM: Small craft lie moored off the inner shore of Dar es Salaam harbor. On City Drive, flanking the harbor, the tall spire of Roman Catholic St. Patrick's Cathedral reaches skyward. At right is the modern Standard Bank building where, on the fourth floor, the U.S. Embassy has its offices. Docks of the busy capital port jut into the harbor beyond the cathedral.

scious that he was drafting, too, the design for his own future. He personally was influenced, at the age of thirty-two, by the writings of Lincoln, Gandhi and Nehru. The history of Roman power had absorbed him; he had translated Shakespeare's *Julius Caesar* into Swahili verse. He was dedicated to the idea that in politics there could be both honor and historical purpose. He said at the time: "There is nothing—or, certainly, there should be nothing—inherently dirty or dishonest in politics as such; for the just management of the affairs of society should appeal to the best in man, and should attract the best members of society."

Shortly before making the decision to enter politics, young Nyerere had taken two other steps which were to influence his life. He had married Maria Magigi, a lovely girl of the Musimbili tribe, and he had become a Roman Catholic. While a student at Tabora Secondary School he had met a mission teacher, Father Walsh, and had become interested in the Catholic faith. Nine years later, as a teacher at St. Mary's School in Tabora, Nyerere had joined the Church. So it was a stable, literate and dedicated young man who in 1954 set about molding the hopes and fears of the territory's heterogeneous tribal people into a unified nationalist movement.

On July 7 of that year, the Dodoma constitution was presented to the annual TAA conference in Dar es Salaam. It called upon members to fight for Tanganyika's independence, to resist tribalism, to fight for local and national elections "with African majorities," and to fight against racial discrimination. Oddly, membership was limited to Africans only, a contradiction that was not corrected until eight years later. The organization was to have a president, a national executive committee which would meet quarterly, and a central committee in Dar es Salaam which was to meet weekly. These provisions and many others were unanimously adopted.

To better encompass the reforms it was undertaking, the organization changed its name to the Tanganyika African National Union. And July 7 became "Saba Saba" (Seven Seven), the first national birthday. From that date "TANU" became the busiest word in the European and Swahili vocabularies.

For some years there had been murmurs for political freedom among the tribal unions and occasionally from the TAA, but TANU had hardly been organized when it was given a prime opportunity to put the demand for independence before the world at large. This was brought about by the arrival of the UN Visiting Mission in August 1954.

The Mission entered Tanganyika by way of Bukoba and Mwanza, on Lake Victoria, and immediately heard tribal complaints about land alienation. At Musoma they heard an appeal to stop immigration, for settlers were still coming in to take over prime farming land. They heard the story of the Meru evictions, for at Arusha, Kirila Japhet was already installed as TANU's first provincial president. In Dar es Salaam, the UN team met with Nyerere and other TANU leaders and heard nationalist objectives for the first time cogently presented.

The meeting had abundant results. When the Mission's report came out in January 1955, it noted not only that its members had been impressed by TANU's "moderation and sense of realism" but it suggested that there should be a timetable for political development in the territory that would conclude with an African-controlled government. This not only was recognition of TANU as the responsible voice of the people but notice of the fact that independence was only a matter of time.

TANU was elated but official Tanganyika definitely was not. The Governor, Sir Edward Twining, the Colonial Office and the British press let it be known that the strongest representations would be made at the UN Trusteeship Council hearing against accepting the Mission recommendations. Their representation was indeed formidable. The British government sent Sir Alan Burns to speak for the Administering Authority. The Tanganyika Legislative Council sent a delegation led by Sir Charles Phillips. The Tanganyika government sent a special representative, Mr. A. J. Grattan-Bellew. TANU decided to send Julius Nyerere. A collection was made in Dar es Salaam and other party strongholds and £600 was raised for his travel expenses.

The New York hearing was in late February 1955. One after another the government spokesmen condemned the Mission report. They complained that the recommendations were based on insufficient knowledge, that they imperiled the economic stability of the territory, and would plunge the country into political and financial chaos. Nyerere, his voice as usual mild and carrying its trace of

Edinburgh, defended the report. Any assertion that the vast majority of Tanganyika's inhabitants opposed the Mission's views was, he said, false. If constitutional changes were not made, non-Africans in the territory would continue to be inspired by false hopes and the Africans by false fears. He said that TANU shared his own hope that Tanganyika, though racially heterogeneous, would be nationally homogeneous. TANU regarded Asians and Europeans who had made Tanganyika their home as much Tanganyikans as Africans born in the country. The Trusteeship Council adopted the 1954 Mission report in its entirety, making it a matter of record for the General Assembly.

Returning home, Nyerere began building TANU into a national party. He was joined in this by the union's energetic young general secretary, Oscar Kambona.

The pair, having acquired a battered Land Rover, went on an organizing tour through the country. In green bush shirt, slacks, and waving an ivory-tipped cane, Nyerere addressed thousands of village meetings. He spoke for freedom to be gained through support of TANU, but he spoke against violence. He talked informally, never above his audience's level, often bringing his dry humor into play. He argued discreetly for national unity as against tribalism, for he and Kambona had agreed that a prime target in TANU's membership drive was to bring in the tribal unions. The drive was successful. In 1954 there were twenty TANU branches, mostly in towns along the rail line; by the end of 1955 there were scores of others.

Communications in the territory were so meager that it was difficult to keep track of the burgeoning membership. Here the apprehensive government helped out. In 1955 a Societies Ordinance was passed which required registration of associations of all complexions. TANU headquarters in Dar es Salaam, by checking at the government registry office in the capital, enrolled each new branch as official registrations poured in.

TANU's own headquarters was a low, mud-walled building on Livingstone (now Lumumba) Street, deep in the Asian section of Dar es Salaam. Here, in a dimly-lit office with a dirt floor, Nyerere received his committee chairmen, branch leaders, visitors and occasional members of the press. In June 1955, a bit of the office was partitioned off as space for the party's new Women's Branch, and a remarkable woman stepped onto the TANU scene. Bibi Titi Mohamed, a plump, short Moslem grandmother, was the party's first woman member and she was now defying all Moslem precepts by personally heading a door-to-door drive for party members. She was also busily learning English, with every intention of becoming one of Legco's first woman members.

These were lean days financially for Nyerere himself. After resigning his teaching post at Pugu he and Maria moved into Magomeni, the drab African quarter that lay to the west of Dar es Salaam on the road to Morogoro. TANU paid its president what it could but that was not very much or very often. To help, Maria started a *duka,* a tiny native store, in the sprawling compound, and also took in sewing.

Earlier in the year Nyerere had been earning $28 a month at the Maryknoll mission near Musoma. This was for translating the New Testament into Swahili, but that job was now done.

Much of the money TANU could raise was spent on trips made by Nyerere into the country to put down political brushfires started by some of the party's local leaders. At Kondona, TANU members were not allowed to register as a branch because they were organizing resistance to cattle-culling regulations. Nyerere made the tiresome overland trip north to urge support of the conservation program. He went to the Uluguru hills where the British district commissioner had publicly charged that the TANU branch was holding a "court" and levying fines. Nyerere proved that the "judge" was not even a TANU member and won a letter of apology from the government.

Nyerere was not so successful in the northern province of Tanga. There, at Korogwe, TANU's chairman was convicted of sedition for announcing that TANU was now the government and agricultural rules were no longer effective. The government not only would not allow Nyerere to visit the area but closed down all party branches in the province.

In the capital, however, TANU and UN pressures finally prodded the colonial administrators into action. It was not that these officials opposed eventual independence; in fact many, including Sir Donald Cameron, had done much to lay its foundation. But they wanted political development to go according to their own careful design. Indirect rule had to be replaced gradually by democratic local government which, to their way of thinking, required many more years of African experience and education.

Since World War II the government had been deliberating over constitutional government but had done little about it. This policy of postponement moved a group of prominent Europeans, Asians and Africans to publish a memorandum in the *Tanganyika Standard* in 1949 protesting that in spite of more than 25 years of British trusteeship no significant progress had been made toward representative government in the country. True, Legco had been enlarged in 1945 to 29 members, fourteen of them nominated and not officials. Of these, seven were Europeans, three were Asians and four were Africans. Someone noted to Julius Nyerere that here was a beginning of African representation. "Nonsense!" he replied. "Has anyone among you seen or met with a member of Legco? None, I can say. Those members are representing only their own ends. I saw one of them visiting Tabora. He drove straightaway to the Provincial Commissioner's house. Later I saw him in Dar es Salaam, where he drove to the Governor's house. Therefore I conclude that he is representing the views of the PC [Provincial Commissioner] and the Governor."

A new constitution in 1955 hardly improved the situation. Legco was further enlarged to include 71 members, of whom 30 were not officials: ten each from the European, African and Asian communities. Opening the Council session Governor Twining claimed: "This ensures equal representation of all three races, and diminishes the possibility of domination by any one race." It was an empty claim: not only did the government retain an official majority, but European members remained in the over-all majority and, worse than that, every one of the 71 members was still being appointed.

TANU responded by increasing its demand for national elections and for African majorities on all representative public bodies. In 1956 Nyerere appeared again before the United Nations in New York and called for universal adult suffrage and a definite timetable for constitutional advance to independence. This new aggressiveness by the party had the effect in Tanganyika of changing European indifference to TANU activities to an attitude of fear. The *Tanganyika Standard* now described TANU as an extreme nationalist organization and noted: "The more ambitious see themselves as presidents, prime ministers and ministers with fantastic salaries."

Perhaps because of this reaction and partly because of the prospect that elections eventually would have to be faced, the community of over 20,000 Europeans in early 1956 started its own political organization. Called the United Tanganyika Party, its nucleus was the group of unofficial members of Legco and its creed was multiracialism. It called for continuance of the political status quo "until such time as the main races are more nearly formed into one whole as responsible citizens of Tanganyika." Ivor Bayldon, its new chairman, took little time in elaborating the party's stand. He accused TANU members of acting "like cheap imitations of American gangsters" and of introducing a reign of terror. He spoke darkly of TANU's "subversive activity." He urged "responsible" Africans to join the UTP.

Nyerere responded by charging that the UTP hoped "to entrench and perpetuate racialism" by continued control of Legco. He called the UTP "the Governor's Party." As for the charge of gangsterism, he said that although TANU was determined to obtain freedom for Tanganyika regardless of how long it would take, the struggle for freedom would be by lawful and peaceful means, since "the way of the jungle was not good for people claiming to be civilized." He called anew for elections.

Surprisingly, in April 1956 the government agreed. The country's first elections would be held in two phases in late 1958 and in 1959. There would be ten constituencies, each to have one African, Asian and European member. This parity representation was more of the government's multiracial formula but TANU accepted it as the best that could be expected at the time. Voters were to choose one candidate from each of the three racial categories. A voter had to have high-school standing or an income of at least $50 a year.

This was the signal for months of hardfisted political campaigning. And the choice was not between TANU and UTP alone, for another party joined the race. This was the African National Congress, formed by Zuberi Mtemvu, TANU's secretary in the Eastern Province. Mtemvu broke away because of TANU's moderate racial policies. His party, he said, would be an African party for Africans, charging that TANU's nonracialism smacked too much of the UTP's multiracialism.

It was soon obvious that the UTP was in fact the government's party. It attacked the United Nations for "interfering" in Tanganyikan affairs and reminded voters that until independence came the final responsibility for the territory rested with the British government and not with the UN. It claimed that throughout the country the tribes were loyal to the government and not to TANU.

TANU protested that the UTP was taking advantage of its position in Legco and called upon the Governor to dissolve the Council. Julius Nyerere made another trip to New York and so impressed the UN General Assembly's Fourth Committee that it passed a resolution that Tanganyika "shall be guided toward self-government or independence and shall become a democratic state in which all inhabitants have equal rights." When this was reported in Dar es Salaam, the English-language press hotly denied Nyerere had the authority to speak for Tanganyika's African millions.

Two months later the government refused to permit TANU to hold open-air meetings because of the "inflammatory nature" of its president's speeches. Thus muzzled, Nyerere started the first party newspaper, *Sauti ya TANU* (Voice of TANU) which soon began nationwide distribution. The government responded with a tract entitled "Some Comments on Mr. Nyerere's Speech at the Fourth Committee of the United Nations." The government began to refuse registrations of new TANU branches and those in eleven districts were banned. Nonetheless, the party prospered. Membership increased to nearly 200,000. In 1957 there were 48 branches. By 1958 there were 134.

In apparent recognition of this strength, the government suddenly lifted its ban on TANU and, as Nyerere had demanded, dissolved Legco to appoint a new one. Even more surprising, the Governor named Nyerere a member to represent the Dar es Salaam constituency. But Nyerere resigned three months later, charging that Legco was too patently a rubber-stamp body. "I came to the Council expecting a little of the spirit of give and take," he said. "That spirit is not there." Another new African appointee, who was to rise high in TANU affairs, was Rashidi Kawawa, then general secretary of the Tanganyika Federation of Labor.

The arrival of a new Governor in 1958 abruptly changed the political climate. Sir Richard Turnbull, Twining's successor, had just completed three years as Chief Secretary in Kenya, where he had a reputation for improving race relations. Dar es Salaam at once learned

why. Addressing the large crowd on hand for his swearing-in ceremony, Turnbull spoke first in English, then repeated the entire speech
in Swahili. The delight of the Africans was increased when he said
that the 1959 portion of the forthcoming elections would be advanced
from September to February.

Julius Nyerere responded in kind. Because of an article in his
Voice of TANU charging a provincial official with fabricating evidence against his party, he was found guilty of libel in July 1958.
Rather than go to prison for six months he chose to pay the fine. To
have played the martyr, he explained, would have seemed like defying
the new Governor.

Besides, there were the elections. The first half affected five provinces, with 28,500 voters registered. It was TANU's first test of
strength and Nyerere wanted an overwhelming victory—which
TANU did win. Three of the fifteen seats were uncontested, but
TANU candidates swept the other twelve. Julius Nyerere himself
polled three times as many votes as his opponent.

Ivor Bayldon, campaigning for the European seat in the Southern
Highlands, lost to a woman candidate: Marion, the Lady Chesham,
who, until she entered the national political race as an independent,
was unknown to the leaders of TANU. She was, nevertheless, to play
an important role in Tanganyika's future development. An American
from Philadelphia, this remarkable woman had first come to Tanganyika in 1938 as the bride of Lord Chesham, who had launched a
cooperative settlement project in the country four years before and
returned annually to check its progress. After war service in England
during World War II, the titled couple returned to make Tanganyika
their permanent home. They began developing Rungemba Estate in
Iringa, in the Southern Highlands, principally to raise cattle, and became popular figures with the Hehe tribesmen who inhabited the
area. When Lord Chesham died in 1952, Lady Chesham took over
management of the estate and became active in community affairs.
She had joined the new United Tanganyika Party but resigned a few
weeks later when she decided its multiracialist policies were fraudulent
ones. Partly to combat them, she had entered the election with
TANU's support. And she had won.

Mtemvu, the TANU rebel, polled a total of 53 votes and forfeited his $75 deposit. The election in the other five provinces that followed in February 1959 was as decisive. Only three seats were contested and again TANU swept the board.

When the 30 new members took their seats in Legco, the opening speech by Governor Turnbull virtually told TANU that the fight for political freedom was won. It was right and proper, said Sir Richard, that the African majority take over both legislature and the government, "a government to which Her Majesty's Government will be able to devolve its trust as being a government under which responsible people of all races would feel secure."

Replying for the elected members, Nyerere said: "We have always waited for a governor of this country even to indicate it was the government's policy that, when self-government is eventually achieved, the Africans will have a predominant say in the affairs of the country." He said in a statement two days later: "It is said that Tanganyika has 120 tribes. I suggest that the way to democracy is to say we have 122 tribes in Tanganyika, the youngest and relatively the most educated being the European and Asian tribes. Let us then have tribal but not racial problems, if we must have problems at all." He added, "We did not like this parity election: ten Africans, ten Europeans, ten Asians. But TANU fought and won it and we sit here today not ten Africans, ten Europeans and ten Asians but 30 Tanganyikans."

Sir Richard named five of the new Legco members, including three Africans, to his cabinet. Nyerere declined an appointment so that he could lead the opposition as chairman of the new Tanganyika Elected Members Organization.

Also, there was the problem of consolidating his party. TANU was growing so rapidly that there was danger of its getting out of hand. The party was now five years old and claimed three million supporters, a half million of them dues-paying members. With the election victory, many party enthusiasts were convinced TANU had taken over rule of the country. Sukuma tribesmen around Lake Victoria would not believe otherwise and marched by the thousands from Geita to Mwanza for an explanation. Elias Kisenge, now TANU's general secretary (Oscar Kambona had left to study in London), hurried to the provincial capital to put out the fire. Nyerere followed a few days later.

Addressing a throng at Mwanza airport, Nyerere told them a TANU card did not mean that they could refuse to pay taxes, open shops without a license or generally ignore the law. In fact, he said, self-government, when it came, would mean greater discipline and higher taxes because there were so many schools and roads to be built.

To emphasize the message, Nyerere on his return to Dar es Salaam changed the party slogan from *"Uhuru"* (Freedom) to *"Uhuru na Kazi"* (Freedom and Work). Members throughout the land were urged to improve their homes and villages on a do-it-yourself basis. Branch leaders were told to encourage communal road-building. Group farming was proposed. The party encouraged education. Night literacy classes were organized. The first TANU school was opened in Lushoto by John Rupia, the party's new vice-president. Plans were made for a middle school for every province. Here, as early as 1959, was the beginning of the self-help plan which was later to dramatize Tanganyika's national development program.

Meanwhile, constitutional development proceeded at a rapid pace. In August 1960, another general election was held which was to effect "responsible government" for Tanganyika. The new Legislative Council would still have 71 members but all would be elected. Fifty seats would be open to all races, eleven reserved for Asians and ten for Europeans. The franchise was considerably widened, though far short of universal suffrage.

The results showed that Tanganyika was already in effect a one-party state. TANU won all but one of the seats, 58 of them without opposition. The lost seat went to a former TANU member who subsequently rejoined the party. Tanganyika's government thus changed from white to black. The new Legco had a majority of 52 Africans.

Julius Nyerere was appointed to head the new administration, with the title of Chief Minister. Most of the men he named to his cabinet were from TANU. Oscar Kambona, back from England with a law degree, became Minister for Education; Rashidi Kawawa, Minister for Local Government. The others: George Kahama, Minister for Home Affairs; Paul Bomani, Minister for Agriculture; Chief Abdullah Fundikara, Minister for Lands; Derek Bryceson, Minister for Health and Labor; Amir Jamal, Minister for Communications and

Works; Sir Ernest Vasey, Minister for Finance; M. J. Davies, Minister for Information Services; J. S. R. Cole, Attorney General.

In a radio address, speaking for the first time as Chief Minister, Nyerere told the nation of the struggles ahead: "It was the character of our people which made inevitable our achievement of responsible government and which again renders inevitable the achievement of our complete independence. It is the same character which ensures our success in the struggle against ignorance, poverty, disease and fear—a struggle in which I am proud and privileged to lead you."

TANU leaders realized now how quickly political advance had taken place and the enormous burden the party soon would be bearing in taking over government of the country. For an organization hardly six years old, the prospect was sobering. A first step, taken in the interests of party unity, was to form the TANU Parliamentary Party, made up of the successful election candidates. Significantly, an Asian and a European were named to the TPP's executive committee: Al Noor Kassum and Lady Chesham. Their appointments hinted that TANU membership would be opened to all races.

To strengthen the party nationally (once self-government was actually achieved), it was planned to replace the ten provincial commissioners of the colonial system with regional commissioners, and the British district commissioners with area commissioners. These appointments were to be made from TANU ranks. The commissioners would join with the central committee in the capital to form the national executive.

The new government had been only a month in office when Governor Turnbull announced in Legco that a constitutional conference would be held in London in March 1961, to arrange for self-government and full independence later in that year. Julius Nyerere's most urgent thoughts were on the problem of finances. TANU already had an economic development committee planning the nation's future, but the need primarily and inevitably would be for capital. So Nyerere sped off on a fund-raising trip to London, Bonn and Washington. He wanted—and eventually got—loans of $10 million each from West Germany and the U.S. and $30 million from Great Britain.

It was a sign of changing times and emerging nations: a self-effacing, dedicated man from a rude hut in the African quarter of Dar

es Salaam, shopping in the capitals of the Western world for multi-
million-dollar loans for his people. For Nyerere had insisted, even
after taking office as Chief Minister, on keeping the little house in
Magomeni. But his friends and followers would have no more of that.
While he was on this trip abroad, a group of them plucked Maria
Nyerere and her children from the hut at Magomeni and moved them,
furnishings and all, to a modest house they had found at Seaview, on
the north shore of Dar es Salaam. On his return, Nyerere had no
choice but to move into his new home.

The constitutional conference was not held, as planned, in London.
Rather, Colonial Secretary Iain MacLeod came to Dar es Salaam in
March with a small staff and, with Governor Turnbull, Chief Minister Nyerere and other ministers, sat down to business. The meeting
took place in Karimjee Hall, where Legco held its sessions. Instead
of laboring through weeks of discussion, the Colonial Secretary announced two days later that self-government would begin on May 1,
and full independence on December 28 of the same year. There were
no reservations, no minority reports. With the realization of what
this meant, the hall exploded with cheers. Crowds outside burst in
and garlanded the conference leaders with flowers. Nyerere was lifted
to the shoulders of his supporters. A victory procession streamed
through the capital.

Three months later, amid formal pageantry, Julius Nyerere was
made Prime Minister, head of a government that was authentically
Tanganyikan. But for him there could never have been a moment to
equal that in Karimjee Hall when independence was announced. At
that moment, after years of hope and struggle, TANU's goal was won.
A whole period of history was ending. The nation was in the hands
of its people.

Nyerere's compelling task, in those final months before full inde
pendence, became the mobilization of party leadership for the busi
ness of government. There was no doubt now that TANU *was* the
government. Before, the party had symbolized a national movement
its principal purpose the political goal of independence. The fiery
sentiment and the party slogans had to be replaced by concrete poli
cies and programs.

Changes began to emerge. One involved the TANU constitution

The primary aim had been the goal of self-rule; now it called for 'consolidation of the freedom of the country and its people." Premier Nyerere elaborated on his one-party policy. When a government is building a country, he noted, there is no room for difference or division. "Tanganyika is going to war against poverty, ignorance and disease so we must regard this as a time of emergency." After a meeting of the national executive, Oscar Kambona announced that the official government policy was to be a socialist one, "to suit Africans," but there would be no nationalization of industry. A special council, representing TANU, the Tanganyika Federation of Labor and the nation's cooperatives, would draft a national economic program.

That summer of 1961 TANU dedicated its handsome new $200,-000 headquarters on Lumumba Street. Funds for the construction had been slowly accumulated from branches all over the country, and the party was proud of its achievement. Premier Nyerere, though he cut a tape officially opening the building, announced that TANU would continue to use its old building farther down the street. This new edifice, he said, would be used as the nucleus of the university that his government was starting. It was time, he pointed out, for Tanganyika to have a college of its own. The party and all the country applauded the move.

Another task before the final take-over in December was appointment of the regional and area commissioners who would be the government's and the party's political supervisors throughout the country. Nyerere also revealed how TANU would unite all the people behind the nation-building effort that was being planned. Every one of Tanganyika's seven thousand villages would have a TANU chairman and committee, he said, "to act as a two-way, all-weather road along which the purposes, plans and problems of the government can travel to the people at the same time as the ideas, desires and misunderstandings of the people can travel direct to the government." This, he stressed, was the job of the new TANU.

The enormity of the burdens ahead confronted the loyal band of followers Nyerere had around him. Young men of limited experience and education were taking over, from a veteran corps of colonial administrators, the task of guiding a nation of nearly ten million. For years they had fought for the power of leadership and now, almost in haste, it was being thrust upon them. The months immediately ahead would tell how ready they were and how worthy of their country's trust.

CHAPTER FOUR

THE PLANNERS

The men grouped around Julius Nyerere in 1961 to form a government found themselves in somewhat the position of Great Britain when she took over Tanganyika from the Germans after World War I. It was a sudden and difficult inheritance, for the Tanganyika of 1961 was 350,000 square miles of problems—many of them the legacy of 76 years of colonial neglect.

There was the nation's health, for example. Derek Bryceson, the new Minister of Health, summed it up grimly soon after taking office when he said: "Two out of every five children born in Tanganyika never grow up." They would die of bilharzia, malaria, smallpox, dysentery or any one of a variety of diseases that plagued a country infested by the mosquito and the tsetse fly. In the preceding year—and this in a country almost touching the equator—there had been 27,-071 known cases of pneumonia. The number of unknown cases could not be calculated. In its 1958 annual report Tanganyika's colonial administration had to admit: "No accurate health and epidemiological statistics are available for the territory."

63

Nor were there doctors to cure the diseases. When white government gave way to black, there were only fourteen Africans who had been trained as medical doctors. Altogether there were 520 physicians for a population of nearly ten million. There were 29 dentists in the country, not one of them African. There were no African pharmacists.

In education the picture was as bleak. More than half of Tanganyika's African population—about four and a half million—were children under fifteen years of age. Of this total, only 435,721, or about one out of every ten, were in school in 1961. Hardly 1 per cent of those who received any schooling at all reached secondary or high school. This was illustrated in school attendance figures for 1960. There were 386,267 children in Grades I to IV of primary school. There were 44,789 in Grades V to VIII and 4,645 in grades beyond that. At that time there were only four schoolgirls in the whole country who had gone through the secondary classes.

Under the colonial system, by contrast, nearly 50 per cent of the European and Asian pupils in Tanganyika went on to secondary school. In 1960 an average of $30 a year was spent for each African pupil; $450 was spent for each European in school. Another academic statistic: in 1961 Tanganyika had not one institution of higher education.

Communications, so basic to the national economy, were hopelessly inadequate in 1961. There was no such thing as an internal network of roads. A visiting economist described Tanganyika's road system as probably the poorest in Africa. Measuring on the basis of so many road miles per square mile of land area, he estimated that the ratio was approximately half that of neighboring, penny-poor Uganda. Tanganyika's railways had deteriorated, instead of improving, since the German occupation. A branch had been added to the central line in 1934 but was abandoned after World War II. Two lines had been started as part of the Groundnut Scheme. One, to the plantation at Kongwa, was abandoned in 1956; and the other, from the new port at Mtwara to Nachingwea, helped to market agricultural products of the Southern Province but was operated at a loss. A post war communications survey of Tanganyika noted: "Few railways in the world had to operate on so meagre a traffic."

Because industries had not been developed, Tanganyika by 1961 hardly had a working class. Of the country's ten million, 315,252 were employed, and 199,021 of these were on agricultural plantations. Another 86,237 were in public services. Of the total 315,252 employed Africans, 215,055 were unskilled. Only 6.5 per cent of the total received more than $30 a month. The vast majority of the country's population, engaged in subsistence farming, were not classed as labor.

There was one class of worker which demanded immediate attention: the civil servants. And for Julius Nyerere they were his worst early problem. During the 1960 session of Legco, Governor Turnbull had noted that there were 3,403 civil service officers, all but 506 of them from Britain or elsewhere overseas. A great many of them wanted nothing to do with an African government, and wanted to leave with a "golden handshake," compensation for loss of their career positions. Nyerere realized that if they left en masse, the country's administration would be crippled. Some TANU leaders, on the other hand, insisted that they leave regardless of the harm done, so that Africans might supplant them. Others groaned at the prospective cost of the severance pay. The compensation for 1,700 claimants totaled $30,000,000. Individual officials were demanding up to 28,000.

Weeks of negotiation in both Dar es Salaam and London resulted in a compromise. Three hundred officials agreed to stay on under contract appointment. Junior African officials would be moved up to replace the others. The millions in compensation would be paid over a period of five years, with financial assistance from the United Kingdom.

Much of the burden of working out such problems of finance fell on the shoulders of Paul Bomani, the able Nyerere lieutenant who served as Minister for Agriculture throughout most of 1961 but became Minister for Finance with independence later that year. One of the gifted graduates of Tabora Secondary School, Bomani came from the Sukuma tribe around Mwanza. Long active in the cooperative movement in the lake region, he became manager of the Victoria Federation of Cooperative Unions after attending Loughborough College in England. He was nominated to the Legislative Council in

COTTON BLOSSOM TIME: Ideal growing conditions in the lake region of Tanzania have made cotton the republic's second most important export. Virtually all of the crop is processed and marketed through the cooperative system. This young woman of the Sukuma tribe is picking cotton in her family's field near Mwanza. From her village cooperative the cotton will go to the giant Victoria Federation of Cooperative Unions for marketing.

1954 and won a Legco seat in the 1959 selection. His brilliance in business and economic matters made him the obvious heir to the finance portfolio after the resignation of Sir Ernest Vasey, last of the colonial administrators in the Tanganyika government.

Derek Bryceson, the Minister of Health, was the only European left in the cabinet but Bryceson hardly could be called a colonial. An elected member of Legco, he became a citizen of Tanganyika and a member of TANU as soon as both steps were possible. Trained in agriculture at Cambridge, Bryceson had flown for Britain's R.A.F. during World War II and had been seriously wounded at El Alamein. Nyerere usually turned to him when there were problems or legislation in the fields of labor, health and agriculture.

Closest to Nyerere in these formative days was Rashidi Kawawa. Minister without Portfolio, Kawawa was regarded by most of TANU as deputy premier. One of TANU's most diligent workers, he was also its most colorful leader. Dressed always in robe and sandals, Kawawa added flair to public occasions, recalling earlier days when he had been an actor. While working in the Social Development Department he played in *Muhogo Mohunu,* a South African film hit, then starred in a number of Swahili productions. One of his official roles had been as overseer of a Mau Mau detention camp at Urambo. Another of Tabora's graduates, he joined the Tanganyika African Civil Servants Association and later became its general secretary.

In 1954 Kawawa brought other union officials together and formed the Tanganyika Federation of Labor. A year afterward he resigned from the civil service to be a full-time general secretary of the TFL. At the same time he joined TANU, which as a civil servant he could not do before, and in 1957 was nominated to Legco. He won a seat, representing Dar es Salaam, in the 1958 election and resigned his TFL post in 1960 to join the government. Just before resigning he had been convicted and fined for running an illegal union lottery. In an earlier brush with the law, he was convicted of intimidating two clerks who had refused to join a brewery union strike. Neither case harmed his popularity; indeed, after paying the intimidation fine, he was borne from the court on the shoulders of union admirers.

Oscar Kambona, who had been a schoolmaster at Dodoma, was given the task of reforming the school system as Minister for Education, later was shifted to the more sensitive post of Minister for Home

Affairs. With Kawawa, Kambona was closest of the TANU group to Julius Nyerere, politically and personally. When Kambona was married in London in 1960—in the first African wedding ever held in fashionable St. Paul's Cathedral—Nyerere flew over to be his best man. Kambona, too, was an indefatigable worker, both for government and party. Europeans in Dar es Salaam regarded him as ebullient and competent, a handsome man, in appearance a darker Tony Curtis.

Four other ministers filled out the group around Nyerere which studied the country's backward condition and began fashioning a development program. George Kahama and Jeremiah Kasambala, Ministers respectively for Commerce and Cooperative Development, were, like Paul Bomani, graduates of Britain's Cooperative College at Loughborough and both had long been in the cooperative movement. Nsilo Swai, who became Minister for Development Planning, had the most impressive academic background of the TANU circle. Educated at Makerere College in Uganda, the University of Bombay, University of Delhi and the University of Pittsburgh, he had been graduated from Delhi with an honors degree in economics and had received an industrial development certificate at Pittsburgh. He became executive draftsman for Tanganyika's planning. Amir Jamal, the Minister for Communications, Power and Works, was the only other non-African besides Bryceson in the Nyerere cabinet. A studious Indian, he was the most articulate spokesman in urging the Asian community to play a larger part in public life. An economics graduate of the University of Calcutta, he gave up his business career to accept a succession of government offices.

With Paul Bomani as chairman, this group met formally as Tanganyika's new development committee. They had at once the benefit of a highly expert blueprint: the report, published in November 1960, of a nine-man team of economists sent to Tanganyika by the International Bank for Reconstruction and Development. Spending nearly a year on the task, the World Bank Mission found that if there was one thing Tanganyika lacked, it was planning. In the past, they said, the government had been run on a year-to-year basis and any planning had been both confusing and lacking in continuity.

The Mission report, *The Economic Development of Tanganyika*, made no less than 282 recommendations. Basically, they were for the improvement and reform of the country's peasant agriculture. Unless the government effectively marshaled the nation's limited resources, the team warned, Tanganyika would be in serious trouble. As a beginning, a three-year development plan was strongly urged.

This was the task Premier Nyerere assigned to the Bomani committee. Further underlining its urgency, he said: "When you have a country with a small section enjoying a high standard of living and a large section, comprising the vast majority of the population, living on a subsistence economy, you know that such a country is sitting on dynamite. When such economic divisions are also identical with racial divisions the dynamite can be even more explosive. This is one reason why we must plan to raise the standards of the mass of people to a decent level in the shortest possible time."

For weeks, at meetings that often lasted far into the night, the ministers went over department and bureau estimates. Projects were proposed and rejected. Statistics of water surveys, agricultural and livestock production, training facilities, road construction and hundreds of administrative procedures were charted and studied. Even such items as the prospective needs of Tanganyika's future foreign service had to be reviewed.

The mass of information was gradually refined into a working draft and finally, in mid-May 1961, the finished result was published. *Development Plan for Tanganyika, 1961–64* was a 96-page pattern for progress. An introduction to the plan cautioned that even if realized, the objectives of the plan would not necessarily result in immediate and substantial increases in output and income. Rather, it noted, they would lay the foundations for future growth.

At that time government expenditures were about $60 million a year. The development plan called for spending another $70 million over the next three years in what could be called pump-priming projects. Agricultural and communications projects would get more than half the total. Education was next in priority. Far down on the list of priorities was an item listed as "Community Development." Its allocation was $700,000. It is worth noting because, of all the millions appropriated, this was to turn out to be the blue-chip investment.

Where was the $70 million coming from? Under "Sources of Funds" the plan noted that $12 million was hoped for from the British government and $9 million from other governments in the form of outright grants; $12 million from internal and $34 million from external loans, and $3 million "from miscellaneous local revenue."

A few weeks after the plan's publication, Julius Nyerere went abroad on his fund-raising tour. In London the response was not encouraging. Colonial Development Fund officials pointed out that there were areas of much greater need and unrest than Tanganyika. Nyerere complained of this in a press interview. "Our very stability is being used as an argument why we should not get assistance," he said with some bitterness. But Governor-General Turnbull also went to London to follow up the application. He returned to Dar es Salaam in August with the announcement that the United Kingdom was coming through with both the grants and loans requested.

Not only did foreign government aid begin to arrive but private investors abroad now became interested in Tanganyika's future. Italy's largest oil group wanted to build a refinery at Dar es Salaam. British money went into a $4-million .cement plant just outside the capital. Danes financed a sugar plantation and refinery at Moshi. Israelis began a plastics factory. A Japanese company began production of nylon fishing nets at Dar es Salaam and Mwanza, and Chinese textile interests planned a mill near the capital. Kahama, the Minister for Commerce and Industry, reported that others were planning tire, aluminum and plywood factories. For a country where industry had been almost nonexistent, Tanganyika was beginning to look modestly commercial.

In agriculture most of the investment was going into the development of water supplies and into training an army of agricultural instructors to work with the country's farmers. There would be 80 senior field officers, 230 field officers and 22,000 field assistants. There already were agricultural schools at Ukiriguru and Tengeru, and a college would be built at Morogoro.

To furnish Tanganyikan farms with water, the agricultural plan called for expenditure of $3 million annually. This included everything from a million-dollar dam on the Pangani River to boreholes for individual farmers. The largest single agricultural project was the opening of a 25,000-acre sugar plantation and refinery in the Kilombero Valley between Dar es Salaam and Lake Nyasa. With $10 million in British, American and Dutch capital behind it, the plantation expected eventually to supply the sugar needs of the country.

To direct the Three-Year Plan's $10-million development program in education, Premier Nyerere had assigned the president of the Council of the Chagga tribes, Solomon Nkya Eliufoo, as the new Minister of Education. He was richly qualified for the task. A graduate of Makerere College in Uganda, of Bethany College in Kansas, U.S.A., and of England's Bristol University, he had taught at Makerere and had been an education officer.

Chief Eliufoo announced at once an end to school segregation. The colonial racial system of education would be abolished as quickly as schools could practicably be integrated. As an example, the Chief reorganized the Ministry itself, which had been divided into African and non-African sections. They became the primary, secondary and technical education sections. The Minister also decentralized the system, turning over to local authorities much of the responsibility for schooling in their own areas.

The plan called for emphasis on secondary education so that Tanganyika could train a pool of administrators and educators. Chief Eliufoo promptly gave his Ministry the goal of increasing high-school enrollment by 1964. To get higher education underway he earmarked $2.5 million for a new University College in Dar es Salaam. Construction was to begin as soon as architects' plans could be drawn. In the meantime, classes would start immediately in temporary accommodations.

The youngest and lowest-financed ministry taking part in the Three-Year Plan was the Ministry for Cooperative and Community Development. But burly Jeremiah Kasambala served immediate notice that it would have a vital role in the campaign against ignorance and poverty. "We will be the government's commando unit," vowed Kasambala. "On the cooperative side we will be spearheads in the struggle, translating into economic terms our leader's philosophy of African socialism. In the sphere of community development we will bring literacy to the people and show them that self-help can be a major factor in the building of our nation." His Ministry received $150,000 to build a training center for development workers at Tengeru, at the foot of Mount Meru, and $75,000 for community centers. Another $200,000 was for materials—cement, lumber, tools—for village self-help projects.

Much of the Three-Year Plan was already in effect when Tanganyika became formally independent on December 9, 1961. The event called for celebration and there were stirring ceremonies, but, politically, little was expected to distinguish the new period from the months of self-government just passed. The ceremonies included the handing over of the colors of the Tanganyika Regiment of the King's African Rifles to the newly formed Tanganyika Rifles, and placement of the new green, black and gold flag of independent Tanganyika on the summit of Kilimanjaro, while, at the capital, the Union Jack was lowered. Prince Philip was in Dar es Salaam representing the Queen and Mr. Duncan Sandys was there for the Colonial Office. There were no racial or political incidents to mar the day.

That same week Prime Minister Nyerere and his Minister without Portfolio, Rashidi Kawawa, flew to New York and heard both the Security Council and the General Assembly approve of Tanganyika's application for membership in the United Nations.

Nyerere spoke briefly at the UN of his country's aims: "The basis of our actions, internal and external, will be an attempt, an honest attempt, to honor the dignity of man. We believe that all mankind is one, that the physiological differences between us are unimportant in comparison to our common humanity. We believe that black skin or white, straight or curly hair, differences in the shape of our bodies, do not alter or even affect the fact that each one of us is part of the human species and has a part to play in the development of mankind."

That statement was pure Nyerere. So, too, was the action he took one month later, though it startled the world and most of his own people. On January 22, 1962, Nyerere abruptly resigned as Prime Minister. Rashidi Kawawa, he said, would be the new Premier.

Nyerere quashed before it could get started any speculation that he had been forced out of office. He had resigned, he said, to work full time on making TANU the instrument through which Tanganyika could attain its national objectives.

"We know," he said in a statement, "that it is unusual for a Prime Minister to step down from his position as a leader of the government to undertake the leadership of a party. But we do not believe it is necessary for us to copy the institutions of other countries. We believe that we must work out our own patterns of democracy and that the step we have announced today is the best way to proceed at the present."

This was not only an article of faith in the power and place of

TANU, but it was one of Nyerere's first pronouncements of his belief in the validity of a democratic, one-party state. In subsequent statements he elaborated on the policy. He contended that where there is one party, identified with and endorsed by the nation as a whole, as in Tanganyika, the foundations of democracy were firmer and the people had more opportunity to exercise a real choice than where there were two or more parties, each representing only a section of the community.

Once a single party had been fully accepted, he argued, it was best to dispense with the disciplines of the multiparty or factional system, because such disciplines limit freedom of expression. For instance, under the factional system, a party member had sometimes to swallow his own convictions and, for the appearance of unity, publicly follow the "party line." This, said Nyerere, elevates the party line to the category of dogma. He wrote:

And this is not unlike what has befallen our friends the Communists. They have made their policies a creed and are finding that dogmatism and freedom of discussion do not easily go together. They are as much afraid of the "other party" as any government in a two-party democracy. In their case the "other party" is only a phantom, but a phantom can be even more frightening than a living rival! And their fear of this phantom has blinded them to the truth that, in a one-party system, party membership must be open to everybody and freedom of expression allowed to every individual. No party which limits its membership to a clique can ever free itself from the fear of overthrow by those it has excluded.

A national movement which is open to all and identified with the whole nation has nothing to fear from the discontent of any excluded section of society, for there is then no such section. Those forming the government will, of course, be replaced from time to time; this is what elections are for. The leadership of our movement is constantly changing; there is no reason why the leadership of the national should not also be constantly changing.

Any member of the movement, which means any patriotic citizen, would be free to stand as a candidate if he so wished. And in each constituency the voters themselves would be able to make their choice freely from among these candidates; they would no longer be obliged to consider a party label rather than an individual. Of such elections it could truly be said that they were for the purpose of letting the people choose their own representatives. If that is not democracy, I do not know the meaning of the word!

The claim is made that a factional party candidate once he has been elected should represent *all* his constituents impartially. How the poor fellow is expected to "represent" that section of his constituents whose main interest lies in hoping for the early defeat of his party by their own party is not quite clear!

Try to imagine an eighteenth century Scottish Covenanter politely listening to the problems of a group of Jacobites, and agreeing "to take the matter up" on their behalf, and you will see what I mean!

But an advocate of a one-party system, in which the party is identified with the nation as a national movement, can admit the identity of the government with the movement without any embarrassment at all. And if he happens to be an MP he is spared the necessity of turning mental somersaults on every journey between his constituency and the Parliament!

It can be assumed that Julius Nyerere did not take these refinements of his policy out into the country as he went about his task that year of strengthening the TANU structure nationally. Rather, he met everywhere with the new regional and area commissioners and concentrated on party organization. In villages he helped form TANU committees and elect local chairmen. It was as a result of Nyerere's painstaking, almost evangelical, tour of the bush that TANU later could boast of party representation in every one of the country's 7,500 villages and hamlets.

Back in the capital Prime Minister Kawawa announced that he would carry on with much the same cabinet that had been formed after independence. In many ways, he let it be known that Julius Nyerere was still "Father of the Country" and "Our Commander-in-Chief." He recalled that in 1957 when he and Nyerere were nominated to Legco and Nyerere subsequently resigned, he himself remained to exert pressure on the Council from inside while Nyerere worked politically from the outside. Now the partnership was operating in much the same way.

Kawawa also revealed that his government was taking steps toward making Tanganyika a republic. As such, he said, she would remain within the Commonwealth. Details for establishment of the republic were debated in the National Assembly in February. It was decided that the republic would have an executive president, to be elected first by national popular vote but later to be linked with the National Assembly elections so that he might have the support of the legislature.

There was no doubt in Dar es Salaam who the first president would be.

When it was announced that formal declaration of the republic would take place on December 9, 1962, Nyerere returned to Dar es Salaam for the presidential elections in November. There was one other candidate—the African National Congress die-hard, Zuberi Mtemvu, who had attracted 58 votes in the 1958 election. But Nyerere won the presidency as though by national acclamation. He took more than 98 per cent of the 1,100,000 votes cast.

It was time for a firm hand to take the helm. It wasn't that Kawawa, whom Nyerere at once appointed as his republican vice-president, or any of his ministers, had been deficient. Rather, it seemed that the fates had determined to wreck their Three-Year Plan. Nature, in particular, had turned against them. The 1961-62 crops were hit by the worst drought of the century. Maize crops, upon which the nation depended for its very survival, had shriveled almost to nothing. Lack of this basic food affected all agricultural production. Thousands of head of livestock died on the hoof. A half million people went on famine rolls.

Funds that were to go into development projects went instead to feed the hungry—six million dollars already had been spent. Food was sought from abroad. The United States gave $2 million worth of corn and more than a million in powdered milk. The Tanganyikan government spent another half million importing maize from neighboring Rhodesia and Nyasaland.

The results of natural disaster spread into the beginning years of the republic. Finance Minister Bomani ruefully reported that for the first time he must present a deficit budget. He said the growth of national income was less than one tenth of normal. He reported that export trade had been crippled, that sisal and coffee export values were badly cut (coffee by one third). There was a diminishing world market for cotton, and prices on the Tanganyika auction were the lowest ever. The mining industry was declining and there was talk of the Geita gold mine closing down for good.

President Nyerere faced other trouble. The civil servant problem continued to plague him. As rapidly as seemed safe he had allowed Africanization of government offices. But the pressure to accelerate the pace was constant. He resisted it not only because he feared a breakdown of services, but because it had the ugly smell of a new racialism. "It would be wrong for us to continue to distinguish between Tanganyikan citizens on any ground other than character and ability," he told impatient TANU followers. "We cannot allow the growth of first-class and second-class citizenship."

Some of the party faithful grumbled that this was only feeding fuel to groups like the old African National Congress, which had extreme views about nationalization. Another group, calling themselves the People's Democratic Party, demanded that the government legislate all lands to Africans.

The labor unions, too, were restive. The Tanganyika Federation of Labor chided the government when legislation was proposed to govern labor relations. The new TFL general secretary, R. J. Magongo, published a protest in which he said: "We appreciate and are well aware of the government's duty to protect and develop the economy of the country. But such onus rests not only on the government but also on the employers, workers and citizens as a whole." At a TANU national executive meeting the TFL demanded not only that Africanization be speeded up but that something drastic be done about increasing national wages.

Then the military acted. Two years after freedom, the 1,600-strong Tanganyika Rifles were still under British officers and they, more than anyone, wanted Africanization. They felt that Nyerere's policy could mean indefinite postponement of promised promotions to officer rank. The soldiers were in a mood for rebellion.

On the night of January 12, 1964, as if to light the fuse, revolt broke out in Zanzibar, the tiny spice island twenty miles off the coast almost opposite Dar es Salaam. Rebel Africans, held down by the ruling Sultan and the Arab-controlled Zanzibar Nationalist Party, seized the police armory and government offices. The Sultan fled the island. Five hundred Arabs who resisted were killed and the Afro-Shirazi Party took over. It appeared very simple.

Men of the Tanganyika Rifles, at least, seemed to think so. Eight days later they tried the same tactics, though fortunately their aims were more modest. Soldiers from Colito Barracks, five miles outside Dar es Salaam, moved in on the capital, commandeered government buildings, the airport and the radio station. Once they had occupied these places of importance, the troops took no further action.

It was then realized that they did not intend to take over; they wanted only to negotiate. Oscar Kambona, to his credit, went to deal with them. Most of them returned to their barracks when he promised that their demands for better pay and replacement of the British officers would be considered. Some, however, stayed in town and touched off rioting and looting of Asian shops that night that resulted in seventeen deaths.

For the rest of the week the government tried to come to terms with the troops, but, apparently regretting that they had already passed up an opportunity to seize power, the soldiers were now demanding conditions that amounted to blackmail. After a night conference with his ministers, Nyerere reached the painful decision to request British troops to come and help. They came at once. Landed by helicopter, a force of Royal Marine Commandos surrounded Colito Barracks and disarmed the mutinous battalion. The Tanganyika Rifles were disbanded and reorganized with recruits drawn largely from TANU youth and with African officers in command. Though the whole country and neighboring states had rallied around to assure the government of their support, it had been, in Nyerere's words, "a shameful experience."

These untoward events of early 1964 had focused world attention on East Africa. The foreign press speculated particularly on the meaning of the Zanzibar take-over. Missions from Russia and East Germany already had arrived there and were busily negotiating projects on the island. Some of the Afro-Shirazi Party leaders were making statements derived unmistakably from Communist sources. In Washington and London the question was asked: "Is this island going to be Africa's Cuba?"

Julius Nyerere did little to comfort them when only weeks later, on April 25, he made his first appearance before his National Assembly as President, and announced blandly that Tanganyika and Zanzibar were joining in a united republic. Asking the Assembly to ratify the agreement, he said that history and geography argued for the union, though foreign governments might not. The agreement was ratified, with cheers.

Thus the old dominions of former Arab sultans were brought together again and, despite the apprehension in Western quarters, the union appeared a harmonious one in the months that followed. Rashidi Kawawa, man of many portfolios, took another post. He became second vice-president of the Republic of Tanzania, for that was the name later agreed upon for the union. The Zanzibar chief of the Afro-Shirazi Party, Sheikh Abeid Karume, formerly an island boatman, became first vice-president. President Nyerere reshuffled the cabinet, naming three Zanzibarians as ministers. All of his TANU circle remained in key posts.

For the latter group, at this juncture, the affairs of Zanzibar rated, at the most, only secondary consideration. They were too much absorbed in planning. Lights were blazing late at night again in Ministry offices. This time it was something so big that other government matters dwindled almost to unimportance.

The Three-Year Plan was over and it had failed; that was conceded. Most of the development goals had not been met. Many of the projects were now seen as having been unrealistic. The vagaries of nature had not been sufficiently accounted for, though it was agreed that the plan failed principally because it was based too much on colonial concepts. It had been primarily a compilation of ministerial programs, which did not involve the nation enough. Where it had, where the people had been called upon to share in nation-building, there had been success, sensational success. "There has been a quiet revolution," said Julius Nyerere, describing it, "and its heroes are the people."

This was the element that excited the planners in 1964. They were completing a fresh design for the country's future, but this time it was based on bold new concepts. It was a people's plan. It was called the "Five-Year Plan for Economic and Social Development" but now not ministries but the nation would be wholly committed.

President Nyerere emphasized this on May 12 in presenting this plan to the National Assembly. "This is as vital to the future of our union as the attainment of independence itself. Independence asserted our dignity and established our opportunity. This opportunity has now to be used and it will require the active participation of every member of our society. This plan is a declaration of war and every one of us is a soldier."

The scope of the plan was enormous. It was a $700-million program that reached into every corner of the country. It involved a corps of engineers, an army of educators, technicians and professional people —the bulk of them to be imported. It called for vast construction projects, rural resettlement and urban industrialization. But most important of all, it involved the people. It would reach down to the inhabitants of every town and village and mobilize them into a national force that would be the final and decisive factor in whether the plan and the country were going to succeed or fail.

A heavy investment was being made in the technique supposed to effect this popular mobilization. The technique was a relatively new one, but it had made some parts of the Three-Year Plan glow with promise. The technique was called community development. To understand fully the formulation and the spirit of the new plan it is necessary to know some background of the technique itself.

CHAPTER FIVE

THE TECHNIQUE

Opinion on community development ranges from rhapsodic praise to rudest contempt. The 1960 U.S. Social Work Report spoke extravagantly of its accomplishments in America: "Community development is one of the most significant and far-flung economic and social movements of modern time, or in fact, of human history." In Tanganyika, Jackson H. Saileni spoke bluntly for the opposition. General Secretary of the African National Congress, Mr. Saileni, during a speech in Mwanza in 1962, described self-help, which is the essence of community development, as "forced labor."

The truth lies somewhere in between. Jeremiah Kasambala, President Nyerere's Minister for Cooperative and Community Development, had a practical and simple definition: "It is a process by which small communities can be induced to set about the task of improving their standards of living by their own efforts and under their own leadership, guided by trained staff and assisted where necessary by technical and material aid."

The operative word is "induce." Development in every case involves change and it is the CD worker's job to induce it. As the agent of change he deals primarily with tensions, for it is tension which makes people act and the reduction of tension which produces satisfaction. The CD worker's role becomes somewhat Machiavellian: he increases tension by heightening people's dissatisfaction with their existing circumstances so that they become conscious of their wants; then he helps them find ways of reducing the tensions thus aroused. Usually it is an alteration in custom that is involved and this is always a sensitive operation, for the future of a community, sometimes of generations of people, can be affected by such changes.

The case of the Yir Yoront aborigines is an example of social change that backfired. The steel ax was introduced to the aborigines who lived in Queensland, Australia, and whose most important tool had been the stone ax. The stone ax was made only by male elders and was presented at initiation feasts and other ceremonies. Axes remained the property of the older men and a symbol of their authority. Younger people had to come and borrow; it gave them respect for the aged. Then a Queensland mission brought in a wholesale lot of steel axes which were distributed at Christmas either as gifts or in return for work done. Most of them went to the young folk, who found them sharper and longer-lasting than stone. Even women and children had some and did not need to borrow from husbands or fathers. Generally, ownership became less identified. Stealing became commoner. Initiation feasts lost their meaning as the granting of stone axes was no longer a ceremonial climax. This in turn weakened the structure of their totemic religion. There resulted a serious cultural disintegration and individual demoralization. All because of the new ax.

A happier illustration was the change effected in a Rhodesian village. A community development worker found a seriously high child mortality rate in the village and traced its cause to a polluted well. The village had no latrines and rain waters were draining into the well. Before urging the villagers to build a new one the CD worker asked questions. He found the old folk adamant against any change; they had been drinking from this well all their lives. The worker knew that the young people, when the situation was explained to them, would insist on a new well. But this could create a village schism and disintegration of the community.

The CD man found projects on which all the village would agree. They decided on a new road, and technical aid was arranged to help them. Old and young worked together on a new school. Then came an epidemic of pig cholera. The CD worker brought in an extension agent to vaccinate the pigs. When their pigs were saved and other villages lost theirs, the old men said: "If we can save our pigs, why not our children?" They asked for help in rebuilding the well. The area around the old well was filled in, proper drainage was provided, and laundry facilities were added to the well, which was now sanitary. Resistance to change had been overcome without damage.

Another case, reported from the Sudan, was less successful. In a campaign to stamp out a disease which could be traced to the vermin-infested tents of rural villagers, the government prepared to move a whole community into rows of mud houses erected for them. It took both force and persuasion, but the move finally was effected. The authorities, pleased at first, were later confounded when it was discovered that the community had indeed moved in toto: each mud hut had the occupant's old tent erected inside it.

One of the earliest proponents of community development was Mahatma Gandhi, who recognized that India's greatest resource was the people who lived in villages and tilled the soil. He urged the nation to rebuild, with its 558,000 villages as the foundation. It was on the 84th anniversary of Gandhi's birth—October 2, 1952—that Pandit Nehru launched what he himself described as "the most gigantic effort in human history consciously to change the life conditions of a nation by democratic means." It was the attempt to unite India's 400 million villagers with government for a physical and social rebuilding of that ancient land. It was all to be done through community development.

A Ministry of Community Development was created and a central committee, with the Prime Minister as chairman, appointed to guide the plan. But it was appreciated that the success of the plan rested with the *panchayats*, the hundreds of thousands of village councils. In the *panchayat* the key man was the *gram sevat*, the CD worker who lived in the village. He promoted the principle that the village was a vital unit of society, to which government services should be delivered in a coordinated, integrated way rather than as separate functions of the health, agricultural, education and other official departments. Much of the CD worker's task was to gear the specialist services of these departments into village life as intimately and effectively as possible.

Administratively, each hundred or so villages, with a total population of about 65,000, was regarded as a block, for which there was a development officer and specialist staff. The blocks were grouped into districts, with a district development committee chaired by the government collector, who was the ranking official in the district. The districts, in turn, came under a state development committee headed by a commissioner of development. The commissioners carried out the directives of Premier Nehru's central committee.

Ten years after the program's conception Nehru described India's community projects as "the bright, vital and dynamic sparks from which radiate rays of energy, hope and enthusiasm." He said it was the most important thing being done in India. Knowledgeable observers agreed, but were less ecstatic about the results. The great bulk of village India had not yet caught the vision of the leaders. The CD workers were meeting resistance from the technicians who favored a more bureaucratic approach to village services. The nation-wide organization was bogging down, too, under bureaucracy. But there was evidence that the gap between philosophy and practice was closing and a genuine partnership between government and people was being realized.

Two years after India's program began, the Philippines embarked on a brave CD program. President Magsaysay appointed a dynamic individual, Ramon P. Binamira, as Presidential Assistant on Community Development. The program was a success from the start. Binamira organized a corps of 1,600 CD workers whom he called his "peaceful bandits." He demanded that they be noisy, cocky and aggressive. Their first assignment was to go into the *barrios* and join the villagers in digging ditches, planting rice and in other everyday jobs. The CD workers later sat on the *barrio* councils and it was largely through their efforts that these village councils were incorporated in 1960 as legal bodies and *barrio* assemblies, made up of all the local villagers. This brought authentic local government into 23,000 villages—a striking community development achievement.

In the fifties and sixties experiments in CD were going on elsewhere in Asia, in South America, the Middle East and other corners of the globe. In some areas they were abundantly successful, in others unimpressive or even disastrous. But there was little question that the technique of community development had achieved world-wide recognition.

A process such as CD was readily adopted in a land like Tanganyika where communal philosophy had long underlain its way of life, and where group endeavor had been practiced throughout history by most of the tribes. Among the Hehe (where community development was known as *lutananu*), when a village agreed to work on a project everyone participated or was penalized. A nonworker's goats might be slaughtered on the spot and the meat distributed among the villagers who were working.

In Swahili it was called *ujamaa*. "In the African's own structure of society," explained Julius Nyerere, "the individual is a member of a kind of fellowship. His community for him is an extension of his family. He regards all men as brethren—as members of his ever-extending family. *Ujamaa* is familyhood."

It was a spirit that permeated all tribal life. When a family's hut was destroyed in a storm or by a falling tree, villagers pitched in to rebuild it. When a family sat down for a meal and a stranger appeared, he was invited to join in. This was *ujamaa*. It was akin to the clan spirit of the Scotsmen, of Irish tribes, and of American pioneers. But the Bantu's *ujamaa* was violated by the slave trade and colonial rule. In Tanganyika, Nyerere hoped to revive *ujamaa* as part of the new spirit of nationhood—and community development was the ideal method.

Tanganyika's history of community development began in 1945 when a three-man social welfare office was set up to organize community centers for the 68,000 returning African war veterans. For construction costs, a grant of $150,000 was received from the Colonial Development and Welfare Fund.

By 1946 there were large centers in Dar es Salaam, Tanga, Tabora, Ujiji and Mwanza, and smaller ones in twenty other communities. Most were staffed by local volunteers. Unfortunately the centers did not attract many veterans, for they preferred to return to family, tribal and village life. But others, principally clerks and urban workmen, did gather and the centers became lively places. The canteens were leased out to enterprising Africans, and beer began to flow.

Music, dances and performances were offered. Most popular were the *vichekesho,* spontaneous stage sketches that lampooned tribal and racial manners. It was a type of buffoonery recalling the Elizabethan stage. When these performances began to include *nach* dances, sensuous posturing accompanied by bawdy songs, the welfare officers hastily forbade them.

More constructively, adult education classes were started, with government schoolteachers and clerks as voluntary instructors. Women began to use the centers, gathering for sewing classes in the afternoons. In 1950 a Social Development Department was organized under the Ministry of Local Government to direct the expanding recreational program. Headed by a commissioner, the department was staffed by five European officers (two of them women) and twenty-three African welfare workers and assistants.

In 1952, one of the department's officers, an Irishman named Hugh McGairl, led a significant breakthrough in the Dar es Salaam program. Claiming that the programs at the centers were not attracting urban workers, he decided to bring the classes to them. He went to the townships where they lived. Classes were organized in nine areas, with groups of 50 or so enrolled. For a nominal fee the workmen received a primer and pencil. Courses lasted from four to eight months.

At Kinondoni, just north of Dar es Salaam, a class of 36, which met under the trees, completed their Swahili course and then wanted to continue with one in English. They built a school and furnished it with seats. Later a radio was installed and it became a township listening post for courses broadcast by the Social Development Department. Another class at Kinondoni, made up of dock workers, built a larger school. They used it from 5 to 6:30 P.M., and allowed classes for women and children to be held there during the day. Another township group was made up of craftsmen—carpenters, blacksmiths and masons—who could read some Swahili but wanted to learn some arithmetic for use in their trades. Classes were started and they also learned simple geometry and the use of drawing instruments.

All this was a happy revelation to Mr. McGairl. In a project report at the time, he was inspired to write: "Becoming literate as an adult in this African society is a spiritual experience in some ways related to the emergence and growth of personality. People are uplifted by it, and are made aware of their power to alter their environment by individual and group action." McGairl's could be a charter statement for the community development movement of any area.

By 1954 the literacy classes were being used throughout the country to spearhead various development projects. Groups of women, now literate, joined sewing clubs, crafts and domestic science classes. In the men's classes, the social development workers occasionally led the villagers to ask themselves why they had not repaired the bridge or a well or why they hadn't extended their road to the one in the next village. They provided the answer by proceeding to work on the project.

The preceding year the Social Development Department had stationed an officer in Pare, a mountainous habitation between Dar es Salaam and Moshi, to conduct a pilot community program. By the end of 1954, twelve roads had been built in Pare, averaging five miles each; 37 wells had been hygienically protected; 1,272 literacy certificates awarded to students, with thousands more having achieved rudimentary literacy. The women had organized thirty-five clubs, and a district newssheet, teaching better land usage, was being published. Many of the village's young girls, upon reaching puberty, would by tribal custom have remained hidden in dark huts until they were given in marriage. Now, as club members, they attended classes in arithmetic, child care, music and other studies.

The best proof that the self-help technique was being recognized and accepted came when native authorities began to appropriate funds from their slim reserves to aid the projects. In 1956, the Chagga Council appointed a Committee for Social Development and budgeted $13,000 for self-help supplies. The Masama Council voted to forego a government allotment of $350 for entertainment beer and to re-budget the money for CD work in the chiefdom. The people of four tribes in the Moshi district contributed funds for materials and joined in building an embankment to divert waters of the Kiluletwa River to irrigate their land. The fine hand of the local community development worker could be detected behind the project.

In nearby Arusha, the CD worker inspired a settlement of Masai warriors to plan and build a bridge across a river that isolated them from farmers who could supply them with honey. For several months afterward the district was beguiled by the sight of the haughty Masai (who normally had only contempt for such labor) carrying stone, sand

and cement for a sturdy, two-span bridge over the turbulent river. Such victories were indeed sweet to the CD workers in the field.

Further evidence that the community work principle was winning acceptance came when the cattle-breeding Turu tribe around Singida (just south of Masailand) requested a literacy campaign amongst its people. The social development commissioner in Dar es Salaam might well have had some reservations about sending a team of his young officers, for the Turu were a quarrelsome, murderous lot, living on the barest of subsistence levels. But in mid-1958 four CD workers presented themselves to the district commissioner at Singida. The DC, at the behest of the tribe, had already appointed an advisory district committee to supervise the project. The committee included the six Turu chiefs, some mission workers in the area, and prominent tribesmen. The CD team leader became executive officer of the group.

There were a total of 88,292 adult Turu in the six chiefdoms, living in 300 scattered villages. Each village was made up of three or four hamlets of about 100 inhabitants. Although the Turu spoke their own Bantu dialect, there was a mixture of Nilo-Hamitic and even Hottentot blood in the tribe. It was the Turu system of inheritance that caused much of the friction and quarrels. Though men of all the hamlets claimed a common local ancestor, brothers inherited land and cattle unequally according to whether they were the senior, junior or middle sons of one wife; or, even more markedly, according to whether they were the sons of senior or junior wives. This gave each hamlet a different footing, and, combined with the scarcity of good grazing land, produced friction that often led to assault and murder. Otherwise, they were a cheerful, even gay people, fond of dancing and singing.

Perhaps as a relief from their resentments, the Turu welcomed all strangers. The villagers knew that witchcraft operated only within the tribe, so that anyone coming from outside, together with the food he brought, was regarded as harmless. So the CD team found themselves greeted at Singida with delighted curiosity, invited into homes and urged to embark on long accounts of their recent experiences.

The team's first task was to recruit teachers. These were found among young men of each village who had had at least four years of schooling. Given a short training course by a CD assistant, the teacher would take a class and receive fifteen shillings (about two dollars) a month. Each student was supplied with a literacy kit, consisting of a reader, *Twende Tusome (Let's Go and Read)*, a writing primer and exercise book, and a pencil with eraser attached. For these each student paid 25 cents. The reading primer was the product of ten years of experiment. It presented whole words or phrases, broke them down into syllables and then re-formed the syllables into different patterns of words or phrases. The syllables were introduced according to their frequency rate in Swahili. The teachers were also equipped with a guide containing lesson notes and hints on teaching adults.

Most of the classes were held in the open air under trees. Soon, however, each hamlet had its own *banda,* a flat-roofed building of mud and wattle, where the groups of thirty or forty pupils gathered. The women students far outnumbered the men. This was not surprising for in many ways the women dominated the life of the tribe, partly because of the importance of fertility: a woman's status was measured by the number of her children, especially sons.

As intended, the literacy classes led to other study groups, particularly among the women. But tribal superstition often stood in the way of progress. In teaching simple nutrition, the CD assistants had to overcome the Turu prejudice against eating eggs. The tribe's women raised chickens by the thousands but sold the eggs in the market. They believed that if they ate the eggs and then failed to bear children, they would be accused of witchcraft. So eggs were out. They also had household beliefs that defied rules of sanitation. When water was short in the dry season, one practice called for cleaning cooking pots with cow urine. These were typical of the tasks facing CD workers at Singida.

A staff worker's account of one of the first cooking classes at Singida is included in the Social Development Department's annual report for 1959. The description is somewhat reminiscent of the garden party in *Alice in Wonderland:*

At an early hour the firewood and water were ready, brought by a group of excited women, who had also brought small quantities of peanuts and beans and their own cooking utensils. About a dozen older men sat a little way off, talking and smoking water-pipes.

When the staff arrived it was found that the shelter was too small, and the men were asked to enlarge it before the next lesson. They replied that they preferred to do it at once, and women and utensils were scattered while the roof was pulled down over their heads and re-erected.

An attempt was now made to divide the women into groups so that all could see the demonstration and take part in the cooking, but the shelter was still too small for the eighty-odd women who had arrived—many of them not from the literacy group at all—and while different dishes were being demonstrated by the three different instructors they all wanted to see how to make each dish. In consequence, there was much running to and fro in order to see every process for every dish. In addition, the headman's wife, possibly jealous of an unwonted lack of interest in herself, decided that this was the time for a private literacy lesson.

Meanwhile, the crowd was continually being added to by both men and women from other villages, who because of the open nature of the country could see what was happening from far on the horizon. They were greeted heartily and also crowded around, but when they found they could not see they turned away and started spontaneous dancing groups to while away the time.

While the staff struggled through the crowd to show the finished products, women who wished to demonstrate to the others how wide their acquaintance was among the visitors, rushed forward and flung their arms around them, shouting "My friends!" The visitors showed no reluctance to try the food; indeed it proved difficult to save any for the women, who started to complain loudly that this was their business, not the men's.

Every scrap was quickly divided and vanished, before some of the class had even had a chance to study or sample it. Comments on the small quantity of food were now passed and everyone looked puzzled and expectant. It was now clear that the group had considered the demonstration as something of a work-party, after which the workers should be abundantly rewarded with food. Indeed, one woman demanded the distribution of the balance of stores intended for future demonstrations. It took some time to explain, but it ended happily, with everyone promising to return for the next lesson. We on the staff had already decided that next time some different methods would be attempted.

Nevertheless, the Singida cooking lessons proved highly successful. Women of the villages were amazed to learn of the many things that could be done with the lowly peanut. For one thing, when pounded into a paste it made an ideal substitute for butter, which they were always reluctant to eat because it was used for religious rites having to do with fertility, and because it was much favored as a cosmetic.

Two of the CD team were at nearby Nkhava one day for a cooking class and pointed out that the village dam had gone nearly dry and was dirtied by roaming cattle. They warned the women of the danger in using this water. A village elder heard this and called the men together. Forty of them went to work and in a few weeks the village had its first deep well.

At Dung'unji, a village near Singida, the cooking classes pointed up the need of a village center. The people decided to build a meeting hall and a resthouse for strangers. In August they began making mud bricks for the buildings, with the women carrying the water in gourds from the well and the men working the clay. An elder provided the workers with beer brewed from millet. The CD staff arranged to have roofing materials provided by Singida authorities. By December the buildings were in use.

Another result of the cooking classes was the planting of new crops to provide vegetables the women needed for the new dishes. Two of the tribe's warriors, who had taken the literacy course, offered to go about the villages to determine what seeds were wanted and how much could be raised to buy them. The warriors set out with a notebook in one hand, and a spear in the other. They were proud to show off their new talents and for weeks went about making their census. Using his companion's back for a table, one would ceremoniously write the order, as a villager gave it. In November they turned in a list that included most of the foods introduced—garlic, tomatoes, eggplant, spinach, European potato, cabbage and a dozen others. A total of ninety dollars had been pledged for seed which was bought and distributed in time for the February planting.

There were many other results reported at Singida. A census of the classes showed that 40,395 had taken the literacy courses; 12,710 men, 27,685 women. Many groups had gone on to "advanced learning" classes. Some studied arithmetic, history and geography; a few studied English. Three thousand women had taken the cooking courses.

Probably most important, because they found continuing reasons for staying together, were the literacy groups, which for the first time provided the Turu with a somewhat permanent institution at the hamlet level. The building could also serve as a common point of reference for the whole tribe, since it took virtually the same form in every place. Thus the classroom *bandas* had become centers in a hamlet-network of radiating tracks. For this restive tribe, the groups had become a healthy, cohesive factor.

In Dar es Salaam the next year, 1960, official recognition was given to the contribution that work in communities such as Singida could make for national government. The Social Development Department became the Community Development Department and was made part of the Ministry of Local Government. A definition of its work was put into the records:

> Community development includes all the processes by which the efforts of the people themselves are united with those of the central and local governments and voluntary bodies to improve the economic, social, political and cultural life of the communities, and to integrate these communities into the life of the nation and so enable them to contribute fully to national progress.

The Three-Year Plan from 1961 to 1964 provided the new department an opportunity to show what a key role community development could play in the young nation's hopes for the future. But while the potential was convincingly demonstrated, the investment was so meager that it could at best be only a demonstration. The department, allotted merely 1 per cent of the Three-Year Plan budget, had a total staff of only 144 workers who were reaching only fifteen of the country's 57 districts.

In 1962 there came a major breakthrough. Jeremiah Kasambala was assigned to reorganize both the cooperative and community development programs, which he would thenceforth direct as a new ministry. In the National Assembly budget debate that June, he announced that the government would double the size of the Community Development Department, with an additional half-million dollars provided for expansion. Personally, he was utterly confident about what CD could accomplish. In a typical Kasambala statement, he told fellow MPs: "We've got a box of matches here and we're going to set the country afire!" Announcing the rapid expansion of the CD training program at Tenguru, the Minister paid tribute to the workers already in the field "laboring untiringly in the dust and discomfort of remote places."

A second tribute to what CD was accomplishing was paid by Vice-President Kawawa when he announced, at the same Assembly session, the new national plan for village development. Each of the 7,500 communities in the country was being asked to organize a village development committee to guide local improvement efforts. These, Kawawa emphasized, would not be merely local groups carrying on isolated self-help projects. Rather, they would be part of a national network which would promote agricultural production, health education, school attendance, public works and all activity that would make for improved living.

Planning and services directed by the village committees would be coordinated by district development committees, the district programs in turn by regional committees, and the over-all national plan by President Nyerere's Economic Development Commission. To service this complex network, Kawawa said, there would be community development officers at regional, district and, so far as possible, village levels. "But in the last analysis," the Vice-President told the National Assembly, "this is a people's plan. Without everyone's effort it is nothing. We are calling upon every villager to join with the government as a team in undertaking this task of building the nation from below."

Still further recognition of the promise of CD came later in the year when organization of the privately financed Tanganyika Community Development Trust Fund was announced. The driving force behind the new program was a remarkable and imaginative woman— Marion, the Lady Chesham—who had also seen community development as the soundest base upon which Tanganyika's future could be built.

Certain of this vision, Lady Chesham had plunged wholeheartedly into the work of demonstrating what CD could do. With funds raised largely in America, Lady Chesham assisted pilot CD projects in rural areas, gearing her plans to the government program. In 1963 Lady Chesham turned over her magnificent home and 500 acres of the estate in Iringa to the Community Development Department for a training school for women CD workers. The following year, she turned over the remaining 1,000 acres and all the farm buildings and equipment to her farm laborers to be run as a cooperative venture for themselves.

But with all these advances the years of the Three-Year Plan continued to be, as it were, a training and demonstration period for the gigantic community development effort that was to come. It was rather like a great military force being mobilized, armed and trained with the expectation of combat soon to be faced.

The big CD push finally came the day in June 1964 when Julius Nyerere announced Tanganyika's $700-million Five-Year Plan and revealed to what a tremendous extent it was based on the principle of community development.

It was an exciting but sobering challenge to put to a staff of workers so freshly recruited and trained, and a dramatic test for a principle that could be regarded as still in its pilot stage. But the die was cast. In mid-1964 the CD army moved into position for the crucial campaign.

CHAPTER SIX

THE PLAN

As Minister of the new Directorate of Development and Planning, Nsilo Swai presented the Five-Year Plan to the National Assembly in May 1964. Following Swai's formal presentation, President Nyerere rose to summarize the program and to remind the MPs of its audacity: "Few countries," he pointed out, "have tried to do so much from such a poor base." He noted that the estimated yearly income per person in Tanganyika was then $57.84; by 1980 it was to be raised to $126. Non-Tanganyikans then were doing all the professional and managerial work in the republic. By 1980 Tanganyika would supply her own trained manpower. The life span of the people was barely 35 years. By 1980 it must be 50. Though here was the first of three five-year plans, it indeed took a great stride toward these objectives.

To achieve them, said Nyerere, the biggest requirement would be increased production of agricultural crops, of manufactured goods. "If we produce more meat our people can have a better diet. If we catch more fish the people's health will improve. And if we produce more sisal, cotton and coffee we get more money from overseas with which to buy the other things we want." There were two routes, he said, to increased agricultural production.

One was the "improvement approach," a joint campaign by agricultural extension and community development workers among the nearly ten million peasant farmers. The CD worker would "by adult education, exhortation and example enlighten both men and women on possibilities of attaining a different, higher and more satisfying standard of living." This cultivated desire of the farmer for a better life would be translated into efforts to acquire the money income to satisfy new material and social needs. The farmer would look to the extension workers for the technical advice to improve productivity, to government agencies for agricultural credit, and to the marketing facilities offered by cooperatives. Thus farmers might be elevated from a subsistence to an income life.

The other route was the "transformation approach." This called for the regrouping and resettling of farmers in the most favorable production areas, and introduction of a system of private and collective ownership, supervised crop rotation and mixed farming.

"These would be new village settlements to be established all over the country," Nyerere explained. "By 1980 we expect to have about one million people living and working on them. Half a million of them, particularly people from the more densely populated parts of the country where land hunger is beginning to show, will be engaged in opening up the Kilombero, Pangani and Wami River basins. These are fertile lands, now lying almost unused. The effect of such settlement will be far-reaching, for planned settlement does not mean only farms. It also means roads, commerce and some local industries, as well as schools for the children and health centers to help people enjoy the new life they are creating."

A total of $100 million would be poured into the development of these two approaches, Nyerere said, for they were the heart of the Five-Year Plan. The President added that private estates and plantations, owned largely by foreigners, would also have a vital part in the agricultural plan. These properties occupied less than 1 per cent of the land but accounted for 40 per cent of the value of Tanganyika's exports. "These estates have both the capital and the technicians that are needed to increase output," Nyerere pointed out, "and we need an increase from them."

Noting that except for foods Tanganyika still imported more than 80 per cent of its consumer goods, Nyerere said much of this was unnecessary. "We export our sisal and then import ropes and mats made with it. We export our cotton and import cloth, export our coffee and buy tinned coffee from abroad. We buy shoes, biscuits, enamelware from other countries, having first exported some of the basic elements of these goods." To remedy the situation, he said, Tanganyika would promote its industries at a pace double that required of agriculture. A massive investment in manufacturing was called for in the Five-Year Plan. When Tanganyika produced consumer goods needed in the domestic market, people would be receiving wages that would allow expansion of that market.

As for the general marketing of Tanganyika's products, Nyerere explained, national produce boards would be established to carry out the marketing of all primary crops, both at home and abroad. The cooperative societies made up of African farmers would serve as agents of these boards. By 1970 a total of 1,600 cooperative societies would be in operation.

A new role for the African cooperatives would be in the field of retail trade, dominated completely in the past by Asian interests. There would be a national chain-store system including twelve urban department stores, 250 retail shops in rural trading centers and 50 mobile shops. In addition, small African-owned shops would be supplied by COSATA, the Cooperative Supply Association of Tanganyika. The plan called for the cooperatives' taking over 10 per cent of all retail trade by 1970 and at least 30 per cent by 1980.

One measure of the progress of modernization was the 12 per cent increase in annual electricity consumption. To keep up with this pace, the plan allotted $30 million over the five years for new power plants and expansion of old ones. Power supply was now an all-state operation: the formerly private Tanganyika Electric Supply Corporation having been bought by the government.

The nation's long-neglected communications were another problem. At a total cost of $35 million, the next five years would see the completion of a network of trunk routes, with a grid of three roads crossing the country from north to south and three running east to west. This also included the construction and improvement of thousands of miles of feeder roads. Another $35 million was to go into the improvement of railways and harbors between 1964 and 1970.

Outlining the $33-million program for educational development, President Nyerere described the difficult decision to be made between providing school facilities for the young or for the grownup. National needs, he said, were clear: "We must educate our adults first. Our children will not have an impact on our economic development for five, ten or even twenty years. The attitudes of the adult, on the other hand, have an impact now. The people must understand our plans for development, for they must be able to participate in the necessary changes."

The emphasis, then, was to be on adult education—$8 million would be spent on new and expanded secondary and technical school facilities. Millions more would go for teacher training. Nyerere noted that Tanganyika had only twenty African graduate teachers in all its schools. The plan called for the training of 1,500. And by 1969 there would not only be higher education for the first time, but there would be 528 students enrolled at University College, Dar es Salaam.

The plan's main objective in the field of health, Nyerere said, was to extend medical services into disease-ridden rural areas. As local bases for these services, 83 new health centers and 300 dispensaries would be built throughout the country. Until doctors and health officers could be trained, a new grade of health assistant was being created by the Ministry of Health to help man these medical outposts. Urban and rural hospitals would be enlarged so that there would be one hospital bed for every thousand of the population. Formerly Tanganyika had no psychiatric beds; by 1970 there would be 200.

President Nyerere concluded his summary with words that were to become a rallying call:

"The Five-Year Plan which I now present to this House is a challenge to the nation. It is as big a challenge as that which we faced in order to achieve *uhuru* [freedom]. This plan, and its successors, can be the means through which we shall obtain independence from the worst of the poverty our country now experiences. It is a declaration of war, and every one of us is a soldier. Our weapons are our hands and brains, our ammunition is our discipline and our determination.

"Mr. Speaker and Honorable Members, it can be done; play your part.

"On the land, in the factories, in the classrooms, in the hospitals; all of us—politicians, civil servants, soldiers, policemen, men, women and children—let us say: 'It can be done, play your part.'

"Mr. Speaker, Sir, I commend this plan, and ask for the support of this House."

He won his support. The entire membership of the National Assembly rose to their feet with cheers of acclamation that roared through Karimjee Hall. The public, too, was caught up in the enthusiasm. Announced that evening over the radio and in the press, news of the plan sped through the streets, into shops and homes. There was a curious drama about it. Everyone seemed involved. Perhaps this was because the expenditures appeared enormous to a people for whom so little like this had ever been done. Or that the plan was their own undertaking and contained something for each of them. Whatever the reasons, the reaction seemed total. People were visibly, audibly moved. For days the event dominated conversation not only in the capital but, gradually, through the rest of the country.

Further evidence of public interest came with the release a few days later of the published plan. In sets of two red-covered volumes, copies were delivered to bookstores, to go on sale at ten shillings, fifty pence a copy. For both volumes, this was nearly three dollars. Yet the government printer, undoubtedly for the first time, had a best seller in hand. Merchants, students, clerks and office workers emptied the shelves of the first deliveries, and for weeks there was a widening demand for copies.

This reaction was what Julius Nyerere intended. He had told his ministers and the members of Parliament to study the plan and describe it to others. He told the Ministry of Information to give top priority to publicizing it. He called in the seventeen regional commissioners from all over the republic for a seminar, and for four days he and his ministers went into every phase of the plan, particularly it local application.

"Our problem now," he told the commissioners, "is to define the operational steps that have to be taken by the leaders of our society in providing all the producing units in our economy with concret indications of what the nation expects from them during the plan period in production and investment."

The President revealed for the first time at this seminar one of the organizational steps to be taken to implement the plan. The country was being divided into eight economic zones throughout which standard solutions to development problems could be applied. In each zone there would be appointed an Assistant Director of Development, to be the "economic lieutenant" in the area. This officer would be responsible for seeing that the plan was being followed at all levels and for bringing to the attention of Nsilo Swai's Directorate of Development and Planning any bottlenecks, inconsistencies or policies which might be prejudicial to the expansion of the economy.

The planning officer was to work with the regional commissioner and the regional and district development committees in setting and attaining local production targets. For this purpose a handbook, prepared by the national planning directorate, would be provided for calculating regional investment and production figures. The handbooks also denoted other data that should be prepared for each zone so that for the first time the nation would have a firm statistical base upon which to prepare development plans.

At this point in the seminar, President Nyerere offered a few cautionary words:

Although I am urging you to plan and program in as detailed a manner as possible, you must not let the plan, national or regional, become a fetish for the people. It does not suffice to put down on paper impressive production and investment targets and leave it at that. Figures on paper are one thing; tons of maize, rice and cotton of high quality, construction of roads, schools and buildings are quite another. Hence machinery will have to be set up to control production and investment so that you and your development committees be kept periodically informed of the extent to which regional, and consequently national, targets are being reached or surpassed.

Following a seminar in Dar es Salaam, Nyerere set out on what was to be a series of provincial tours to promote the plan. Like his earlier trips to organize TANU, they took him to every corner of the country. One trip took him west to Kigoma, on the shore of Lake Tanganyika, where 800 farmers, carrying hoes and axes, staged a parade as a pledge to work their hardest for the plan. He told a rally of 10,000 at nearby Ujiji that nation-wide action was required; otherwise the plan would exist in nothing but book form. He inspected two communal farms, one run by Mwanga tribesmen, the other by Ujiji. He went to Tabora to lay the foundation stone for a new TANU building and, when checks for $5,000 from the Asian community were handed to him for the building, he directed that they be used instead to assist development projects. He went to Iringa, to Tanga, Mtwara, Songea and Mbeya, telling countless audiences of the plan.

His ministers followed suit. With almost evangelical zeal, they crisscrossed the nation to describe and sell the plan. Bibi Titi Mohamed, who had not only achieved her goal of election to Parliament but was also named Junior Minister for Community Development, told schoolgirls at Kilimanjaro that they should volunteer for literacy teaching and for self-help projects. Addressing a public rally of 3,000 at Moshi, she condemned drunkenness as an obstacle to Five-Year Plan goals and called upon tribesmen to give up drink and join adult education classes. Job Lusinde, Minister of Home Affairs, exhorted students; Richard Wambura, Junior Minister for Communications, addressed government workers; Austin Shaba, Minister for Local Government, spoke to government trainees.

TANU branches throughout the country threw their massive influence behind the promotion. The plan was described at regional and district conferences and at village meetings. Seminars were held at regional and district levels at which both commissioners and TANU delegates discussed the plan with teachers, cooperative officials, agricultural agents and health workers. And the TANU women's and youth units further spread the word.

The promotion took many forms. From Mwanza came word that Sukuma bards, who told the history and legends of the tribe in song, had composed a lively tune describing the goals of the Five-Year Plan. At Mahembe the area commissioner began a promotional campaign he called "One man teach one man"—about, of course, the plan. The Ministry of Commerce organized a clinic for African businessmen to tell them how increased trade would promote the plan. Farmers at Moarika were told by their regional commissioner that their part in the Five-Year Plan began with maintaining a better and healthier home. The regional commissioner at Dodoma called upon the unemployed of his area to go to work on communal farms to aid the plan. At the other end of the scale, large landowners who failed to submit development plans for their farms were warned by the Commissioner of Lands that further delay might mean forfeiture of their property.

The plan was becoming part of the life and fiber of the people. But it was going to require more than such acceptance. How, for instance, was the plan being received by the investors—the foreign governments and private financiers? By the end of 1964 Nyerere could report favorably on this. The government grants and loans were coming in, he announced, and private investment was surpassing expectation. The first to aid were Great Britain, the United States, West Germany and Israel. Approximately $6 million a year was already being received from the United Kingdom in technical assistance when Paul Bomani returned from London in August to announce that Britain had agreed to a $22-million development loan and $11 million more in technical assistance.

The United States—mainly through the Agency for International Development—had already subscribed nearly $30 million. This began with $1.5 million from the U.S. Development Fund, to be used at the discretion of the Tanganyika government. The remainder was largely on generous repayment terms: no payment for nine and a half years, during which three quarters of 1 per cent interest was charged, then 30 years of half-year installments with interest of 2 per cent.

West Germany's *Kreditanstalt* followed with a $3.5-million loan for agricultural development, to be repaid between 1968 and 1982. Israel helped out with two loans: one of $2.5 million for a government hotel in Dar es Salaam, another of $300,000 for irrigation projects. International aid came from the World Bank (which had made two loans totaling $17 million), and the Commonwealth Assistance Loan Fund ($6 million for bridge- and dam-building).

Nonaligned Tanganyika now turned to the East to match this considerable bounty from the West. In June Vice-President Kawawa and a ten-man economic mission went to Peking to sit down with Premier Chou En-lai and Foreign Minister Chen Yi. They returned to announce a $45-million interest-free loan agreement, to be granted in both cash and equipment.

By the end of 1964 the Chinese appeared to dominate the aid scene, possibly because of the nature of the gifts. In September a freighter arrived from China with a cargo of automatic weapons, rifles and farming implements. A few days later some of the agricultural equipment—ploughs, harrows, cultivators and wheelbarrows—were publicly presented by the Chinese at Arnautoglu Hall, but there was no public glimpse of the military equipment. Later it was announced that the Peking agreement would include the building and equipping of a $10-million textile mill, largest and most modern in East Africa, at Ubongo, outside Dar es Salaam. The mill was to be named after Mao Tse-tung. The Chinese would also finance a 5,000-acre state farm on the Ruvu River, below Kidunda, with an investment of $1.5 million. Still another project financed from the loan would be a farm implement factory, also to be built at Ubongo, which would turn out 500 tons of hand tools and animal-drawn implements annually.

Two months after the visit to China, Rashidi Kawawa and his economic mission went in the other direction: to Moscow, Warsaw and Prague. In less than a fortnight they were back to announce more massive aid. Russia, Poland and Czechoslovakia had agreed to $45 million in aid to finance a variety of building and technical assistance projects. Russia would make a geological survey, to promote prospecting for solid minerals, oil and raw components for cement production. The U.S.S.R. would also establish a fish-processing plant, a meat-packing plant, a cotton-linting mill and a spinning mill. Poland, which had separately signed a trade agreement with Tanganyika, would, under the loan agreement, help establish a sugar estate and refinery at Wami and make a study of electrification needs in Zanzibar. The Czechs agreed to provide finances for factories producing automobile tires and tubes, shoes and ceramics, and for state farm development.

Having been overlooked by the Kawawa mission in August, the Yugoslav government in September dispatched four experts to Dar es Salaam to make arrangements for building a tractor factory.

During the year following, loans and grants continued to flow in. A $10-million military aid treaty was signed with West Germany under which a transport and communications squadron would be equipped and trained for Tanzania's projected air force. By November 1964, the first Tanganyikan flying trainees were taking pilot courses. The government at Bonn also agreed to provide building materials worth $2.5 million for the Tanganyikan Ministry of Housing's slum clearance program. Another West German gift of $150,000 went toward a 200-bed hospital to be built near the foot of Kilimanjaro.

With West Germany helping to build an air force, Canada came forward in late 1964 with an assistance program to rebuild the United Republic's army. The aid, announced by the redoubtable Mr. Kawawa, would include funds for a military academy for officer training, equipment and Canadian army instructors.

There was even the tiny beginning of a Tanzanian navy. In mid-December the West German ambassador formally turned over to Vice-President Kawawa four patrol boats as a step in securing Tanganyika's 500 miles of sea border. The flag of the United Republic was raised for the first time on Tanzania's own vessels: the *Rafiki*, the *Papa*, the *Salama* and the *Uhuru*.

More United Nations aid was announced. Among UN Special Fund projects announced: $900,000 for a faculty of science at the new University College; $800,000 for a national institute for productivity (to advise on Tanganyika industry); $800,000 for an experimental sheep-raising program in the Southern Highlands.

To cap an impressive first year of fund-raising, President Nyerere announced in December 1964 a $20-million capital loan agreement with Britain to cover cash needs for the first two years of the Five-Year Plan. The agreement was particularly appreciated, the President said, because it would help his government meet the local costs of many of the aid programs, the finances for which usually covered only the import costs. The British loan, he said, would help implement 217 specific projects.

At the 1964 annual dinner of the Dar es Salaam Chamber of Commerce in September, Minister of Finance Bomani happily recited a list of the loans and grants coming in. He commented: "We hope that in the United Republic, the East and West will meet in a constructive effort to help with the development of our economy." He also mentioned that, on his recent visit to Europe, investors in both Paris and London had expressed keen interest in the private sector of Tanganyika's economy.

Shortly afterward, in an address before all the Chambers of Commerce in Tanzania, the new Minister of Commerce, Abdulrahma Babu, underlined the same point with a slogan: "Trade, not aid, is Tanzania's best hope in the future." Mr. Babu, one of the Zanzibarians in the cabinet and an unabashed spokesman for all-out socialism, charged colonialism with dividing the world into developed and undeveloped countries. "The developed countries' population is barely 10 per cent of the world total," he told the Chambers of Commerce, "but they control 90 per cent of the trade. All the poverty and misery the developing countries have been subjected to stem directly from this frightening imbalance." He claimed that developed countries had set up systems of "productionism" that excluded certain tropical products by high import tariffs while subsidizing their own agriculture. Therefore, he said, Tanzania would have to struggle to create a healthy and aggressive trade of her own if she hoped for productivity.

To encourage foreign investment, the government passed the Investment Protection Act which allowed a number of concessions, including tax relief measures and guarantees of the repatriation of capital and profits. This may have induced the releasing of once-reluctant private capital, for by the end of 1964 new investment was building up into many millions. Most important, the money was going into processing ventures that added an industrial look to the burgeoning economy.

One such venture was the construction by an Italian syndicate of a $15-million oil refinery on a 280-acre site alongside Dar es Salaam harbor. The refinery would produce annually, from crude oil, an estimated 600,000 tons of petroleum, kerosene and other by-products —enough not only for the domestic market but allowing, too, nearly a 50-per-cent surplus for markets in other countries of Africa.

Another enterprise was instituted by the Tasini Textile Co. Ltd., a Dutch firm which had been manufacturing cotton cloth in Tanganyika since 1955. They set out to build a $2-million spinning mill twelve miles out of Dar es Salaam. Moving quickly, apparently to forestall Chinese proposals to move into the industry, Tasini's managing director went to Europe in November 1964 to order machinery. The mill built, Tasini expected to spin virtually the entire output of Tanzania's cotton plantations. In 1964 Tasini Textile manufactured four and a half million yards of cotton cloth for East African markets, though this was done with a million dollars' worth of cotton yarn imported from India and Israel. The new mill, first in the country, would well serve Julius Nyerere's purpose of promoting home manufacture of home produce.

By the end of 1964, the Kilombero Sugar Co. Ltd., backed by British, American and Dutch capital, reported the production of nearly 13,000 tons of sugar for the year. This was the first step toward the target of 105,000 tons annually by 1970—enough to meet the country's entire need.

In the dominant sisal industry, not only were first steps being taken to process the product but significant strides were being made to Africanize the industry through mutual agreements between private growers and the government. In 1964 the government made two moves to participate in sisal production. One was a $4.5-million partnership with British industrialist Sir Isaac Wolfson to buy out the Ralli Estates, one of the largest sisal producers. The other was a tripartite agreement between the government, the Rural Settlement Commission and the Amboni Estates to open up 20,000 virgin acres in the Handeni area in northeast Tanganyika to sisal farming. The Amboni group, already among the largest producers, would cultivate one half of the new land and would train 250 African farmers to operate the other half.

Earlier in 1964 Julius Nyerere had bemoaned the fact that Tanganyika exported sisal and then bought it back in the form of rope. By the end of the year the country had its first baler twine factory, designed to turn out 4,000 tons of twine a year, which would be enough not only to supply all East African needs but to include surpluses for shipment to overseas markets. The new plant, opened in October, was a subsidiary of British Ropes Ltd., world's largest ropemakers, which had been purchasing annually 100,000 tons of Tanganyika's sisal fiber (about one third of the total crop).

The products of two other industries being financed with a goal of self-sufficiency were matches and beer. At Moshi, a group of Tanzanian businessmen, African and Asian, established a match factory to begin production in June 1965, with an annual target of 450,000 boxes of 50 matches each. Timber for both the matches and boxes would come from the slopes of nearby Mount Kilimanjaro. And to expand the country's beer production so that the domestic demand might be met, the Tanzania Breweries Ltd. embarked on a $2.5-million modernization program at its Dar es Salaam plant.

Miscellaneous projects offering more proof of Tanganyika's economic boom included the projected $6-million Dar Hilton Hotel to be built on the site of the old Kaiserhof on Dar es Salaam harbor. (The Kaiserhof, since World War I known as the New Africa, had been bought by the government's National Development Corporation.) A hundred yards down the waterfront stood the soaring 200-room Kilimanjaro Hotel, built by the government with Israeli aid. Besides the Dar Hilton, other Hilton hotels would be built in partnership with the government on Zanzibar and at Arusha.

Proudest project on the 1964 industrial front was the launching of the $15-million Hale hydroelectric scheme on the Pangani River near Tanga. Most of the financing for the huge power plant was provided by a Commonwealth Development Corporation loan which could be paid back in annual foreign exchange savings. At the project's opening ceremony, President Nyerere explained that the electric power from the Hale plant would replace that provided by plants at Dar es Salaam and Morogoro for which $700,000 in diesel oil and other fuel had to be imported each year. "Instead of foreign exchange we shall now use our own water," he said. The power taken by "borrowing" five miles of the Pangani River to drive giant generators housed in a cavern 275 feet below the river bed would supply the coastal area from Tanga down to Dar es Salaam.

About 600 miles farther up the Pangani River, near Moshi, another project in the plan that recruited the forces of nature was launched in September 1964. This was the start of the $3-million Nyumba ya Mungu Dam, to be the largest in East Africa. The dam would form a lake surface of 57 square miles and it would irrigate 55,000 acres of land. A hydroelectric plant below the site would provide 6,000 kilowatts of electric power for communities from Moshi to Korogwe.

Here again the financial aid would come from Britain, and Julius Nyerere paid wry tribute to this assistance. At ceremonies which he opened by setting off a booming explosion to start dam construction, he addressed an international audience:

I want to say thank you to the British government. Before we became independent I used to say we wanted independence because we wanted to develop. I said that when we became independent in ten years we would do more for the development of this country than the British did in their 40 years here.

One would have thought the British would say, "Very well, we shall go away, stay away for ten years and at the end of that time we shall see if you have fulfilled your promise."

They have not done this. Instead they have said, "We will send you technicians to help, and pay for them. We will also give you loans and grants to help you show that you can do in ten years what we failed to do in 40." Nothing could be more generous. I want, most seriously, to express the gratitude of this country to the government of the United Kingdom.

Certainly at this juncture Tanganyika had cause to be grateful for the aid coming from so many sources. And it seemed fitting that the country turn now to its own people, that they might give evidence, as it were, of this gratitude. In December 1964, Minister of Finance Bomani announced a $3-million issue in National Savings Bonds for public subscription. The bonds could be bought for as little as one dollar and were redeemable in seven years at a tax-free gain of 40 per cent. "These bonds," said Bomani, "are a form of self-help. The more we raise, the greater will be our independence of overseas borrowing and the quicker will we be able to implement our whole program of development." As 1965 began, the people were responding loyally. To most of them even the minimal one-dollar bond was out of reach. But in offices, in shops and on farms, groups of workers clubbed together to buy small lots. Steadily the bond sales climbed toward Bomani's $3-million target.

But it was not through bonds that the people would make their major contribution to the Five-Year Plan. Rather, it was to come from the nearly ten million on the farms who, as Julius Nyerere had told the National Assembly, must be spurred to the desire for improvement and to the effort to attain a better life. This was the assignment given to community development. This was the great and demanding task of the corps of CD workers now moving out into the field.

CHAPTER SEVEN

THE PLAN IN ACTION

One pioneer member of the CD in the work so vital to the success of the Five-Year Plan was Fikirini Y. Sanze—a lowly private in the small CD army in the field in 1964. He was a community development assistant assigned to the villages of Mgeta, Tangeni and Mlali in Morogoro district. Morogoro lay 130 miles west of Dar es Salaam, on the trunk road crossing Tanganyika to Tabora and Kigoma. It was high country, dominated by the Uluguru Mountains and through it ran the Mgeta River which, joining the wider Ruvu, ran eastward to the sea. Here lived the poor but energetic Bantu tribe, the Waguru.

Fikirini Sanze, a short wiry man, was one of the tribe. He had only eight years of schooling at Morogoro, but he was an expert in such practical lore as crop planting and rotation, village sanitation and building construction. He worked with affectionate impatience among his people, gently persuading them to try new things. His own village was Mgeta but he spent several days each month at Mlali and Tangeni, walking the twenty or so miles that separated the three villages. He was a familiar, friendly figure in the area.

108

Sanze was a devout Moslem, but whenever he passed the Catholic Mission School at Tangeni, run by a Holy Ghost priest from Holland and four Waguru nuns, he always was hailed by the children. They called *"Mwini! Mwini!"* (Good Sir! Good Sir!) from the schoolyard or, meeting him by the path, welcomed him with the ancient Arabic greeting *"Shikamgou"* (I kneel and dust your shoes), to which he would smilingly reply, *"Shikamo, Marahaba"* (I dust yours seven times). He had a special affection for this tree-shaded village in the hills. Tangeni's huts were grouped on both sides of a stream that tumbled down the valley to join the Mgeta below. The villagers diligently planted all fertile ground in the area and did well with their crops. They grew maize, rice, cassava and bananas for themselves, and coffee and vegetables for cash crops. Sanze had arranged for their joining nearby cooperatives: the Mlali and Mgeta Coffee Growers Societies and the Mgeta Vegetable Growers Society. They came to look upon him as a village adviser.

Sanze was, in fact, an official adviser. At least twice a month he attended meetings of Tangeni's village development committee. With him on the committee were the TANU leader of the village, as chairman, and the Tangeni headman, as secretary; also one of the school nuns, the rural health officer, an agricultural field assistant and three elected villagers. Sometimes a man from the Mgeta or Mlali cooperatives would join them, particularly during the planting or marketing seasons. Sanze also attended VDC meetings at Mgeta and Mlali.

At a Tangeni VDC meeting in 1964 the villagers had spoken of more schooling for their children. The little mission school had five grades and there now were children who had passed through all these. The villagers asked Fikirini Sanze if he could arrange help for them in building a new schoolhouse with classrooms for Grades VI and VII. He said he could, and in August they began building. The farmers joined in teams of four, working afternoons after a morning in the fields. From an abandoned mission church down in the valley they carried a supply of old brick. Sanze requested a mobile CD field unit serving the Morogoro region to come to Tangeni and instruct the villagers in making new mud bricks.

The mobile unit, one of those then located around the country, was a traveling workshop, operated by a former building contractor, Carlos Fivawo, who had been recruited by the CD division in Dar es

Salaam. Fivawo, an old friend of Sanze's, drove the truck over one day, brought a hand brick press, and showed how to make mud bricks with a small mixture of cement. The villagers were delighted with this modern touch. The year before they had built a small community center, using the traditional mud on wattle, and the building was already deteriorating. Carlos Fivawo had also trucked over a dozen wooden roof trusses he had made in Morogoro as a CD gift to the project. The cement and some corrugated iron for the roof were also bought with CD funds.

Fikirini Sanze wrote a report on the school project, which was finished in October. The report went from Tangeni to the district development committee at Morogoro and from the regional CD office there to the Community Development Division headquarters in Dar es Salaam, to be added to the growing file of projects accomplished. It was typical of CD work being done by now in hundreds of villages. And Fikirini Sanze was typical of the corps of CD assistants whose work in the field was directed from a complex of low frame buildings fronting on Azania Drive in Dar es Salaam.

Here was the home of the reorganized Ministry of Community Development and National Culture. It was headquarters for the small army of CD assistants who, like Fikirini Sanze, were spreading the idea of community self-help into all corners of the country. From this national base the program was being organized on regional, district, village and hamlet levels. Because it was a new ministry, promoting a relatively new idea from which so much was expected, the best talents available were being recruited.

A new leader was appointed. In late 1964, Jerry Kasambala had been appointed Minister of Commerce and his cooperatives had been incorporated into that ministry. To succeed him as Minister of Community Development, President Nyerere recalled Tanganyika's delegate to the United Nations, Erasto Mang'enya, a chief of the Mbondei tribe, who earlier had been deputy speaker of the National Assembly. A teaching graduate of Makerere College in Uganda, specializing in agriculture, he was a forceful, although soft-spoken man, who accepted his new portfolio eagerly.

"I am privileged to lead this work which has been accomplishing a silent revolution in our country," he told a press conference after arriving from New York. "Community development is bearing tangible results and our people have become increasingly aware of the move toward progress."

Chief Mang'enya found a veteran CD headquarters staff working heroically, but Cleopa Msuya, the Ministry's hard-driving permanent secretary, told him the big problem was recruitment. The CD Division now had 336 trained officers, supplemented by an equal number, mostly untrained workers, attached to local authorities. The goal of the division was to have two trained CD assistants for every ten village development committees, or a total of 1,500 for the 7,500 villages in the country. Already underway, the build-up would mean doubling the combined staffs, a goal fixed by the Five-Year Plan. Msuya, of the Pare tribe in the northeast, had been in community development work since graduating from Makerere University. After working in the field, he rose fast to the top administrative post in the Ministry.

Recruitment and training of staff was the responsibility of the new commissioner of community development. F. J. Mchauru, a stocky, pipe-smoking former field officer, was another progressive CD veteran. After leaving the London School of Economics he went into teaching but turned to community development work in 1946 to become one of the key figures in the program.

There were two phases of training. One was officer training at Tengeru College, near Arusha, where recruits received a six-month basic course in CD principles and in the administrative aspects of serving village committees and providing assistance for projects. They then went into the field for six months and returned for another four months of classes, after which they were qualified as CD assistants. The Tengeru training center had been started in buildings borrowed from the Ministry of Agriculture, but in mid-1965 a $200,000 "campus" was being completed with dormitories and study buildings for 128 trainees. The principal at Tengeru was G. M. Mkwawa, a grandson of the legendary Hehe chief who had harassed German military forces in colonial days.

Two training centers for women were also operated by the division. One was at Musoma, financed by the Swedish government and the UN's Food and Agriculture Organization, which would train women in home economics so that they could return to their villages and demonstrate what they had learned. The other was at Rungemba, the

Iringa estate that Lady Chesham had turned over for the emergency training of women CD workers during 1964–65. After that it was to become an adult education institution for women.

Another, more ambitious training program was under the direction of Kime Petro, a senior CD officer who had been both a teacher and an army medical assistant before joining the division in 1957. As director of adult education, Petro was charged with establishing a network of district training centers all over the country. These, Petro explained, would be run by CD officers and would provide short, intensive courses for local leaders, both men and women, in all matters fundamental to the understanding and achievement of local development targets.

"They will give courses in agriculture, basic health and local government, and have classes in small business operation and in trades," he said. By the end of 1964 six of these were in operation: at Handeni, Iringa, Jombe, Geita, Singida and Mwanza. The Five-Year Plan called for 30 more. Eventually there would be one in each of the country's 61 districts. During the Five-Year Plan, $1.5 million would be spent on them.

Kime Petro's section was responsible, too, for the mass literacy program, in which CD workers served as organizers and advisers of local committees and recruited paid and volunteer teachers. The program was bolstered by a policy incorporated into the Five-Year Plan requiring all secondary-school graduates to serve six months as teachers in the literacy campaign before entering the university or going to work. This would provide a new teaching force of 1,000 annually.

In charge at division headquarters of the work of the six mobile construction units in the field was Elijah Suluja, a rangy, bespectacled building specialist whose professional and private goal was to effect a revolution in Tanganyikan home-building. By 1969 the six units would be increased to seventeen, one for each region. For their use Suluja had prepared a construction handbook suggesting scores of ways to improve native houses. Suluja saw with dismay the corrugated tin roof replacing thatch on Tanganyikan huts. The tin sheeting was being used, he said, because it was a lazy way of building and because it could be easily transported to a new site when the mud walls of an old home began to come down. Thatch, he insisted, was more beneficial for it allowed some ventilation in windowless mud and wattle

of the tribes rejected windows in the belief that it was
m that spirits entered. Also, tribesmen did not like to be
om the outside. Many of them, Suluja said, still had the
ng that a house was a place to hide in safety, as in a cave,
ess was the symbol of safety.

had designed a model three-bedroom house which incor-
indigenous materials and many traditional features, but he
it would be a long struggle before anything like it would be accepted. At present his field units were emphasizing the need to replace dirt floors with stone or cement. He noted wryly that when
tribesmen took the trouble to install stone or cement it usually was not
with a regard for sanitation, but because such floors were a symbol
of prestige and wealth.

Women's work of the division was directed by Miss Bassilla Renju,
who in two years had completed a three-year diploma course in public and social administration at Oxford University in 1954. She had
taught school at Moshi on her return, then joined the CD division. She
was enthusiastic about what CD was doing for the distaff. "Our
women, especially in the rural areas, are losing their traditional feeling of inferiority," she said. "They're eager to show they're not stupid."
She noted that in 1964 a total of 66,096 women had joined 1,440
self-improvement clubs organized by CD. "There has developed," she
added, "a great awakening on the part they have to play in our national effort."

To provide teaching materials for CD workers in the field, the division had a visual aids section at Dar es Salaam headquarters, with
T. N. Nshiku, a trained commercial artist, in charge. Its activities included the showing of documentary films and the production of posters, graphic materials for lectures, and other training supplies.

At Dar es Salaam, and in five other towns as well, CD continued
to operate community centers with social and educational programs
for urban dwellers. At a cost of nearly a quarter of a million dollars,
these centers were to be renovated and six new ones built as part of
the Five-Year Plan. They were to be staffed by CD officers and volunteer personnel.

Such was the structure of the headquarters organization that Chief
Mang'enya took over and began to rebuild in 1965. The new Minister
served notice at once that because the success of the CD program de-

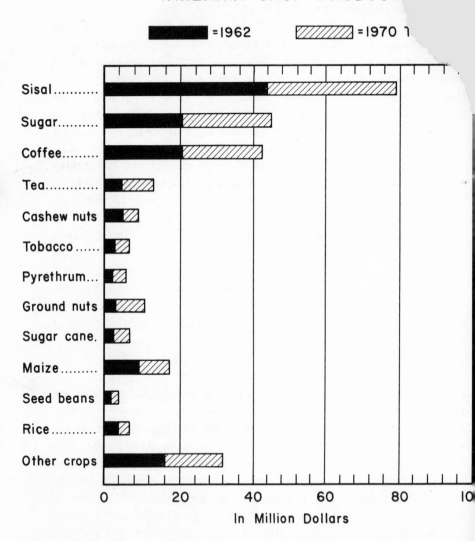

TANZANIA CROP PRODUCT

■ =1962 ⊘ =1970

In Million Dollars

pended on those in the field, he intended to spend m⟨...⟩
inspecting the network of regional, district and village offi⟨...⟩
projects. This was a policy which heartened the CD workers,
knew that anyone who wanted to really know what CD was ⟨...⟩
and what it could do—had to go into the field.

Typical of the CD field programs in the seventeen regions was t⟨...⟩
one in Mwanza. The capital of Tanganyika's cotton trade and once a
station on the slave route, Mwanza was a bustling port on the south
shore of Lake Victoria, a thousand miles northwest of Dar es Salaam.
It was nearly as inaccessible overland in 1965 as it was in 1857 when
Burton and Speke took five months to reach Tabora from Dar es
Salaam and Speke another month to make his way north from Tabora
to Mwanza. There was no direct road to the town, which had to be
approached from the south via Mbeya or even by the wide swing
through the north via Nairobi. Only in the very dry season could it be
approached somewhat directly, via dirt roads through Dodoma. Today
the best route to Mwanza is by air.

Except for the low plain where the town was built, the land rises
abruptly from the lake shore and is studded with massive, rounded
boulders of granite left by the glaciers. The town and surrounding villages are shaded by towering mango trees that were planted by the
Arab slavers. The Arab influence was still visible in the look and dress
of the people, most of whom were Moslem, though the area was dotted
with Christian missions. Shabby, one-story shops kept by Arabs or
Indians made up most of downtown Mwanza.

But in 1965 there were signs of vitality and change. A modern post
office was being completed in the shopping area and, by the waterfront, two handsome stone buildings to house the regional court and
the police department were nearly complete. On the far side of the
town park, in startling elegance, stood the headquarters of the Victoria Federation of Cooperative Unions. Here was a multistoried structure of granite blocks and glass that might have been moved from the
New York skyline. All the lake region regarded the VFCU building
with pride.

Near the modest Mwanza Hotel and among the retail shops, two
offices stood side by side. One was TANU headquarters, the other
the Mwanza community development office. In the latter was a large
reception room ornamented only by some metal files, a table and some

TANZANIA MINING PRODUCTION

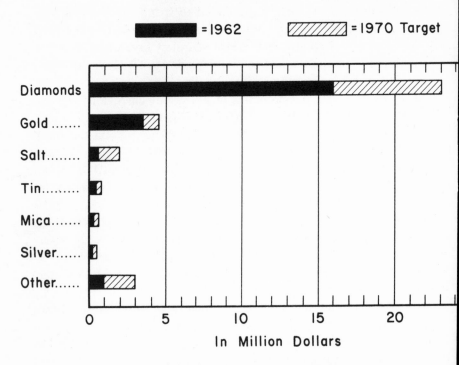

TANZANIA LIVESTOCK PRODUCTION

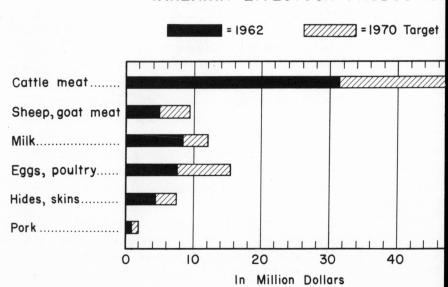

chairs. Behind it were two small offices. One of them belonged to the regional CD officer, Hussein Minja, a compact man of nearly forty, with high cheekbones and a neat moustache.

Minja was one of CD's veterans. He had gone to school in Pare and Moshi, then to the government school at Tabora. In 1949, after two years in Pare as a Ministry of Agriculture agent, he joined the old Social Development Department. Working among the Samba tribe in Lushoto, he had learned how effective the community development approach could be.

Part of the job in the Mwanza region was to induce cotton farmers to adopt proven methods of increasing their crops. Although Mwanza produced most of the country's annual 35,000-ton crop, there were no large plantations; all the cotton was produced on small family farms and taken to the cooperatives. It was a problem of educating thousands of individual farmers. "They produce only 400 pounds an acre," said Minja, "whereas by proper cultivation they could produce up to 3,000."

In his region Minja had a scattered team of 49 CD workers, nineteen of them division staff and 30 appointees of local authorities. Mwanza was made up of four districts: Mwanza itself, and Geita, Kwimba and the island of Ukerewe. It covered 20,000 square miles. There were already 340 village development committees in the region, all served by his staff.

Minja himself worked with the regional development committee, chaired by the regional commissioner. He also met regularly with his district CD officers and they, in turn, met with the village workers. In late 1964, Joseph Nyerere, thirty-eight-year-old younger brother of the President, succeeded John Malecela as Mwanza's commissioner. Malecela, appointed to take Chief Mang'enya's seat at the United Nations, had boasted in 1964 that Mwanza would achieve the goals set for it in the Five-Year Plan within three years. "I'm going to keep you people to that boast," said Joseph Nyerere at his first meeting with the regional committee. "You've got work to do."

Besides Minja, other committee members included the regional health, education and agricultural officers, area commissioners of the four districts, and two delegates from the cooperatives. Joseph Nyerere (who had recently completed organizing a national youth program) told the committee that Mwanza had the potential for being the country's richest region. This committee, he said, could do much to make it so. Part of his own dream for opening up the area, he explained, was a plan for a great canal from Lake Victoria to Lake Eyasi that would provide irrigation and communications for the land resources of the vast Maswa plain in the southeast Mwanza region.

At the time of Joseph Nyerere's arrival, Minja was conducting a series of seminars on the Five-Year Plan. These were held at the tiny TANU college in town, with Barbro Johansson, Mwanza's European member of the National Assembly and a staunch TANU supporter, as speaker. Miss Johansson, a Swede, spoke Swahili more fluently than most of her audience. Brought in from all parts of the region for month-long sessions, groups were made up of teachers, agricultural extension agents, health officers, local officials of the cooperatives, TANU village chairmen and women leaders.

This was the administrative side of Minja's regional CD role. What was more important was the work in the field, which he summarized as follows: In 1964, there were 613 literacy groups active in Mwanza, with 33,158 attending. There were 79 women's clubs with 2,178 members. During the year, eleven schools had been built in Kwimba district, two in Mwanza, seven in Ukerewe. Eight dispensaries had been built in Kwimba, seven in Ukerewe and four in Mwanza. One hundred and thirty-five miles of road had been built or repaired in Geita, 104 in Kwimba, 87 in Ukerewe and 73 in Mwanza. Geita had built three community centers, Kwimba a youth hostel and Ukerewe a new bridge. All this had been done on a self-help basis. The projects had cost the central and local governments a total of only 279,912 shillings, or about $20,000, in materials.

"It shows," said Hussein Minja, "what can be done by CD. Yet it is only a beginning. It is just a start in our five-year goals." He spoke for the region. Geita, one of the smaller communities, offered an illustration of CD work at the district level. The town lay a hundred miles west of Mwanza on a winding dirt road that in another hundred miles crossed over the border into Urundi. The journey to Geita began with a long ferry ride across Mwanza Gulf, then the hundred miles of dusty road.

Geita had little in the way of a town center, merely a cluster of low, wooden buildings housing local government offices: the police, the court, the area commissioner. These structures were unpainted, forlorn. The air of torpor was, however, deceptive. Most of the offices inside were crackling with action. The central one was that of the area commissioner. The office on the left was the court's. Charles Adam Mtowa occupied the room on the right.

Charles Mtowa was senior CD assistant in charge of the Geita district, a sprawling collection of hamlets, or *gungulis,* administered as nineteen divisions, each with three to five subdivisions. Mtowa was directing CD work in three of the divisions on a pilot basis, with six local CD assistants. Most of the *gungulis* were ten and twenty miles apart, and transportation made it impossible to cover more than three divisions at the time. And Mtowa, the only worker who had a vehicle, had a bicycle.

A stocky, serious man about forty, Mtowa is a Bemba, one of Zambia's tribes. He came from Rungwe, not far from the Zambia border, where a migrant Bemba group lived. At the time he went to school at Rungwe and later to secondary school at Iringa, Zambia was known as Northern Rhodesia. In 1948 Mtowa joined the Ministry of Health and worked for ten years as a rural medical assistant. He joined CD in 1961.

One typical day, Mtowa emerged from his office and mounted his cycle for the half-hour ride to Nyamalembo, where he had an appointment with Elikwa Sylva, the village's TANU and VDC chairman. Sylva, a lean farmer in worn shirt and trousers and bare feet, was waiting to tell Mtowa that the water project was finished. He led the way downhill past a few scattered huts to a clump of trees. Mtowa had first seen the watering place weeks before. It consisted of a spring bubbling from the ground into a small, open pool that was muddied by cattle and stray dogs. The source of Nyamalembo's water, it was the reason for the hamlet's location. During his first visit, Mtowa had suggested that if he could obtain some cement, the villagers could improve their spring. And he had described how it might be done.

Now it was finished. The men of Nyamalembo had dug a large pit around the "eye" of the spring and with brick and cement had built a bulkhead to house the supply of water. From this bulkhead it was piped to a covered cement reservoir from which the clear cold water flowed continuously through two pipe heads. The women were delighted by the project, so it was planned now to fence in an area below the reservoir and build a stone and cement surface where the women could do their washing. Sylva asked for and was promised more cement.

Sylva also wanted Mtowa to see the site chosen for the first plantings on the communal farm, a project decided upon at the last meeting of the VDC, which Mtowa had attended. Ten villagers, the medical assistant and a division officer representing the area commissioner also sat on the committee. The villagers decided that in addition to the crops on their own modest two to five acres they would join in a communal venture. There were fertile, unused acres lying to the west of the hamlet that would be ideal for cultivation. They were the property of the Geita Gold Mine Ltd. But since the mining was done deep underground by the British operators, Mtowa received permission to make use of the 200 acres of land on a "shilling-a-year" basis.

It was decided, Sylva told Mtowa, to farm 25 acres the first year and plant cotton, maize and groundnuts. Two hundred and twenty farmers had agreed to join and already some had begun clearing the bush. The communal crops would be marketed through the nearby Mukarani Cooperative Society.

Things were generally looking up in Nyamalembo, Sylva added. He told Mtowa that the village's two-room *pombe* shop, for example, was going to be converted into a community center. Everyone gathered there on Saturday and Sunday, to drink, dance and sing. There was a bin in the corner of one room where some millet and maize flour was stored. These were mixed and cooked into a mash from which the drink was brewed on a rough hearth. The adjoining room was a bar where the *pombe* was served, on week ends only. This room, Sylva indicated, would be enlarged into a hall so that classes and clubs could meet. Mtowa promised to help organize an activities program for the center and to recruit volunteer leaders. He knew that heavy *pombe* drinking was customary, largely because there was so little other recreation. The club and class activities might compete with some success against the rowdy week-end sessions.

Mtowa returned to his office that afternoon. With a CD assistant he examined the needs of the big building project going on at Nyanghwale. This was one of his pilot CD divisions where the villagers had embarked on self-help building. They had already built a community

center and a small office building for the CD assistant and were working now on a dispensary with a ward for in-patients. A separate group
was making mud bricks for a new TANU office in the village.

Mtowa must guide such projects with care. Sometimes the villagers
are over-zealous in their planning and abandon a project when it is
hardly started. This was emphasized at VDC meetings: work should
be thoroughly planned, particularly as to the availability of materials.
Sometimes there would be plenty of ready labor but a project would
be left half-done because there were not enough funds for materials.
And each time a project was given up it became more difficult to interest the people in new ones.

In late 1964 Mtowa had 32 projects going in his three pilot areas,
in addition to literacy classes and club programs. Within another year,
he promised, with more CD workers coming from both the division
and local authorities, his staff could move into some of the other sixteen divisions. With a man like Charles Adam Mtowa on the scene,
it could be predicted that Geita in the next few years was going to be
a lively nation-building district.

To meet and work with people at the village level, probably no CD
worker went so deeply into the back country as Prisca Batundika, a
cheerful young lady the CDA had assigned to Hussein Minja's regional office. Prisca, member of the Bahaya tribe from the area west
of Lake Victoria, had attended, at Kashasha, the only girls' secondary
school in the entire lake region. As her first CD assignment she was
given the isolated village of Nyaluhande on the wide Maswa plain
southeast of Lake Victoria. To reach Nyaluhande one followed the
broad lake road running from Mwanza to Musoma, then struck off
halfway to travel southeast across the plain. Settlements became thinner and thinner. Lion, zebra, leopard and other game stalked the bush
just out of the settlements. The dirt road had virtually disappeared by
the time Nyaluhande was reached. Prisca stayed at the hamlet most
of the time, making the trip back to Mwanza only once every few
weeks.

It was the women of the village who had requested CD aid. They
had formed a local unit of the women's section of TANU, and were
eager to learn and pass on to others all these new ideas for living that
they had heard CD was teaching. So Prisca gathered a selected group
of women members for a series of courses. One was on nutrition, show-

ing how a healthful diet could be followed with food available locally. Another was on handcrafts and another on infant care. (Much of the high child mortality rate was due to improper feeding.) Another course was specially requested by the village women: they wanted instruction in being hostesses. The women wanted to know how to greet guests and entertain them, how properly to serve a meal. The request was very touching, Prisca felt, coming as it did from these women who lived in mud huts with their pathetic possessions and modest aspirations. Too, Prisca saw their request as a pledge to the future from the women of Tanganyika. The "hostess" course became her favorite class.

The lessons completed, the Nyaluhande women wanted to invite someone from Mwanza and entertain for the day as they had been taught. Members of the class would be joint hostesses. With Prisca, they decided to ask Barbro Johansson, the Mwanza MP, who was coming out to neighboring Busega the following week to meet with the local VDC on the Five-Year Plan. She would be the ideal guest, for she had met most of the women, could speak both Swahili and their own Sukuma language, and she was intensely interested in CD work.

On the day of the visit a delegation of Nyaluhande women in brilliantly hued party dress met Barbro and escorted her to the UWT chairman's home. It was one of the larger mud huts, which had been coated with a wash of lime white. Barbro was seated in the single chair. Two club members served fruit refreshment while others, sitting on the floor against the walls, asked politely about affairs in the regional capital. There were animated questions about Joseph Nyerere as the new commissioner, for the ancestral Zanaki home of the Nyereres was not many miles distant from Nyaluhande, toward Musoma.

Barbro was then taken on a guided tour of the village, particularly to inspect the poultry run that the UWT had started as part of a program, sponsored by Julius Nyerere's wife Maria, to encourage the inclusion of more meat and eggs in the national diet. Prisca had brought the agricultural agent in from Mwanza to help launch the club project. Barbro was next shown Nyaluhande's water supply—a stagnant pool formed by a spring at the bottom of a clay pit. An ancient Moslem villager was bathing himself in the pool as they passed, and a woman with a gourd dipper was filling a petrol can with water.

Prisca assured their guest that the villagers were already thinking of doing something about the spring.

Back at the chairman's house, a great meal had been prepared with a variety of dishes. Barbro took her seat of honor and was given a separate plate and spoon. The others, using their fingers, ate from common platters. A versatile staple of the meal was the peanut, or groundnut. There was groundnut soup, subtly flavored. There was a paste of banana and groundnut. Fried fish was served with cassava leaves cooked like creamed spinach. A pot of baked soybeans had a peppered sauce of tomato and onions. There was rice cooked in oil and chicken also fried in an onion sauce. There were shelled boiled eggs. Barbro watched as some of the women ate them, in defiance of an old superstition which claimed that eggs affected a woman's fertility. (One woman admitted to Barbro that she couldn't overcome her feeling. "If I try to eat one," she said, "I vomit.")

After the meal there was a small reception at the council house where Barbro told the women something of the Five-Year Plan. The day ended when the club presented their guest from Mwanza with a small handbag made from leopard pelt.

The report of Prisca Batundika's Nyaluhande courses was another item added to the headquarters file of projects accomplished. By mid-1965 reports like hers were coming in by the thousands. Some were accounts of impressive construction projects, some were group educational accomplishments, some told of patient victories over superstition and ways of neglect.

The people of Kibosho, for instance, had built a 160-bed hospital.

Pupils of Chingutwa School, in Mtwara region, built a staff residence for their teachers.

Sixty-four inmates of Isangi Central Prison were awarded certificates for completing the CD literacy course.

In Dar es Salaam, a CD team spearheaded a campaign that built a rehabilitation home and center for destitutes.

Four villages in the Ilemela division of Mwanza joined in building a dispensary.

In the Kilimanjaro region, eighteen miles of new road were constructed. At Dodoma the villagers of Chihanga built a seven-mile road linking the village to the main Dodoma-Arusha highway.

In Nzovwe, in Mebya region, a new community center was built entirely by women, and the women in Matagoro village in Songea built their own school for adult classes. This was one of many such projects for which funds for materials were provided by Lady Chesham's trust fund.

People in Tunduru district, Ruvuma region, completed seven primary schools, 25 cooperative warehouses, four community centers, two medical clinics, twelve bridges and 300 miles of road repairs.

As Hussein Minja had said, it was all just a beginning but the results were convincing evidence that the total effect of thousands of projects, seminars and classes could amount indeed to a transformation of the life of the people. The "improvement approach," as implemented by the growing corps of CD workers, was well on the way to attaining Five-Year Plan goals.

But there were other forces, besides community development, making tremendous headway in the drive toward the plan's goals. One of them was Tanganyika's burgeoning cooperative movement.

CHAPTER EIGHT

THE COOPERATIVES

In the colonial period, the African may not have been deliberately excluded from business affairs, but he certainly was not noticeably active in them. When Tanganyika became independent in 1961, the number of Africans in responsible commercial or industrial positions could be counted on the fingers of one hand. It was apparent, in the days before independence, that the European businessmen did not cherish—any more than did the Asian—the idea of African partnership in company, shop or office affairs.

This was no proof, however, that the native Tanganyikan was incapable of doing business, nor evidence that official colonial policy held him back. On the contrary, by joining in a viable partnership of their own, the African and his colonial mentors demonstrated that he African was fully capable of business management. This partnership was, of course, in the cooperative movement.

For more than a century, cooperatives had been capturing the imagination and support of societies where an economic revolution was needed to improve the lot of the common man. The success story of cooperatives in Britain, Israel, Nova Scotia and Scandinavia was well-known and impressive. But in no other part of the world had the

125

cooperative movement so quickly and so completely effected social and economic change as it has within the past generation in Tanganyika. It also served the vital purpose of grooming leadership for the country, while other channels—in business and in government particularly—were being denied to them. From graduates of such training and experience in cooperatives, Julius Nyerere was to recruit the nucleus of his cabinet and his government department heads.

In Tanganyika, primarily an agricultural country, the cooperative movement first concerned itself with the marketing of crops. When this became a working plan, the movement turned to other production and services: societies were organized for the livestock, dairy and fishing industries. Bus lines and trucking firms serving the whole country began a cooperative transportation system. Even gold and diamond mines went into cooperative production. From the producers of goods, the movement turned to the nation's consumers. The Cooperative Supply Association of Tanganyika, or COSATA, was created to put retail trade on a cooperative basis. A national credit union and a national cooperative bank were organized. Small manufacturing firms, now beginning to emerge, were cooperatively managed. As larger industries developed they, too, would be cooperative enterprises. Tanzania was entrusting its economic future almost totally to the principle of cooperative effort.

The first crop cooperatives dealt with coffee. Coffee had long been grown in Tanganyika, having been brought by the Haya tribe in the sixteenth century from Abyssinia to the western shores of Lake Victoria. Speke and Grant found the bean growing there when they explored the lake region in 1862. When the Germans arrived at Bukoba in 1885 they found that the Bahaya chewed the bean but made no drink of it. In the nineties, German priests of the missionary Holy Ghost order showed the Chagga tribesmen in Moshi, on the slope of Kilimanjaro, how to cultivate the plant. It soon became an export crop. By 1925, more than 6,000 tons valued at nearly $1.5 million were being exported.

In that year the first cooperative, the Kilimanjaro Native Planters' Association, was organized by Chagga growers at Moshi. Other Chagga groups also formed societies. The move was partly protective. European planters were opposing African coffee plantings, protesting that the Chagga crops threatened the Moshi product's reputation for quality. Also, they felt that if the Chagga became independent growers it would be difficult to recruit estate labor. But the Chagga persisted and fortunately they had a champion in the district commissioner, Major Charles Dundas.

Dealing directly now with the London market rather than with local traders, the societies sold the cooperative crop at much higher prices. From the increased profits, they voted a levy of two cents per pound of coffee and put their cooperatives on a business basis. They reorganized as the Kilimanjaro Native Cooperative Union and a full-time manager was hired. The new manager, A. L. B. Bennett, trained Andrew Shangarai, an African, to succeed him.

Coffee exports by the Kilimanjaro union alone reached 7,910 tons in 1953, the year of peak coffee prices, and sold for more than $10 million. With such profits, the grateful tribesmen built a magnificent KNCU headquarters at Moshi, including a school of commerce, and donated $300,000 for a secondary school for the area.

As other cooperatives began to form, the government gave official endorsement to the movement. In February 1932, Tanganyika's Legislative Council passed the Cooperative Societies Ordinance. Based on similar acts in India and Ceylon, the ordinance provided for registration, audit and financial supervision of the societies. The first societies registered were the twelve making up the Kilimanjaro union.

Government recognition became more constructive in January 1951, when the Department of Cooperative Development was organized, with a commissioner and a staff of inspectors appointed to promote the movement. This was the early partnership which put the African producer into business. It was to the lasting credit of the colonial administration that these inspectors were sent out to tour the bush and help organize primary societies of all kinds. The "Cooperatives," as the inspectors were known to the farmers, became a familiar sight around the countryside where they traveled by motorcycle to hold meetings and inspect books.

Coffee growing—and coffee cooperatives—spread to other parts of the country. In 1947 the Mwakaleli Coffee Growers Association and four other coffee cooperatives joined with four rice cooperatives to form the Rungwe Cooperative Union. Again, it was German missionaries who had started coffee growing in Rungwe, far down in the Southern Highlands, and a man who was to become one of Julius

Nyerere's first Ministers managed this cooperative. Jeremiah Kasam
bala's union helped to make Rungwe famous for its high-qualit
Arabica coffee. RCU production rose to 1,663 tons by 1959. Tha
year Jeremiah Kasambala left the cooperative post to become Parlia
mentary Secretary to the Ministry of Agriculture. He was first of th
cooperative "alumni" to join the government.

In Bukoba the industry was advancing to the extent that in 1950
group of 48 coffee societies formed the Bukoba Native Cooperativ
Union, which was to become another of the giants. The BNCU sen
staff abroad for special training, built an impressive headquarter
building and a hostel at Bukoba and operated its own coffee-curin
plant. One of the overseas trainees who returned to become secretar
(later general manager) of the BNCU, was C. George Kahama. I
1959 he, too, left his cooperative post to join the government as th
first Minister for Social and Cooperative Development.

On the slopes of Kilimanjaro's sister mountain in the north, Moun
Meru, another five coffee societies joined together in 1957 as the Mer
Cooperative Union with young Nsilo Swai as general manager. Bu
Swai was also to leave to join the Nyerere government. In 1959 h
left for Dar es Salaam to become Minister of Commerce and, late
National Planning and Development Director.

While coffee was the first product in Tanganyika to be markete
cooperatively, it was outshone by the development of the cotton socie
ties. The beginnings of cotton in Tanganyika offered an intriguin
puzzle. It was known that cotton was first cultivated 5,000 years ag
in both India and Peru. Fragments of cotton cloth of that age wer
found in both countries. When the Germans moved into Tanganyik
in the late nineteenth century for the first colonization, they foun
tribesmen in the coastal region growing a species of Indian cotto
When they reached the interior region around the great lakes the
found the tribes cultivating a Peruvian cotton, a botanical enigma c
plant migration.

The Germans, eager to promote cotton cultivation, distributed see
free of charge, published Swahili handbooks on cotton raising, an
even gave prizes to stimulate production. They established experimen
stations and seed farms in the Kilosa, Rufiji, Lindi and Moshi districts
In 1911 they put seventeen steam plows to work in the southern re
gion. By 1913 there were 79,000 acres under cotton cultivation, 47,

000 of them by African farmers. Production that year was 12,000 bales. But World War I abruptly halted German sponsorship of the crop.

During the British administration, cotton cultivation became centered in the Lake Victoria region among the Sukuma tribesmen, with Mwanza as capital of the industry. The hard-working Wasukuma were not at the time happy with their lot. They could sell their raw cotton only to local traders whose prices were as low as their scales were weighted. To protect themselves from short-weight the farmers had to hire independent weight checkers when they went to sell their cotton.

In 1951, after studying the methods of coffee cooperatives around Mount Meru, the Sukuma farmers started the Lake Province Growers Association. The next year, Gavin J. B. Green arrived in Mwanza from the Cooperative Department in Dar es Salaam and began promoting further organization. In 1953, largely through Green's missionary effort, 38 primary societies were registered and the mammoth Victoria Federation of Cooperative Unions was formed.

General manager of the VFCU from 1955 to 1960 was Paul Bomani, under whose dynamic guidance VFCU began its astonishing growth. By 1960 there were 360 primary societies, nineteen unions and a membership of 140,000 in the federation. The VFCU by then owned six modern ginneries and had built its elegant headquarters and hostel in Mwanza. In 1960 the federation handled a total output of 170,000 bales of cotton, and that year the VFCU, too, lost its general manager. Paul Bomani went to Dar es Salaam to become Minister of Agriculture and, later, Minister of Finance.

Other areas and other crops were caught up in the spreading cooperative movement. In isolated Songea in the south, a union was formed by four societies to market their tobacco crops. Another was formed to sell the rice and cotton grown by twenty primary societies in the Lake Tanganyika region. Another brought together eight societies in the Pare district to handle rice, cotton, coffee and timber. The Usambara Union, with seven societies as members, marketed coffee and wattle bark for 5,000 farmers in Tanga. Still other unions were formed for the marketing of mica, cashew nuts, fresh vegetables, cattle, mangrove poles, oil seeds and milk.

The cooperatives also took hold in many unlikely spheres. In Dar es Salaam the city's cab drivers decided to run a cooperative taxi fleet.

African prospectors formed a gold cooperative. In Dar es Salaam, a Watch Dealers and Repairers Cooperative Society was formed and in Tabora, a Beekeepers Cooperative Society. In Mwanza one cattle cooperative related itself to the political struggle. It called itself *Idetemye Bageni* (Let Foreigners Quake). Another Lake Province society wa known as *Kiguna Bahabi* (Protectors of the Poor).

By 1961, one quarter of the total value of Tanganyika's exports —produce worth approximately $30 million—was being marketed through cooperatives. This was a proportion unmatched by any other African country and, on a world-wide basis, one surpassed only by Denmark and Israel. There were 760 Tanganyikan societies registered with a total membership of 327,000.

It was at this juncture that the cooperative movement began to be accepted, in government planning, as a major factor in the future economy. In a speech at the time, Vice-President Kawawa put it in these words: "Our government is determined to provide a guide toward the realization of a total cooperative community in our country." And Julius Nyerere said: "The cooperative movement gives economic effect to the philosophy of African socialism. Despite such traditions as the Rochdale principles, cooperation in its real sense has provided the basis of our African society for thousands of years. Our society was one vast cooperative."

There was an attempt to implement these policies in the Three-Year Plan but, as with most of the 1961–64 proposals, the planning and the financing were much too limited. Total allotments of $720,000—or hardly 1 per cent of the $70-million plan—went for cooperative development. The major portion of these funds went to expansion of the Cooperative Development Division of the Ministry of Agriculture. The staff of supervisors and inspectors was nearly doubled, from 158 to 286. Appropriately, an African officer, B. Maharage Juma, was appointed as commissioner of the division. Beginning his service as a cooperative inspector in Mwanza in 1940, Juma in 1949 became the first of the African staff to spend a year at Britain's cooperative college at Loughborough.

The Three-Year Plan also provided $120,000 for initiating Tanganyika's own cooperative college, based on the Loughborough pattern. Another $15,000 was to help organize the Cooperative Union of Tanganyika, whose purpose was to unite the country-wide movement

The expanded division staff continued to promote and arrange new cooperatives. By mid-1963 it could be reported that total membership, in 1,045 societies, had passed the half-million mark.

In 1962 the government had created two national organizations to lead the booming cooperatives. One, the Cooperative Union of Tanganyika, had W. R. Kapenga (a veteran cooperative society official) as secretary-general. It was announced that henceforth no society would be registered or allowed to function that did not affiliate with one of the 34 unions. The International Labor Organization dispatched its adviser on cooperative education and training to Dar es Salaam for a year's stay to draft a program of regional courses for society members. The new national union arranged for distribution of 384 tractors purchased for cooperative farmers by the Agricultural Credit Agency.

Managers of the various unions making up the national organization were called into Dar es Salaam for a seminar that was opened by Julius Nyerere with an admonition: "Tanganyika is a backward country, and we must have no misconception about it. The only way to develop our nation is for all Tanganyikans to accept that we know nothing and continue our search for knowledge. I myself am just learning to be a president. All I have in common with the President of the United States is the 21-gun salute."

Thus far the cooperative societies had been concerned, as we've seen, almost solely with crop marketing. The second new organization turned to the nation's consumers. On September 21, 1962, President Nyerere opened the Dar es Salaam headquarters of the new Cooperative Supply Association of Tanganyika. And on the same day he purchased the first twenty-shilling (about $2.80) share in the COSATA retail shop opened at the African township of Magomeni.

COSATA was the government's initial move in its plan to challenge Asian domination of the retail trade. Besides the store at Magomeni, others were planned that year in Moshi, Mbeya, and Ukiriguru. Minister of Commerce and Cooperatives Kasambala let it be known that COSATA was in business for keeps. "Unlike our rural cooperatives," he said, "the consumer cooperatives are faced with intensive competition of a ruthless kind. I am, however, determined that COSATA must be successful, and it is going to be." Vice-President Kawawa was more aggressive. "All who oppose COSATA," he said in a Cooperative

Week address, "are enemies and traitors. We will search out these people and keep them in a certain place."

Representing still another beginning in the cooperative field in 1962 was the creation of five credit unions. By 1963 there were 2,500 members in 26 of these self-help groups, and they were united into the Credit Union League of Tanganyika. Mr. Kasambala hailed this as the opening blow against the nation's "obnoxious pawnbrokers."

In a speech before the Dar es Salaam Chamber of Commerce on July 30, 1964, Jerry Kasambala indicated the extent to which he expected his cooperatives and private commercial firms to do business together. He said there would be a Tanganyika Association of Chambers of Commerce in which COSATA and other cooperative unions would be equal partners with private firms. The Association would be, he added, "an active and effective instrument in the development of the economic commercial life in the United Republic."

He revealed then the major role planned for cooperatives: "In the field of marketing, it is the aim that all produce, with the exception of perhaps sisal and tea, will be marketed through cooperative societies by 1970. This will be achieved by bringing produce handled by the cooperative societies under the control of government commodity boards."

The commodity boards, he said, would not conduct direct sales but a new government organization would be created to participate in the export business. "They will receive no special favor or treatment," he noted, "but will have to compete with commercial exporters."

By 1970 the cooperatives would have, Kasambala added, at least a 50 per cent share in all processing industries, through partnerships with private enterprise. However, the cooperatives would participate in manufacturing only in a minor capacity. As for distribution and import, Mr. Kasambala said, COSATA would be assisted in obtaining appointment as manufacturers' main agent for those commodities mainly consumed by Africans, with government organizations controlling at least 10 per cent of all import and distributive trade by 1970.

Mr. Kasambala said he would assist the government organizations "through import confinement," adding, "I have already done this in the case of jute and sisal products. I intend to do the same for imports of *khanga* cloth, milk products, synthetic fabrics and fibers, and bicycles." He noted that the policy would displace a "number of existing traders, particularly Asian traders, who will be affected by the changes in the distributive system." He advised them to "seek a new outlet in the field of industrial and agricultural enterprises."

A look at the new Five-Year Plan would show how Jerry Kasambala's hopes—some might call them threats—were to be implemented. The plan provided for a massive aid program in the form of low-interest loans to achieve most of the goals outlined before the Dar Chamber of Commerce. The loan program was to be administered by a new National Cooperative and Development Bank, with a credit agency prepared to advance $20 million in loans, almost exclusively through cooperatives.

In the field of agricultural production the plan called for $6 million in short-term credit for cotton farming alone. With 250,000 more acres to be planted, the loans would be made through 500 cotton cooperatives, to be used for tractors, fertilizers, plows and other equipment.

African farmers would be aided in controlling a greater share in the giant sisal industry. Dominated by foreign interests, mostly British, sisal production of 214,000 tons in 1963 accounted for more than one third of Tanganyika's export earnings. At a cost of nearly $5 million, it was planned to finance five African sisal settlements of 5,000 acres each. Credit also would be extended to cooperatives in the Lake Victoria region producing hedge sisal. Goal for sisal production by 1970 was 270,000 tons.

In coffee production, emphasis was to be placed on improved growing methods rather than on increased acreage. Loans of $1.5 million would be available to coffee cooperatives, mostly for copper sprayers, insecticides, pruning knives and other equipment. Target production by 1970 was set at 49,000 tons, nearly double that of the current crop. Annual coffee income by then would be approximately $50 million.

Groundnuts were still a large item of production and the target here was to treble the crop—from 16,000 to 45,000 tons—by 1970. It was an ambitious goal, but somewhat more realistic than the British promoters' 1946 target of three million tons. And only $75,000 was being allotted to help the groundnut farmers.

Loans from the remainder of the $20 million to be made available would aid cooperatives producing maize, rice, cashew nuts, cassava and a dozen other agricultural products. Hundreds of thousands of farmers who had been raising barely enough to live on might now, through the cooperatives, make a new start on a cash income basis.

The Five-Year Plan gave the cooperatives virtually a mandate to revolutionize Tanganyika's cattle-raising industry. In 1964 the country had a cattle population of 8.5 million but these were pitifully lean beasts living on a bare subsistence level. The livestock plan's emphasis would be on greatly increasing average weight of the cattle and on raising them for market and consumption rather than, as the plan noted, "as an idle investment and status symbol." This obvious thrust at the Masai, whose cattle often acquired the role somewhat of family pets, was underlined by the remark: "It is the intention to tackle on a broad front the problem of changing the age-old attitude of the Masai toward cattle."

Reform of the livestock industry would be entrusted to 150 new cattle cooperatives, which by 1970 were scheduled to market 70 per cent of the nation's livestock. More than $3 million would be expended on improvement of the total herd and $600,000 would be advanced to the cooperatives.

To alter the condition of Tanganyikans as almost exclusively the producers of primary agricultural products, the Five-Year Plan budgeted $7 million for the financing of processing equipment for African farmers. The equipment would range from sisal baling presses to mobile abattoirs to fish-refrigeration plants. A rubber-processing plant would be built for the raw product from the new Kilombero Valley plantations. A powdered milk plant would be built in Tabora. There even would be an instant-coffee plant for Bukoba. As Jerry Kasambala had stated, at least 50 per cent of these processing plants would be cooperatively operated.

To increase the cooperatives' share in the distributive field, the plan provided principally for increased credit resources for the established marketing cooperatives, but also made special provisions for the proposed cattle-marketing program and for COSATA and its new retail outlets. COSATA's 250 retail shops in rural trading centers would cost $1 million, the twelve supermarkets including the department store in Dar es Salaam, $1.5 million, and the 50 mobile shops, $450,-000. In the manufacturing sector, at a total investment of $200,000, the plan called only for sponsoring a chain of 50 tailoring cooperatives, twenty handicraft and ten construction societies.

By 1964 the architect's design for the new cooperative college was completed. A 30-acre plot at Moshi was selected and $450,000 allocated for the construction. The college would enroll 372 trainees a year. Basic training would be offered for the jobs of cooperative society secretaries, inspectors and cooperative union staff, and a one-year advanced course for manager trainees. Another indication of the cooperatives' coming of age was the decision to build a network of field offices throughout the country. Thus the touring agents called "cooperatives," many of them still making the rounds on motorcycles, would each have a headquarters.

By 1965, other evidence of the cooperative movement's astonishing growth could be pointed out in almost every corner of the land. None was so impressive, however, as the Victoria Federation of Cooperative Unions. This giant of the cooperatives now had a membership base of 200,000 cottongrowers in the lake region. They were organized into 450 primary societies and these in turn into nineteen affiliated unions. It was the function of the societies to collect the seed cotton from members, to grade, store and bag the cotton and make payments to the individual growers. The nineteen unions transported the cotton from the society warehouses to the ginneries, purchased and issued bags to the societies, and supervised administration of the societies. The federation, as the apex organization, was the policy maker for the cotton producers. It negotiated agreements for producers with the ginner and the government, served as purchasing agent for supplies and equipment, and marketed the total crop.

In 1965 the VFCU handled all the lake region's cotton crop: 250,-000 bales valued at $21 million. The federation owned eleven cotton ginneries, which processed more than half of the total crop. The VFCU also owned three oil mills and two rice mills. It owned a sisal factory at Musoma and had the monopoly on the hedge sisal in the region. It owned 158 tractors and that year bought nearly $2.5 million worth of fertilizer for the member societies.

Except for three European accountants and a few Asians, the federation was completely African, with Emmanuel Bomani (younger brother of Paul Bomani, the Minister of Finance) as general manager. In 1964 the VFCU operated on a budget that was one third the size of the Tanganyikan government's total budget. Its expenditures were three times those of the Ministry of Agriculture, which supervised the trade.

The VFCU's own goals in the Five-Year Plan were to double cotton production; to build ten ginneries and buy nine more to bring the total owned to 30; to buy five sisal factories, five oil mills and four rice mills. This empire, it should be recalled, had started hardly a decade before when a handful of peasant farmers banded together in protest against the greed of local traders. The VFCU is now the largest cooperative in Africa.

In 1964, the government announced that a $1.25-million cooperative center would be built on Lumumba Street in Dar es Salaam. The foundation stone of the fourteen-story center was laid on September 23 by President Nyerere, who described the structure as a symbol of the effort of all Tanzania's people to work together for the common good. The building would house the national headquarters of COSATA, of the Cooperative Union of Tanganyika, the National Cooperative and Development Bank and the new African Cooperative Alliance. This latter, Pan-African, organization had been created at a meeting in Moshi of representatives of the cooperative movement in all parts of the continent. In recognition of his country's leading place in the movement, Secretary-General Kapenga of the Cooperative Union of Tanganyika had been elected its president.

The movement was given voice, too, in 1964. A national cooperative newspaper, *Ushirika (Work Together)* began publication with a monthly issue of 25,000 copies for cooperative society officials throughout the country.

COSATA announced that at the end of its first year of business it had a turnover of $20 million. The National Credit Union announced a goal of 400 new member societies during the next five years. The Cooperative Union of Tanganyika announced that by 1970 it would double the number of cooperative societies—from 1,400 to 2,800.

It was all part of Tanganyika's purposeful mood as the country bustled through the first year of its great drive toward self-improvement. The opening months of the five-year campaign gave evidence that the cooperatives certainly would be in the vanguard of the national effort.

CHAPTER NINE

THE UNIONS ·

The labor movement in Tanganyika, after striving fitfully over the years to achieve a separate identity, became a full working partner of the nationalist government in 1964. Considering the country's circumstances, this was probably as it should be. As Julius Nyerere said: "If a government is a socialist government, representing the working people, then it must be treated and acknowledged as such, not only by the capitalists but by the workers themselves. Once firmly established, the trade union movement is part and parcel of the whole nationalist government."

In a country almost exclusively agricultural, organized labor could expect to make only modest progress and arouse little interest. In 1925 the British Governor, Sir Donald Cameron, created a Tanganyika Labor Department and the next year the department made a national survey. Labor recruitment, shortages, migrations and wages were studied but there was no evidence that labor had ever organized or gone on strike. "Workers did not protest conditions," said one survey member; "they simply avoided unpleasant employers." When Sir Donald left five years later, his labor department was discontinued. It was not revived until 1938.

It took the Groundnut Scheme to create an active interest in the labor issue. The succession of cargo steamers crowding into Dar e Salaam harbor in 1947, bringing men and machines for the project not only built up an army of dock workers, teamsters and truckmen but caused city food prices to rise way beyond the Africans' ability to pay. The dock men went in groups to their employers to demand better wages. They were rejected out of hand, for new labor was easy to recruit. On September 7 the workers held a mass meeting on the dock and refused to unload the ships. The move was not called a strike but it spread to African workmen all through the capital. For a week the city was paralyzed.

Officers of the Labor Department went among the dock men seeking leaders with whom to negotiate, but there seemed to be no responsible spokesmen. Even after the workers returned to their jobs on the promise of better pay, the labor officers continued to seek labor leadership for it was now the government's policy to encourage organization. A Trade Unions Ordinance was passed for the registration of unions Labor officers explained organization and negotiation. Finally, late in 1947, a dock workers' union was organized and duly registered. A few others followed.

At the end of 1947 the Labor Department reported for the first time the proportions of Tanganyika's labor population. Its annual repor announced 324,533 "natives" in regular manual employment, 28,88? in nonmanual employment and 10,709 in casual employment. The trade unions gradually emerged from their ranks.

An inveterate organizer, Rashidi Kawawa, was the first popularly recognized trade union figure. Even while still in school Kawawa had started the United Young Africans Organization to recruit student leaders for adult education. Upon graduation from Tabora Secondary School in 1949, he joined the Tanganyikan African Civil Servants Association and the following year was named its general secretary In 1954, when he was elected president of the association, he interested leaders of the handful of other unions, including the dock workers', in forming a united labor body. Thus was born, in 1955, the Tanganyika Federation of Labor. Rashidi Kawawa agreed to quit the civil service and work full time for the federation as its general secretary.

Kawawa had problems from the start. The colonial government was vigorously opposed to a national labor federation. Its labor officials had encouraged unions so long as they were run by westernized, clerical types who would cooperate with the department, but they frowned upon the new central organization. European employers also resisted further organization. They claimed the budding unions did not authentically represent the workers since only a small proportion of the workers were dues-paying members.

Kawawa realized this was a valid criticism in the TFL's formative years. Most of the union leaders were illiterate "voices of discontent" and membership standards were lax. Most members, having paid the original fee to join, rarely paid regular dues. Yet all were ready to strike when action was demanded and therein lay the union's strength.

This strength was demonstrated within the year. In 1956 the Hotel Workers Union went on strike for higher wages and better working conditions. Other unions joined in their demand. Several employers resorted to a lock-out of workers. The strike became a general one, paralyzing business in Dar es Salaam. Kawawa flew to London to consult with officials of the Trades Union Congress. A TUC man and another from the International Confederation of Free Trade Unions were dispatched to Dar es Salaam. They soon negotiated a settlement that not only improved working conditions but included a minimum wage agreement. Union members now saw the benefits of organization and were more inclined to pay their dues.

The following year the second United Nations Mission visited Tanganyika. In its report it noted "a vigorous trade union movement." The first Mission (in 1954) had reported no unionism at all. The 1957 team found 25 unions registered (fifteen of them members of the TFL) and a total union membership of 35,000.

When he resigned from the civil service Rashidi Kawawa had joined TANU and, as might have been expected, was soon prominent in its affairs. He organized its national Youth League movement and in 1957 was rewarded by TANU with appointment as one of its nominees to the Legislative Council.

Some of the potential of this early alliance of labor with TANU was revealed during the 1958 annual conference of the party at Tabora. Here plans were discussed for a general nation-wide strike if the government did not concede some of TANU's political demands. The strike plan included civil servants so that national administration itself would be crippled. Fortunately, Julius Nyerere decided such action was unnecessary.

By 1960, Kawawa, elevated now to the presidency of the TFL, reported that membership of his 27 unions had tripled to 95,000. The largest group was the Tanganyika Plantation Workers Union, with 25,000 members. Others included the Tanganyika Railway African Union, 16,250 members; Tanganyika Union of Public Employes, 14,-000; Transport and General Workers Union, 10,000; and Tanganyika African Local Government Workers Union, 8,000.

Equally impressive was the Ministry of Labor and Health report that 56 per cent of the working population's terms of employment were now determined by collective agreements. Wages of the 131,699 sisal and 19,277 tea workers were negotiated by the plantation union. There was now a total of 404,742 workers in the country. Their average monthly wage had risen from $9 to $10. Highest paid were urban workers in Tanga and Dar es Salaam who averaged $18 a month.

Other union leaders also began to emerge. Michael Kamaliza, general secretary of the Transport and General Workers Union, publicly denounced Asian companies for refusing to negotiate with his union. He called a strike of 400 workers in Kilosa and, after trucks and cabs had been idle for eleven days, announced a wage agreement that gave a minimum of $11 a month for unskilled workers and $28 for drivers. Kamaliza also did not hesitate to denounce those in high places. When Sir James Farquharson, acting Commissioner for Transport, suggested in Dar es Salaam that the government adopt India's policy of banning strikes by workers in any public utilities, Kamaliza attacked the Commissioner's proposal as "highly irresponsible."

L. L. Ngahyoma, general secretary of the Dock Workers and Stevedores Union, claimed in a press statement that Dar es Salaam's stevedoring companies collected nearly $4 million annually for handling ship cargoes but distributed less than $1 million of this to the dock men who did all the work. He demanded a 40-hour week and $35 a month pay for his union workers. He settled reluctantly for $25 a month and three additional days off with pay.

When Rashidi Kawawa resigned as TFL president in September 1960, to join Chief Minister Nyerere's government, Michael Kamaliza was elected to succeed him. Kamaliza, in turn, appointed J. D. Namfua, secretary of the National Union of Post Office and Telecommunications Employes, as TFL's secretary-treasurer.

Young Mr. Namfua discovered almost immediately that the federation's relations with the new Nyerere government were not necessarily smooth. In December he went north to Mwadui in the lake region to confer with leaders of the Tanganyika Mine Workers Union who had threatened to strike at the Williamson diamond mine. Apparently because the mine was partly government-owned, the new Minister of Commerce, Nsilo Swai, also hurried to the scene. Namfua spoke to union and mine officials and found both sides ready to negotiate. Mr. Swai announced, however, that if the miners did not return to work in 48 hours they would all be fired. He described the Williamson mine as a model employer. An editorial in the *Tanganyika Standard* supported him in this, noting that the miners received an average of $2 a day and housing facilities.

Protesting at what they called government interference, the union leaders thereupon went through with the strike. It lasted eleven days and cost the mine an estimated $320,000. On December 17 Namfua met with the mine management and next day announced an eight-point agreement which included pay increases, compensation for injury and other benefits. Namfua added a statement for the press: "I must warn the government that trade unionism was put on trial at Mwadui. Trade unionism has sustained that trial and trade unionism is here to stay. We do not and shall not take orders from anybody other than from the members we represent."

These strong words were quickly rebutted by the *Standard,* which editorialized: "Mr. Namfua should beware. If he forces the government into a trial of strength he is likely to come off second best." Yet not too long before, the *Standard* had described members of the government as "hotheads and rowdies."

Labor and government also crossed swords on the issue of Africanization of jobs, both in the civil service and in business. During a debate in the National Assembly, Chief Minister Nyerere announced that his government's Africanization policy was to get local people, whether they were Africans or not, into the civil service to supplant expatriate officials. The Tanganyikan Union of Public Employes took angry exception; they wanted no jobs to go to Europeans, local or not. A

INDEPENDENCE DUE: When British Colonial Secretary Iain MacLeod came to Dar es Salaam in March 1961, Julius Nyerere and his TANU leaders knew that their fight for independence was nearly over. And following only two days of discussions in Karimjee Hall it was announced that self-government would begin on May 1 and full independence would follow in December of the same year. Before entering the hall for the historic conference, Nyerere posed outside with well-wishers from various tribal groups. Among them, beaming broadly at his right, was Bibi Titi Mohamed, dynamic women's leader of TANU.

PRESIDENTIAL SMILE: Some of the buoyancy that helped make him beloved by his people is shown in this candid photo of President Nyerere, making one of his informal inspection trips to a community development project at Morogoro. At left is Vice-President Rashidi Kawawa and at right, behind the President, the then Minister of Culture and Youth, L. N. Sijaona.

TUPE press statement claimed that the union could name twenty competent Africans to fill twenty official posts for which the government was recruiting personnel in the United Kingdom. It also noted that in many government departments Africans were doing all the essential work while European officials sat in the departments as figureheads. The statement concluded: "Mr. Nyerere has been misled or misinformed."

In the Legislative Council, members who were also union officials continued the attack on the Africanization policy. They also criticized the government on unemployment: in late December a TFL statement described Chief Minister Nyerere's program to combat the problem as "very inadequate." There was considerable other evidence in the following months that labor leaders were ready to speak out against the government, TANU, or Julius Nyerere himself.

For example, the Dar es Salaam branch of the Tanganyika Union of African Teachers sent a delegation to Nyerere to protest the school salary scale passed by the National Assembly. They urged him to cut the salaries of ministers, members of Legco and non-Africans "earning fat salaries in the Ministry of Education." They charged MPs with being yes men for accepting the Ministry's salary recommendations and threatened to call a teachers' strike if they were not amended.

After the annual dinner of the Tanganyika Sisal Growers Association (at which the association chairman had charged unions with bringing the industry "to a point of collapse"), Victor A. Mkello, general secretary of the powerful Tanganyika Plantation Workers Union, chided the association for not having invited a single African employee to the dinner. And Mr. Mkello chided Chief Minister Nyerere for attending the dinner without checking first with the TPWU on union relations with sisal plantation management.

L. L. Ngahyoma, the docks unionist, threatened that his dock workers would take over the port of Dar es Salaam if the Ministry of Labor did not soon require compulsory arbitration to settle cargo-handling labor disputes. The union did, in fact, call a slow-down strike during which ship handling was reduced 50 per cent. Ships were kept waiting outside the harbor and, with maize imports cut off, areas of the Central and Northern Provinces were reduced to near-famine. After a month the slow-down ended, with the union winning its objective: a 40-hour week.

The TFL itself came under attack during the stormy labor days of 1961–62. Early in 1961 members of the Building Construction and Industrial Union (which was not affiliated with the federation) went on strike in Dar es Salaam where they were building the new high-rise Standard Bank. The union's leaders accused the TFL of undermining the strike by allowing members of its own Transport and General Workers Union to cross picket lines at the bank building. A band of strikers marched to the site and charged the rival unionists working on the project. A police squad forced the strikers back and cordoned off the downtown area. The shouting strikers then marched on the TFL's headquarters. Several marchers were arrested and subsequently fined. TFL Secretary-Treasurer Namfua testified in court that one of the defendants had shouted: "We have given them our votes and now these dogs are becoming corrupt. We shall not tolerate TFL nonsense. There will be blood shed."

Not long after this incident, Namfua resigned his TFL post to become parliamentary secretary to the National Treasury. He was the first of a number of labor leaders to accept government posts. Succeeding Namfua at the TFL was Clemence Rwegasira, a Bukoba unionist who had represented the Tanganyika Railway African Union at a World Federation of Trade Unions congress in Moscow. Taking office, Rwegasira told newsmen: "It is my intention to use my influence to make the TFL as independent as possible from political control."

In March 1962, Rashidi Kawawa, after his surprise inheritance of the premiership from Julius Nyerere, appointed TFL President Michael Kamaliza as his Minister of Labor and precipitated a wholesale reshuffling of the federation's leadership. Into the TFL presidency went Victor Mkello, the fiery Tangan plantation organizer, and R. J. Magongo moved up from the militant Tanganyika Union of Public Employes to be general secretary, with new executive powers. Clemence Rwegasira was retained as a director of the federation. One of the new regime's first moves was to nominate twenty students for the Patrice Lumumba Friendship University in Moscow. They also took under advisement a proposal to nationalize all major industry, made by S. J. Katungutu, general secretary of the Tanganyika Railway African Union who had just returned from East Germany.

The TFL's new general secretary indirectly confirmed the widening divisions between the trade unions and TANU by announcing that a standing relations committee—eight members from the TFL and eight from TANU—was being appointed to promote a united approach on national issues. The committee, for one thing, would support TFL unions and discourage creation of new ones, like the militant construction union.

In June 1962, the government revealed its formula for a labor policy. Minister of Labor Kamaliza introduced two bills in the National Assembly. The Trade Unions Ordinance (Amendment) Act, empowered the Minister of Labor to name the TFL as the "designated federation" to which all unions must belong. It also authorized a "check-off" system by which union dues were deducted from members' pay by employers, and required each union to turn over a proportion of these dues to the federation. The other bill, the Trades Disputes (Settlement) Act, made both strikes and lock-outs illegal unless a complex procedure of arbitration through the Ministry of Labor was first utilized. Unionists could remember Kamaliza once describing a similar proposal for a ban on strikes as "irresponsible." The first law had the immediate result of canceling the registration of nineteen trade unions, which were regrouped into affiliates of the TFL.

Outraged union leaders complained that the government was swallowing up the labor movement. Said a statement of the Tanganyikan National Union of Teachers: "This is a very shameful and shortsighted declaration by the government of their failure to accord fundamental human rights to the working people of the country." The TNUT president, D. M. S. Mdachi, was more specific. "We are fast moving into totalitarianism," he charged. "Why force unions to join in a puppet federation controlled by a minister?"

At a rally held in Dar es Salaam to denounce the bills, Abdullah Mwamba, Tanganyika Railway African Union chairman, called for the immediate resignation of the Minister of Labor. The Tanganyika Plantation Workers Union predicted that the new laws would start a perpetual war between government and labor. The TFL officers were unanimously opposed. Said General Secretary Magongo: "This will hold the labor movement back because both sides, labor and management, recognize that it forces agreements on them." Said Director Rwegasira: "This abominable policy cannot suit the aspirations of the working class." And, more moderately, President Mkello: "I appeal to my fellow president of TANU to see that the country is not divided into two by passage of these bills." Through the summer the bills were debated in the Assembly and disputed at union meetings, but by September both were passed.

Within the TFL itself the dispute split the member unions into several fighting factions. It began at a TFL meeting when General Secretary Ngahyoma of the dockers' union claimed that Mr. Nyerere "had misrepresented the facts" while explaining the two labor bills at a rally sponsored by TANU. TFL Secretary Magongo said the federation would support the anti-Nyerere charge and anyone who did not was "a stooge and a Tshombe." This outburst proved Magongo's undoing, for soon thereafter President Mkello announced the suspension of both the TFL general secretary and of TFL Vice-President Hassan R. Khupe (because the latter had protested Magongo's suspension).

The suspensions were opposed by the Mine Workers Union and the Tanganyika Railway African Union—and they in turn were suspended. Matters appeared to be deteriorating rapidly when the National Union of Post Office and Telecommunications Employes protested the suspension of the two unions. The TFL's General Council halted the process in November when it confirmed the dismissal of Magongo and Khupe, ousted the railways union from TFL membership and lifted the suspension of the Mine Workers Union.

TRAU, now an outlaw union, continued to harass the government. In January 1963, it accused the Ministry of Labor of deliberate delay in handling labor disputes and Africanization of jobs. TANU responded for the government, accusing TRAU Secretary Katungutu of secretly attempting to destroy national security.

Labor affairs in the sisal industry were at this time preoccupying the government. Although, in November 1962, new agreements had generally raised sisal labor wages, by late January 1963 more than 10,000 workers were on strike on fifteen estates. The Ministry of Labor had set up a Central Joint Council for sisal labor-management discussions but Victor Mkello's TPWU refused to accept the Council's role as negotiating machinery. The strikes threatened to paralyze the all-important sisal industry.

President Nyerere acted firmly. Invoking Section II of the Deportation Ordinance, he ordered that Mkello and the TPWU's organizing secretary, Shehe Amiri, be taken into custody. The two were put into detention at Sumbawanga, in the Ufipa district, charged with inciting illegal strikes and organizing opposition to labor legislation. Restrictions were placed on union activities in the sisal country around Tanga, and union officials were not allowed on the estates.

The TFL protested their president's detention and were joined by the Zanzibar and Pemba Federations of Labor in appealing to the President to release Mkello. On February 1 a TFL delegation called on Nyerere at the State House to repeat the request, but again it was rejected.

Meanwhile, a new general secretary, more sympathetic to government intentions, had been appointed by the TFL. He was A. C. A. Tandau, former secretary of the Transport and General Workers Union. Immediately prior to his appointment Tandau had taken the government's side when a visiting official of the International Transport Workers Federation, Walter Townsend, had urged the TFL to re-admit TRAU to membership, even though the railway unionists might occasionally criticize official policy. Tandau was indignant about the suggestion. "I warn all our international friends not to interfere in our internal affairs," he said in a press statement. Nonetheless, less than a month later, Minister of Labor Kamaliza announced that TRAU was, after all, still an affiliate of the TFL even with its membership canceled. TRAU, Kamaliza blandly explained, was still a registered union and as such was still bound by federation rules.

On March 9 President Nyerere lifted the two month-long deportation orders on Mkello and Amiri. Mkello returned to his three official positions apparently without rancor. He resumed work with his plantation union, presided again at TFL meetings and attended National Assembly sessions, having been seated the year before as one of the nominated members. On March 15 he addressed a welcome-back rally in Morogoro and announced he felt no bitterness and would cooperate with the government to help build the country. But later in the year, when the TFL General Council discussed a government proposal to reorganize the federation into more of an official body within the Ministry of Labor, he was among the unionists who put down the suggestion.

In other ways it was made clear that labor was still chary about identification with government. Minister of Labor Kamaliza was confronted with this feeling when he went to the Dar es Salaam waterfront in September to hear dock workers' demands for a provident fund and severance allowances (to be paid when government plans to take over port management in early 1964 went through). Kamaliza listed the good things that the government had brought to the workers but he said that they could not keep their jobs and still get severance pay. The workers booed, hissed and chanted: "We want money, money, money!" They shouted that they would be ending service with old employers and entering new employment when the government took over, so were due the allowances. Kamaliza promised a $30 bonus in lieu of the allowance, but when he left they were still booing.

The Tanganyika Union of Public Employes, too, was impatient. They charged the government's policy of Africanization was leading, instead, to "brotherization," with relatives of African officials getting the prime positions. They said other Africans in key government posts were becoming "black colonialists" who liked to have Europeans and Asians, rather than Africans, working under them. President Nyerere regarded the charges seriously, named a committee including TUPE and TFL representatives to study the situation.

Uglier charges were heard from TUPE officials late in 1963. At a mass meeting of the union in Dar es Salaam one of its secretaries, Rogers Mlangwa, was cheered when he called for nationalization of all industry. He called upon government leaders to go to Eastern countries to learn how socialism really worked. He was cheered again when he said: "Some of our leaders themselves have shares in foreign enterprises in this country."

Protesting the discharge of 25 Public Works Department electricians who had gone on strike, the general secretary of TUPE on January 10, 1964, remarked: "The government should realize that when Tanganyikans fought for freedom and human respect they did so because they wanted these rights to be accorded not to the President, his ministers and other personalities alone, but for all the people of Tanganyika." These were unpleasant words for Nyerere and his followers, but they reflected the mood of at least a part of the nation at the time. And it was then that the mutinous events of the dark month of January 1964 exploded, to cause such national shame.

It was reported that labor had its part in the mutiny plot and indeed it was primarily fear of a labor-military alliance of dissidents that reportedly prompted President Nyerere to call the British troops in. President Nyerere himself announced that TFL leaders and other union officials were among those arrested after the mutiny. The names were never made public nor was disposition of their cases announced, but it was not difficult to identify who was missing.

It was the end, at any rate, of the Tanganyika Federation of Labor, which only three months before had observed its eighth anniversary with a mass rally. On January 27 what was left of the TFL leadership met in executive session and voted the demise of the organization. This, as might have been expected, was sentimentally expressed. On February 8, TFL General Secretary Alfred Cyril Tandau led a procession of hundreds of unionists through Dar es Salaam to the door of the State House. They stood quietly in the sun until Julius Nyerere appeared. He was flanked by Vice-President Kawawa and by Labor Minister Kamaliza.

Tandau addressed the President, to assure him that he and his government had the faith of the nation's labor. Tandau said that labor wanted to help restore Tanganyika's damaged name and was ready to join with TANU, the cooperatives and the farmers of the land in this. Visibly affected, Nyerere thanked the unionists for the statement of loyalty. It was only the "bad ones," he said, who had been picked up after the mutiny. There were 200 in all, he explained, from the trade unions, the police and military, from the general public and even from TANU. This was, after all, "only 200 out of ten million," he pointed out, adding that it was now up to the rest to join in the rebuilding.

Two weeks later, labor was nationalized by a bill introduced in the National Assembly on February 21 by Michael Kamaliza. The Minister began his address with a sober account of recent labor developments in the country. Trade union leadership, Kamaliza claimed, had been administratively irresponsible, financially lax and viciously self-interested. A review of union expenditures, he said, showed that 93.8 per cent of total union income had been used for administrative expenses, including the maintenance of fleets of motorcars. He singled out Victor Mkello's plantation union as an example. In 1962, Kamaliza reported, total income of the TPWU was 1,499,000 shillings, or about $200,000. Mkello and his staff had spent 95 per cent of this on administration. Virtually nothing in the way of benefits had gone back to the workers.

Kamaliza told the Assembly that such conditions argued for reorganization of the trade union movement "in a manner which would unite all wage earners within a single workers' movement which would be an additional instrument of national unity." He therefore submitted for vote the National Union of Tanganyika Workers (Establishment) Act, 1964. The union, Kamaliza explained, would be closely affiliated with TANU and would be known, by overlooking the slight alphabetical inconsistency that would nicely allow the acronym, as NUTA.

The bill creating NUTA not only legally dissolved the TFL but eliminated all other unions. Workers would now join one of the nine sections of NUTA: Docks, Agriculture, Domestics, Transport, Central Government Civil Servants, Local Government Civil Servants, Teachers, Miners, and East African Common Services Workers—including railway, postal and customs employees.

NUTA would be headed by a general secretary and a deputy secretary, both to be appointed for five years by the president of the republic. The general secretary would appoint an assistant secretary to head each of the nine sections. There also would be a NUTA secretary in each of the country's ten regions. The secretaries together would make up NUTA's general council, which would be responsible to an annual congress to which all area branches would send representatives.

The Minister of Labor explained why the power of appointment of NUTA's leadership should be vested in the president: "I realize that the decision may be misunderstood by some critics, particularly overseas. These critics should know that in Tanganyika we have had a trade union movement which has been weakened by conflicts of personalities between union leaders. It is now the intention of government to remove this source of weakness and that a strong labor movement be organized and built up which will assist government in implementing effectively our socialist policies." He added: "We in this country are endeavoring to find a solution to our problems which will be a Tanganyikan solution, and we are not required to copy or be bound by foreign ideas."

NUTA would require all workers in a unionized shop to be members and the check-off system of deducting dues would be continued. This, Kamaliza emphasized, assured NUTA of adequate revenue. He estimated that, with 300,000 expected to be enrolled in the national union, annual income would approximate one million dollars. Not more than 40 per cent of union income, the Minister said, would be allowed to be used for administrative expenses. The balance would go into social services for union members, including housing, and into investment.

The NUTA bill was passed virtually without debate and the following day President Nyerere appointed Minister of Labor Kamaliza as the union's general secretary and A. C. Tandau, formerly of the TFL, as deputy secretary. Kamaliza immediately named the nine union men who would be his section secretaries. And he announced that NUTA had no intention of affiliating with any international organization.

Tanganyika appeared to accept the wholesale labor reform calmly. The press commented politely on the necessity of firm action if restive unions were to be controlled. Kamaliza put the issue forthrightly to the people. He called a public rally in Dar es Salaam and spoke effectively on the aims of NUTA. The talk went over. He even won cheers when he explained that in the future each industry and shop would have workers' committees which would have to be consulted before a worker could be dismissed. He was cheered again when he defended the new union as characteristic of African socialism.

However, Kenyan labor leaders were critical. A statement by the Kenya Railway African Union denounced creation of NUTA as "a defeatist move." The general secretary of Kenya's Federation of Labor said: "It is unfair to have the Minister of Labor as general secretary of the union unless the government also makes him general secretary of the employers' association." He added: "Socialist countries do not go this far in labor policies." Nonetheless, only eight months later Kenya followed Tanganyika's example by dissolving its own Kenya Federation of Labor and the Kenya African Workers Congress and creating the government-sponsored Central Organization of Trade Unions.

But Tanganyika's favorable reaction became enthusiastic as NUTA announced what it was accomplishing for the worker. One achievement was passage of the Security of Employment Act, which legalized the workers' committees Kamaliza had promised. Provisions of the act were based on agreements signed by NUTA and the Federation of Tanganyika Employers on procedures to be followed by the committees. As the Minister explained it, the committees, which were to meet regularly, would make labor and management realize they both had responsibilities that were vital to national prosperity. "This bill will protect the good worker against the bad employer and the good employer against the bad workers," he said.

Other accomplishments included formation of the Workers Investment Corporation and the National Provident Fund. A three-man board was appointed to direct NUTA investments in housing, small industry, and building loans. Union members were made to feel that their total contribution would have a vital part in national development. This feeling was promoted by the National Provident Fund. Approved by the National Assembly, the fund would be built up from contributions by both employers and employees. It would be directed by a board of fifteen: five representing government, five the employers and five the workers, with three trustees to invest funds. It was estimated that $5 million would annually be made available from the fund for development projects.

On the industrial front, NUTA was signing labor agreements for the workers which Kamaliza announced would raise the 1964–65 wage level 42 per cent higher than it had been in 1962–63. In November 1964, NUTA and the Tanganyika Sisal Growers Association signed a contract that established a closed shop in the sisal industry and effected annual wage increases totaling $4 million. A pact was signed in December between NUTA and the major oil companies in Tanzania awarding 10 per cent pay increases. The Tanganyika Textiles Ltd. agreed to a minimum monthly wage of $30 with a $3 annual pay raise. The East African Tobacco Company raised their minimum wage to $35 and agreed to quarterly reviews of the company wage structure. The Tanganyika Electric Supply Company signed a NUTA contract allowing wage increases of 5, 15 and 25 per cent in different worker categories.

A general wage agreement covering most of the country's large agricultural estates was signed by NUTA and the Tanganyika Association of Agricultural Employers. The agreement called for establishment of a national industrial council which would rule on wages, lay-off and severance procedures for agricultural workers. In December a four-man delegation led by Jason Moaga, head of NUTA's civil service section, sat down with a committee in President Nyerere's office to establish a new pay schedule for civil servants.

In its first year, NUTA set a pace that would almost assuredly attain the labor targets set in the Five-Year Plan. And it looked, in mid-1965, as though the labor situation were well in hand. As NUTA moved into new offices not far from TANU headquarters in Dar es Salaam and then laid the foundation for a multistoried office building of its own, there was every appearance that an efficient and dedicated corps of administrators had taken over from the brawling rival unionists of TFL days. The motives, the organizational structure and the financial affairs of the new labor order were now matters of public record. Labor seemed to be marching in step with the rest of the country toward the prescribed national goals. It was too early to tell what restive forces, if any, were still brewing within the labor ranks, ready to rebel against the new discipline.

Those taking the brighter view would have accepted the happy summary that Michael Kamaliza made of labor affairs in a statement to the press in 1965. "The last two years," he said, "have seen the emergence of an efficient and compact labor force which is a key to the success of any plan for economic development and to a plan such as ours which places great emphasis on increasing industrialization."

In speaking for labor and its part in Tanganyika's development plan, Kamaliza still was speaking for only 3.5 per cent of the country's population. There remained the ten million people toiling in the traditional agricultural pursuits and the one million of their number whom the government planners hoped to move into areas of high productivity. The goals fixed for them made up the very heart of the Five-Year Plan.

CHAPTER TEN

THE FARMERS

The success of Tanganyika's Five-Year Plan rested primarily on members of a farming population of ten million that was largely illiterate and seemed discouragingly remote and ill-organized. It was a perilous point of departure for the country's elaborate economic design. When Julius Nyerere stood before the National Assembly in May 1964 to outline the development program, he emphasized again and again that increased agricultural production was the key to the plan. It would not succeed, he said, unless the individual farmer increased his yield, improved his quality and—where necessary—expanded his area of cultivation. The plan, he pointed out, would stand or fall according to the effort of the man with the hoe.

The President explained what this meant in terms of individual production. Each farmer, he said, must increase production annually by 7 per cent, in terms of value of the goods marketed. For every $100 he earned by selling his crops in 1965 he must earn $107 the next year, $114.50 the next and so on. The government, Nyerere added, would do all in its power to help the farmer do this.

A few months later, in his annual report for 1964, Saidi Ali Maswanya, the new Minister for Agriculture, outlined farming goals in terms of total national production. A massive ex-police official of the Nyamwezi tribe, Saidi Maswanya had been assigned the Agriculture portfolio because he himself was a proven producer. He had demonstrated administrative ability both in police work and as a TANU organizer. Like several of his colleagues in the cabinet, Maswanya was a graduate of the government school in his native Tabora.

Maswanya presented a table of five-year agricultural goals which meant in some cases a doubling of production by 1970. "Put in its simplest terms," the Minister reported, "this means that the farmers growing these crops will have to produce one third more sisal, two and a half times more cotton, twice as much coffee, two and a half times more tea, twice as much cashew, two and a half times as much tobacco, three times as much pyrethrum, three times as much groundnuts, three times as much sugar cane, twice as much maize, twice as much seed beans, two and a half times as much rice."

The Minister noted that he deliberately used the word "produce" because in the minds of many people "to grow more" meant to increase physically the amount of land under a particular crop. "What we aim to do, rather," he said, "is to persuade the farmer to adopt new and more modern techniques so that he can achieve most of his production without necessarily increasing the amount of land he cultivates." This was the essence of the "improvement approach" suggested in the Five-Year Plan, as opposed to the "transformation approach."

In Tanganyika, agriculture generally was still practiced under the traditional system of shifting cultivation. This meant that only enough crops were raised to provide the food and subsistence requirements of the family. It involved clearing an area of bush, cultivating it for a period of from two to eight years (depending on the nature of the soil), then moving to a new area to repeat the process. The abandoned land rarely recovered its initial virgin fertility because of erosion and oxidation and the practice of clearing by fire. Fire was used after rough clearing to free the land of debris and undergrowth, but often it swept uncontrolled over vast areas. The combination of shifting cultivation and fire reduced thousands of square miles of Tanganyika and other parts of Africa to desolate scrubland.

Farming methods were primitive. Usually the only implement used was the *jembe,* a stout, short-handled hoe. In cases where livestock was kept by the farmer, grazing was normally in bush pasture away from the cultivated land so that no use was made of manure as fertilizer. Because 60 per cent of Tanganyika was infested with the tsetse fly, it was not surprising that in any one year hardly one tenth of the 178 million acres of land available to the African farmer was under cultivation. Another reason for the low proportion of cultivated land was the fact that approximately 35 per cent of the fertile area was used to graze livestock.

To aid the farmer, particularly the stock raiser, the Five-Year Plan declared open war on the ubiquitous tsetse fly. Tanganyika, in the heart of the tsetse belt that included much of tropical Africa, had suffered great human and animal losses from the infection carried by the fly, which causes the often-fatal sleeping sickness in men and the wasting disease of *nagana* in cattle. In neighboring Uganda, the fly had brought death to 200,000 humans between 1901 and 1906, killing two thirds of the inhabitants in the affected area. By 1964 in Tanganyika, according to Minister Maswanya, the human toll had been reduced to only 500 yearly while the annual damage to cattle in cash terms was estimated at $7.5 million.

The tsetse, which looks like a brownish housefly, carries the infectious trypanosomes from one human or animal host to another by biting and sucking the blood. Because the tsetse can fly a range of barely 300 yards and live only in trees or bush, they can be eliminated from areas of human habitation by clearing all growth from a wide belt outside the area. The government campaign against the tsetse scourge, said Minister Maswanya, would cost $1.5 million and would include purchase of two aircraft for an aerial spray attack on the pest, for a biological control unit at Tabora, and for motor vehicles and spray equipment for ground warfare against the fly.

The Five-Year Plan would aid the farmers' fight against other pests as well. A ministry control unit was already killing 100 million birds a year. Unchecked, the grain-eating birds had consumed an estimated 80,000 tons of crops each year in the North and Central Provinces. The plan included motor vehicles and additional staff for a new control base at Arusha. Other pests were rats and mice which annually destroyed an estimated 25 per cent of crop production. An appropriation of $150,000 was made for the vermin control unit. Another million dollars would be spent to build 500 cattle-dipping stations in the campaign against ticks and tick-borne diseases.

Special education would be provided for the farmer. Under the Three-Year Plan experimental farmer training centers had been so successful that eighteen more, at a cost of $1 million, were to be built in the various provinces during the next five years. Training of agricultural agents was also to be greatly expanded, with additional facilities at the ministry training institutes at Ukiriguru and Tengeru and at the new agricultural college planned at Morogoro. Staff expansion would allow the ratio of agricultural agents of only one to 2,500 population to be increased to one to 1,000.

Here, actually, was the crux of the agricultural improvement approach. If production was to increase annually by the projected 7 per cent, it would depend largely on the success of the agents in the field —both the agricultural and the community development officers—in reaching the farmer in his own environment and persuading him to adopt improved methods. Improvement meant that farming would be more intensive and on more permanent locations.

The transformation approach toward increased production was far more revolutionary than the patient improvement approach. As President Nyerere told the National Assembly in his Five-Year Plan address, this called for the settlement by 1980 of one million farmers in collective villages where high productivity agriculture would be carried out.

The settlement program was made up of two parts. One, the regrouping and resettling of farming families within that one third of the country's area where fertile soil and adequate rainfall favored production. The other, settlements in new, unexploited areas which would be developed by irrigation projects and flood control.

The Ministry of Lands, Settlement and Water Development, and its new Minister, Nangwanda Sijaona, would direct the vast settlement plan. Sijaona was another of the young TANU leaders whose record of party and government service prompted President Nyerere to entrust him with one of the major responsibilities in the achievement of development goals. When only twenty-seven, Nangwanda Sijaona had been the first African to be elected chairman of a town council. That was in

1955 in his native town of Newala, in the Southern Province. He was later elected an MP for Lindi and served as parliamentary secretary to the National Treasury.

The settlement idea had its roots in the 1960 recommendations of the World Bank Mission. The members reasoned that farmers on new and favorable soil would be more receptive to change than if they remained in familiar surroundings. Mission members also reasoned that such farmers would be willing to adopt new practices and abide by rules as a condition of receiving land grants and government aid.

Julius Nyerere had responded to the settlement proposal at once and in 1963 he created the Village Settlement Agency to promote the idea. As agency commissioner he named S. W. Frazier-Smith, a tall, bony former colonial officer of the progressive missionary breed such as those who had nurtured the country's cooperative movement. Commissioner Frazier-Smith was firmly convinced that the settlements offered Tanganyika as bright a potential as the prospering cooperatives. The basic principle of the settlements, he said, was that the community should live as a "gathered" village. Concentrated groups of farmers, in villages rather than in scattered hamlets, made it easier to foster a spirit of group cooperation, and cooperation, the Commissioner contended, was the most rapid road to agricultural progress.

"The grouping of people in villages," said Frazier-Smith, "implies in itself a new pattern of agriculture. That pattern is to allow each farmer to have a homestead plot of approximately one acre within the village, but he would also hold land in one or more different soil-type plots surrounding the village. In this way not only will he have an equal share in the good and poor soils but, by grouping the types of crops grown into large blocks according to soil capability, use would be made of tractors and other modern agricultural aids so that a farmer would not be limited to his capacity to cultivate with the hand hoe. For example, if cotton were the main cash crop it would be possible to plow, harrow, plant and spray economically by machinery a large block within which each farmer would have his individual plot."

The commissioner explained that each settlement would be made up of 250 families. According to one plan, they might live in a single village around a service center, which would include a market, schools, a hospital or clinic, community hall, government and cooperative offices, playing field and village green, police station and reserved areas for other community services. Another settlement design called for three or more small villages around a central service center. Thirty or so families, as services personnel, would be added to each village's farming population. The community area would total 300 acres. With outlying croplands of fifteen to eighteen acres per farmer, the whole settlement would require about 4,500 acres.

Five such settlements had already been started on a pilot basis in 1963. But under the Five-Year Plan a total of 79 would be launched, each to be granted a government advance of $450,000 which the farmers would repay on a long-term loan basis. Financing required approval by the respective regional development committee and a survey of the area's soil and water resources. The settlement agency provided planning officers to lay out the village and farmlands, and agricultural officers to advise on crop selection and production methods. The agency also would assign to some of the settlements a production manager to be in charge until community leaders could take over.

Thus far, Frazier-Smith said, there had been no trouble in recruiting settlers. Yet from the experience of the pilot villages lessons had been learned about settler volunteers. One was that urban dwellers made poor settlers and often deserted the hard life of a farmer. Also, resistance was encountered in moving farmers from some overpopulated areas, particularly on the slopes of the high northern country. This was true of the Wasambara in the Usambara mountain region and among the tribes of the Pare hills, who were urged to resettle in the rich Pangani Valley farmland. They had to be convinced that they were not threatened by malaria in the lowlands.

To anyone who wanted to see at first hand a settlement under development, Commissioner Frazier-Smith recommended a trip to Rwankoma. This was one of the five pilot settlements started in 1963 with a $900,000 loan from the United Kingdom. Rwankoma, a fertile valley lying inland from Lake Victoria, is not far from the great plain making up the Serengeti national park. The wide valley, flanked by a jagged range of low, brooding mountains, is scorched by the sun in daytime, but winds off the lake soften the air at night. The settlement is at the head of the valley.

Rwankoma was to be a community of three villages. One of them was already complete, a second under construction. These were pleasantly sited on one side of a hill that leveled out into the village center.

CD's GUIDING SPIRI¹
Hon. Marion, the Lady Ch[e]
ham, American-born memb[er]
of Tanzania's Parliament, b[e]
came a pioneer leader of t[he]
community development mov[e]
ment which now is the fou[n]
dation for the republic's [na]
tional economic program. La[dy]
Chesham founded and ser[ved]
as secretary-director of t[he]
Community Development Tr[ust]
Fund of Tanzania, which ch[an]
nels private donations i[n]
self-help projects throughc[ut]
the country.

PRESIDENTIAL PUN: No speech by President Nyerere is complete without a sprinkling of anecdotes and puns. The audience is always responsive and here the other speakers and honored guests are obviously delighted, too, by the Nyerere humor. Shown here are Vice-President Rashidi Kawawa, with cane, and, right, the then Minister of Culture and Youth, L. N. Sijaona. The occasion was a Republic Day anniversary meeting at Magomeni, outside Dar es Salaam, in 1963.

It was here that George Harvey, Rwankoma's manager, had his office. A former field officer in the Ministry of Agriculture, Harvey had eagerly accepted a four-year appointment to show what could be accomplished by settlement production. Son of a family distinguished in Britain's world of the theater, young Harvey was admirably cast for his role as guide for these pioneering tribesmen. The 80 families of Rwankoma were his flock. Transmitted to them, his skill might free them from poverty and hunger.

George Harvey spoke with zest of his mission. "We've got 850 acres already cleared or under cultivation. When the other two villages are filled, we'll go after the whole 10,000 acres." He said the primary crop would be cotton, along with maize, wheat and groundnuts. Each farmer would have about eighteen acres in the blocked plots outside the village. On his own one-acre *shamba*, the farmer would grow food crops for the family table.

Harvey told of last season's crop, Rwankoma's first. "We planted nearly 300 acres of cotton. They went about it properly: early planting, fertilizer, careful weeding. You know what they averaged?" He paused dramatically. "Rwankoma averaged 1,200 pounds an acre. This season's crop we're predicting 1,500." (African farms usually yielded about 400 pounds of cotton per acre.)

Under terms of the settlement loan the Rwankoma farmers did not have to start repayments for five years, after which they had twenty years to pay off their advances. The first cotton crop had prompted them, however, to voluntarily contribute 100 shillings each (about $14) as their first payment on the loan. Such decisions were made at village meetings by an elected committee of six, one of them a woman. This committee, or one of its members, was to take over full management of the settlement as soon as possible. The 80 settlers had been recruited from more than 400 applicants, most of them from the Zanaki tribe around Musoma. (This was Julius Nyerere's tribe and the settlement was only a few miles from Muhunda, where the President had been born.)

"One of our biggest recruitment problems," Harvey has said, "was to induce the farmers to come here without their cattle. Until we have a proper cattle dip we're not allowing any cattle into the valley save the few needed for milk supply. But like most tribesmen, the Zanaki regard cattle, and more and more cattle, as the symbol of wealth. We have to show them that it is income, not cattle ownership, that is really wealth. They must be taught that income from cash crops is their best security and a way to an improved life. Believe me, it isn't easy!"

A recent visitor to Harvey's settlement found a cluster of workmen down in the lowlands west of the village center building what appeared to be a series of stone terraces. Broken rock and boulders were being moved into place to form a dam. This would trap waters during the rainy season to provide a settlement reservoir 30 feet deep. The settlers had started it early in the dry season and planned to finish it in time for the October rains. A small pumping station had been built and would not only provide running water for each home in the village but would later irrigate portions of the cooperative plots. The village already had electric lights. A combination windmill and waterwheel by the stream below kept a small generator going and provided enough power to illuminate the square and the main street.

It was a brave sight: the Rwankoma primary school, the two-room dispensary, the bustling market and the tiny frame building of offices, surrounded by the cultivated fields. Hardly a year before, this had been an empty, isolated valley where only tribal hunters occasionally ventured. Now it was the beginning of a new life for 80 families. If Rwankoma can be taken as typical, the settlement movement represents a wise social investment.

The type of settlements planned as great irrigation or flood control developments were less social experiments than engineering projects. But they were to open up the land to the other half million farmers who, Julius Nyerere said, would be contributing to increased production by 1980. It was estimated that there were four million acres which could be thus developed. The Five-Year Plan allotted nearly $30 million to open up 250,000 of these acres in Tanganyika's wide river basins by 1970.

Largest of the projects was the $8.5-million Pangani Valley Development. Through this great valley the Pangani River runs from its sources high on the slopes of Kilimanjaro and down past the Pare and Usambara mountains into the Indian Ocean near Tanga on the north-east coast. A million tribesmen live in the 13,000 square miles of valley, and irrigation of thousands of acres would do much to reduce overpopulation of the Arusha-Moshi region in the north. Construction of the Nyumba ya Mungu Dam near Moshi is part of the valley project.

and it will help to control the river flow, both for the irrigated areas and for the hydroelectric plants being built farther down the stream.

Another $5 million was budgeted for development of the vast Kilombero Valley. This high inland valley is in the headwater basin of the Rufiji River which cuts across the center of the country from its tributaries near Mbeya in the west and flows six hundred miles eastward to the Indian Ocean. Several farming settlements would be started in the valley to supplement the fast-expanding sugar industry there.

The third major irrigation area is in the coastal basin between the Wami and Msangazi Rivers south of Tanga. Here 200,000 acres that would be ideal for sisal and sugar production were to be irrigated in a $2-million project that includes hydroelectric power installations. In addition to these major projects, another $6 million would be spent by 1970 in developing rural and village water supplies.

But the country still faced the immense agricultural problem of transforming its tremendous livestock population into a valuable national asset rather than, as it potentially could be, a serious threat to the master plan for the future economy. By 1965 Tanganyika supported a cattle population of nearly ten million (or one head for every man, woman and child in the republic), and seven million sheep and goats. This vast herd should have represented a living storehouse, as it were, of national wealth. Instead, it had seriously been described by a Royal Commission which had studied East Africa as "a danger and a deficiency." The 1955 report of the commission said: "The danger is that they may turn their lands into a desert; the deficiency that, without management of their herds, and in some cases better usage of their lands than mere pastoralism, they will contribute far less than their lands' potential to the growing needs of the community." A visiting economist of the U.S. Aid to International Development in 1963 put it more directly: "The annual damage by abusive deterioration of pastoral areas is equal to the total contribution of livestock products of pastoral areas." Since cattle had taken over more than one third of all arable areas, these are portentous statements.

Basically, the abuses of cattle raisers stemmed from the fact that the tribesmen owned the land communally but owned livestock individually. Each cattle owner was intent on increasing his herd but took little responsibility for seeing that there was adequate pasture to feed it. No restriction was placed on the number of stock owned by a family or an individual, and tribal families raised as many as possible for a variety of reasons. The cattle were slaughtered for the family's meat or exchanged for grain or other foods. A large herd was supposed to be insurance against drought, on the simple thesis that the more there were, the more might survive. Cattle were needed, too, as payment when buying a bride. Most of all, the larger the herd the greater the prestige. In pastoral country, cattle were the primary symbol of wealth; the weight or quality of the beast mattered little. Breeding was indiscriminate and uncontrolled and stock often deteriorated rather than improved.

Ironically, the Tanganyikan tribespeople, for all their cattle, suffered from a deficiency of animal protein. The 1960 World Bank Mission found that domestic meat consumption was deplorably low and recommended that on nutritional grounds it be increased by 40 per cent—an estimated additional consumption of 100 million pounds a year. Mission members also found that Tanganyika was importing cattle; in 1959 the Northern and Tanga Provinces alone imported 33,000 head of cattle from Kenya for slaughter.

This did not mean that Tanganyika was not marketing a considerable supply of its own cattle. In 1959 meat exports totaled $5 million and at the Dar es Salaam plant of the Tanganyika Packers Ltd., 80,000 head were slaughtered along with 17,000 head at the plant in Arusha. Nor did it mean that the Ministry of Agriculture's veterinary department was not making some headway in educating the tribal cattlemen to the advantages of raising livestock as a cash crop.

By the end of 1964, Agriculture Minister Maswanya could claim in his annual report that the gross domestic product from Tanganyika's livestock industry was $60 million for the year, of which $15 million was exportable produce. Almost in the same breath, however, the Minister bemoaned the fact that Tanganyika was still importing $3 million annually in meat and dairy products.

Under the Five-Year Plan, the Minister promised, some radical reforms would be made. "These," he said, "will include the introduction of improved pastures, the organization of proper ranching schemes, the upgrading of indigenous cattle and a change in the attitude of the farmer toward his cattle."

The section of the plan itself dealing with livestock problems was more explicit. "The long-term goal," it noted, "is to stabilize cattle production at its present numbers but with a significant increase in average weight. To this end enforcement measures will be promulgated if example and exhortation prove unavailing. To date the contribution of livestock to the country's material product has been woefully inadequate; average liveweight of animals is among the lowest in Africa. The government's program has been designed to tackle this problem on a broad front. Assuming a target increase of 10 per cent in the average weight of cattle, the plan assumes that it will be possible to increase livestock production by about 5 per cent per year."

The plan presented a long list of projects which would be financed to help develop the livestock industry: new stock routes for herd movement, with construction of boreholes for water supply; 47 new veterinary centers; stocking of state ranches; vehicles and equipment for disease control; funds for national dairy plants in Dar es Salaam and Tanga; artificial insemination units for all the main cattle centers. Nearly $7 million had been allocated to help reform the backward industry.

In September 1964, the government backed up its livestock plans with the Range Development Management Bill, making changes in grazing and other livestock handling methods mandatory. The National Assembly quickly put it through three readings and made it law. The bill was aimed directly at Tanganyika's worst tribal offenders: the haughty, battle-loving spearmen of the north—the proud Masai.

The bill called for the partitioning of the fourteen million acres of Masailand into ranching districts, each to be served by a regulatory commission. Inventories of stock and of pasture and water resources would be made and cooperative associations set up in each district for cattle marketing. Veterinary department and community development agents would promote improved breeding, immunization and grazing methods, and would help organize the cooperatives.

Much of the legislation was based on the recommendations of an American, Leland E. Fallon, who visited Masailand in May 1963 to make a study of range resources for the AID program in Tanganyika. "Here," Fallon wrote in a report on the situation, "is a region with land resources having a potential of $200 million and an annual cash marketing potential of more than $15 million from livestock and agricultural production." What, in fact, was the area yielding? Fallon estimated it at only $700,000 annually, or about a half dollar per head of cattle.

Fallon recommended that the whole problem be placed under a range management division of the Ministry of Agriculture and that range districts be established. Each district would be broken up into individual range allotments with a limited number of cattle to be raised on each. His detailed proposals were the basis of the 1964 legislation.

It was not the first attempt to regiment the nonconforming Masai. In 1950, the colonial government had made an abortive $750,000 effort to bring order into the Masai system of cattle raising. The money was spent largely on three big dams and on boreholes at Lemuta and Kakesia that pumped 1,000 gallons of water an hour. The Masai elders agreed that not more than 3,000 cattle would be watered at the first two dams and 1,200 at the other. But colonial officials, visiting the scene later, were horrified to see herds of many thousands brought to the watering places, trampling down the troughs and leaving dead cattle behind to putrefy in the dams. Masai herdsmen similarly overwhelmed the pumping stations, intimidating the operators into manning them day and night until sources went dry.

It is difficult for the Masai to forget that their God-given mission is to tend cattle, rather than to dig and raise crops in the soil like lesser men. To the planet Venus they say: "I pray you, who rise yonder, to hear me. Keep my cows alive. Take care of my people." But by 1965 the Masai, too, had shown signs of change. They had been convinced, for example, that diseases like rinderpest could be kept down by regular immunization. Masai elders met with the Arusha regional commissioner at Monduli in January 1965, and agreed to try farming on a settlement basis at Loliondo, Enduland and Kibaya-Kijungu. There was even a group of twenty *morani,* young Masai warriors, who agreed to farm a 600-acre settlement. Masai herdsmen in Waso completed a self-help project that gave the community a new twenty-bed hospital.

More important, the imposing Great Spokesman of the Masai, Edward Ole Mbarnoti, rose in the National Assembly one day and pledged his people's support of the Five-Year Plan. The Masai would rejoice, he said, in the range development program.

"In colonial days," he added, "British rulers failed to control my people because they did not understand the nomadic nature of the Masai. Now, at last, the government has found a solution, because it understands the needs of the Masai before they can settle anywhere: water, grass, and the desire to avoid disease."

With the government allocating $2.5 million for grazing research and services, disease control and water supply to help bring economic order into Masailand, there was now some hope for believing that the long-truculent tribe would join forces with the cultivators of the soil. Not all the five-year goals required quantitative, productive results such as those demanded of the Masai and the farming population. Other results would be measured solely in qualitative terms. Education was one of these, health another. Each was crucial to the success of the Five-Year Plan.

CHAPTER ELEVEN

THE PEOPLE

The basic producing units of the Five-Year Plan remain the people and their needs—education and health needs primarily. These were taken up in that section of the plan antiseptically entitled "Social Infrastructure." The section told of schools needed at primary, secondary and college levels, of the tremendous task of educating adults, of hospitals, clinics and medical services needed to improve the people's health. It told nothing of the people's own participation, of their individual dedication to the total vision of the plan. It was left for the citizens themselves to demonstrate in their own ways how committed they could be to the vision.

There was the gentle fraud, for instance, perpetrated by old Sharif Sepeku out of his resolution to improve himself. Sharif was one of a group of elders attending a literacy class at Bagamoyo. One evening, after having turned in his homework, he confessed to the teacher that the work had, in fact, been done by his son while he, Sharif, went to a religious ceremony. He was most contrite.

There was the more robust report from Singida. Three men were in court there, charged with stealing a bull belonging to a woman villager. They told the chief, sitting as magistrate, that while they had indeed taken the animal, they had done so in their capacity as a committee of the adult education class at Unyamikumbi School. The woman, wife of Matthew Mathame, had failed consistently to attend class, so they had seized the bull as *njughuda,* the traditional tribal fine. The bull had been cut up, they explained, and the meat divided among the class members. The hide was sold to buy a football for the school. The chief fined the three a nominal fifteen shillings.

And in Dar es Salaam there was a report that there were not enough teachers or classrooms to accommodate the thousands lining up for adult education courses.

These were encouraging tidings for those setting the health and education goals of the Five-Year Plan. But by no means could the people's willing spirit delude the leaders into underestimating the enormity of their task. So much had to be done to make up for what Julius Nyerere described as "the years of neglect."

The year 1925, for example. That year the colonial government of Tanganyika had appropriated a grand total of $54,000 for African education. There was the year 1956 when Nyerere reported that in the colonial government's educational budget as much went to teach the children of Tanganyika's 25,000 Europeans as for the children of nine million Africans. In the year 1960 only half of the African children of the territory had a chance ever of seeing the inside of a classroom and in the whole country a total of just 480 had reached high school.

That year, belatedly, the colonial government proposed to do something about neglected African education. It voted a record budget for the Ministry of Education, but the UN Trusteeship Council was unimpressed. Its 1960 report commented: "The Council noted the limited 'crash program' which the Administering Authority had under consideration for the development of secondary education but considered that a large-scale 'crash program' was required as a contribution to the future progress and stability of the territory."

Were it not for the mission schools which had provided the bulk of primary education since German colonial days, the picture would have been bleaker. During the British colonial period, the chief governmental contribution to African education was in the form of financial grants to schools run by the Roman Catholic, Anglican and Lutheran missions. President Nyerere himself taught at St. Francis College in

Dar es Salaam from 1952 to 1955. (After independence, the religious schools still played a significant role. For instance, in 1965 there were more than 250,000 students in about 3,000 Catholic schools.)

So it was left to the young nation, on attaining independence, to take up the slack in education. Drawing up its $70-million Three-Year Plan, the Nyerere government allotted 13.8 per cent, or about $10 million, to education. It added more than $2 million a year to the education budget, earmarking most of the funds for secondary schooling. As the 1960 World Bank report had pointed out, the dropout record of African students, if allowed to continue, would be disastrous for a nation determined to stand on its own feet. In 1960 there were 386,-267 African students in the four grades of primary school. In the four grades of middle school, Standards V to VIII, there were only 44,789 African boys and girls, indicating about a 90 per cent dropout. And in high school there were only 4,645 students from the whole country, still another interval decrease of 90 per cent. Of the nation's students only 1,202 were prepared in 1960 to take the Cambridge certificate examinations which would make them the equivalent of high-school graduates.

Goal of the Three-Year Plan was to increase the number of high-school graduates threefold: from 1,202 certificate candidates in 1960 to 3,275 by 1964. Sights for the higher school certificate group were extensive: a sixfold increase would be attempted. In 1960 there were only 110 who took the Cambridge examination after completing Forms V and VI, which compared to a junior-college education in the United States. The 1964 goal was 620.

To emphasize secondary education, the Minister of Education, as part of the 1961–64 plan, altered the traditional 4-4-4 school system (under which there were the massive dropouts at the end of the four-year primary school and the four-year middle school). Henceforth there would be an eight-year primary course, a four-year secondary course leading to a school certificate, and a two-year course leading to a higher school certificate. Pupils of any race would be eligible to the secondary schools on a competitive examination basis.

In 1960 there were, as the World Bank Mission had pointed out with utmost concern, no facilities for university-level education in Tanganyika. The Bank Mission noted that there were 215 Tanganyikans at the East African University in Uganda, 27 at the Royal Technical College in Kenya, and 77 overseas: 39 in the United Kingdom, twelve in the United States, seventeen in Pakistan and India, three in Ireland, and two each in Liberia, Rome and Ceylon. The three-year planners resolved to do something about this. A sum of $2.5 million would go toward a University College at Dar es Salaam, to be part of the University of East Africa. As a start, the college would use the new TANU headquarters for classes.

These added facilities, limited as they were, were enough to generate a speed-up in the tempo of formal education, which was to increase year after year. But there still remained the adult bulk of the population. Tanganyika's men were 80 per cent illiterate, its women 89 per cent. It was these adults, as Julius Nyerere had said, who must understand and be involved in the nation's plans if the country was to move ahead.

In 1962 Prime Minister Kawawa had explained the dilemma and outlined a plan. "One of the inhibiting factors," he said, discussing the government program, "is the failure of the citizen, and especially the rural cultivator, to identify himself in the broad process of nation-building, combined with a lack of knowledge and an understanding of what is required of him."

He therefore launched what he called "The People's Education Plan." Its aims were to make education, in its broadest sense, available to all adults, especially women. As a first step, literacy classes would be organized close enough to homes so that everyone could attend. Step two: discussion classes would be held in every village center so adults could learn of local and national problems. Step three: in each of the country's 57 districts training centers would be set up where brief courses could be taken in agriculture, health, local government and trade.

All organizations in the country would be recruited as a combined force to help offer these adult education courses: the Community Development Division, the Information Service, the Tanganyika Broadcasting Corporation, the East Africa Literature Bureau, the labor unions and cooperatives, TANU and various voluntary and local government agencies.

The CD workers of the country were given the primary responsibility for the program. They were to encourage formation of literacy classes. They were to induce each village development committee to sponsor village center programs which would be, as Premier Kawawa worded it, "windows to the outside world" for the people. The CD officers were to develop the district training centers. They were to be "wardens" of the centers and responsible for arranging courses in citizenship and general education, using such teaching resources as extension agents and health officers in the district, schoolteachers, district and TANU officials and specialists from regional headquarters.

The Tanganyika Broadcasting Corporation played an experienced role in the mass education program. Low on finances but high in production and ideas, the TBC began, in partnership with officials of the Ministry of Education, to beam lively courses to both primary and secondary level public schools. TBC was on the air for schools two hours daily. Pupils liked the radio lessons in history because they were sometimes dramatized by the TBC staff, and those in geography because they came with recorded background sounds. There also were classes in English and Swahili, in general knowledge, and special news broadcasts for the schools were also included. A once-a-week program, "Calling All Teachers," gave the Ministry of Education an opportunity to explain its policies to faculty members. Community development officers saw TBC's facilities as a prime outlet for the dissemination of material to village and district groups.

During the years when education was a colonial stepchild, the Tanganyikan African National Union tried to shore up the territory's sagging school program. In 1958 at its annual conference in Tabora, TANU decided that one thing Tanganyika needed was an institution which could provide advanced schooling for adult leaders who had had no opportunity to obtain a formal education—an institution similar to Oxford's Ruskin College. In 1960 the party recruited Miss Joan Wicken, a graduate of Ruskin, to work on the project. She was made executive secretary of the Tanganyika Education Trust, founded by TANU to finance the proposed college.

Within a year the trust had negotiated the purchase of an outmoded hotel at Kivukoni, a sandy peninsula forming the outside rim of Dar es Salaam harbor. TANU raised $30,000 for the project; the government granted $20,000 and the Institute for International Solidarity (West Germany), $25,000. By 1962, Kivukoni, "the working man's college," had a student body of 39. These were drawn from TANU, government, cooperative and trade union staffs. Among them they

MUDDY FINISHING TOUCH: With the framework of wattle finished, the next step in home-building is to plaster the walls with mud. The mud quickly hardens in the sun and will withstand a season or two of rains before deteriorating. The rafters will be covered with thatch or, if the family is opulent enough, with a roof of corrugated iron. Community development workers are teaching the tribesmen to mix a small portion of cement (provided by the government) with the mud to make bricks that will hold up under rain.

COFFEE ON KILIMANJARO: On the slopes of spectacular Mount Kilimanjaro in northern Tanzania, members of tribal cooperatives make this a relatively prosperous area by growing coffee, now a primary product of the republic. These women of the Chagga tribe near Moshi gather a rich harvest of beans.

averaged nine years of schooling. But every one had exhibited leadership potential.

On a more modest but much wider scale, and again to fill a gap, TANU ventured into another area of education: it instituted a program of "self-help" primary schools. The idea was born in 1955 when young party leaders induced parents to gather their children at village homes for daily instruction. When colonial officials informed them that the practice could not be permitted, it was suggested that a private organization be legally established to carry on the work. So TANU organized the Tanganyika African Parents Association and got solidly behind the movement.

TAPA, just as TANU had done, spread from the capital to the towns and from towns to villages and hamlets. By 1959 there were 1,320 TAPA primary schools. Most of them were mud huts and some were merely clearings beneath a large tree, but each had a sponsoring parents' committee. Standard teaching programs were organized by district working committees and an education secretary was appointed for each of the seventeen regions. Teachers and secretaries were paid at first with funds raised by the parents' committees but district councils and local authorities gradually began to contribute.

By 1964 TAPA was firmly established on a national basis, operating 2,500 schools with 100,000 pupils. At national headquarters—a whitewashed, mud-walled office on Lumumba Street in Dar es Salaam—the new executive secretary described the dynamic force behind the movement.

"It's really a people's organization," said Timothy Samjela, a trim, brisk man in horn-rimmed glasses. "These schools belong to the parents themselves. The teachers are working for them and their children. They know I am working for them. They are the proprietors."

He said TAPA was governed by a national executive made up of two delegate parents from each region. They had elected Job Lusinde, a TANU veteran and at the time Minister of Home Affairs, as their national president.

Samjela, who had gone to Bagamoyo Seminary but had never himself been a teacher, said that no more TAPA schools would be built until the present 2,500 were brought up to Ministry of Education standards in regard to both physical plant and program. "With the ministry and the local authorities subsidizing us more and more we'll soon be public schools," he said, smiling. "That, of course, is for the best, but I'm sure many of the parents will regret giving up the schools they've worked so hard to build."

By 1964 the government mood for change and improvement had infected most of the population. The desire for adult education became contagious. NUTA reported that its labor sections were organizing night classes with the aim of making every union member literate. Employers were requested to help teach the workers, to discuss production problems with them. The new army disclosed plans for classes that would make every soldier literate. Army units even took on self-help projects: the Fifth Battalion at Tabora started a dairy farm; the battalions at Dar es Salaam and Nachingwea went into poultry, maize and groundnut growing. In Dar es Salaam the new College of Business Education, aided by a $500,000 gift from West Germany, opened two-year courses of training in administration and accounting. The new Institute of Adult Education reported that it was overwhelmed by applications for class instruction. The Community Development Division reported in 1964 that more than 300,000 were enrolled in literacy classes throughout the country.

The year 1964 was in many respects a happy milestone in the history of Tanganyikan education. Besides the great surge in adult education, there were achievements in formal education. The Three-Year Plan had set as its primary education goal the tripling of the number of high-school graduates. In 1961 there were 1,202; in 1964 there were 4,165. The big dropout rate at the end of the first four years of primary school had been reduced. In 1961 only 19,000 pupils went from Standard IV to Standard V; in 1964 more than 45,000. In January 1964, all secondary school fees were abolished. By the end of the year eleven new schools offered facilities for secondary education. On November 30, 1964, Julius Nyerere went to one of the new secondary schools, Mkwawa High at Iringa (named after the redoubtable Hehe chief), and told its first graduating class how vital were Tanganyika's educational goals:

I have consistently pointed out in my visits to secondary schools around the country that pupils are privileged people. Each one is selected out of many hundreds, and then receives the benefit of a secondary education which is denied to a very large number of their fellow citizens. With this privilege there must go a sense of responsibility. It costs approximately $650 to keep each student at Mkwawa High School for one academic year; in a country as poor as the United Republic this is a tremendous burden. It can only be justified if the knowledge which is gained here is grasped by hard and disciplined work, and is later ploughed back for the good of the people of this nation.

The brightest achievement of 1964 was the graduation of a tiny class of twelve from University College, Dar es Salaam. The ceremony was held on the new college campus on Observation Hill, seven miles out of Dar es Salaam, amid imposing blocks of buildings going up on all sides. While classes had been going on in the TANU building downtown in the city, first sod on the campus site outside the city had been turned in 1962. Funds had poured in from many sources, including more than $1 million each from the British government, the Ford Foundation and the Tanganyika government. The Aga Khan, Sir Isaac Wolfson, the Rockefeller Foundation and the Carnegie Foundation added to the fund, and AID provided two major U.S. loans. By mid-1964 the building program had grown to $15 million.

That first commencement day in 1964 was a day of triumph for the class of twelve who received the degree of Bachelor of Laws. These students had, after all, registered at an unproven college. They had attended classes first in an abandoned bank building and had been housed in a Salvation Army camp and a Roman Catholic hostel. They had moved to better surroundings when the assembly hall of the TANU building was turned over to them; then in 1964 they finally moved to the elegant new buildings on Observation Hill.

It was a sentimental day for R. Cranford Pratt, the Canadian educator who had come to Dar es Salaam in 1961 to help the new Nyerere government with its dream of a national college. For three years, Pratt had met and solved the endless problems of building, manning and programming the infant college. Now, most of his job being done, he announced that he was turning the work over to an African educator, Dr. W. K. Chagula.

It was a rewarding day for Julius Nyerere. As Chancellor of the University of East Africa he was there to present the degrees. He spoke of the founding of Tanganyika's own college as part of the political and economic revolution that his government was trying to effect:

All young countries have to be revolutionary in their policies if they are to survive. It is this which distinguishes them from the developed countries, and, indeed, from their own past. But revolutions do not just happen—least of all economic revolutions; they demand scientific and objective thought, and the reasoned application of basic principles to the existing situation, and the deliberate conversion of unpleasant facts into something more palatable. There is no short cut, no easy solution. . . .

The annual per capita income in Tanganyika is $58. The cost of keeping a student at this college will be nearly $3,000 a year. That is to say that it takes the annual per capita income of 50 of our people to maintain a single student at this college for one year. It should not be necessary to say more. It is obvious that this disparity can only be justified, morally or politically, if it can be looked upon as an investment by the poor in their own future.

The Five-Year Plan and the annual budget announced in 1964 reflected the government's unremitting concern for education. In his budget message Minister of Finance Bomani noted that the 1964–65 recurrent expenditures would be $16.5 million, an increase of $2.8 million over the year before. Another $6 million for education would be budgeted from the new development fund. As President Nyerere pointed out, "Judged by any international comparison, this appropriation of 17 per cent of the national budget for education is a fantastically high proportion but unfortunately our inheritance demands it."

In the five years just ahead, $150 million would be spent on education. Based on President Nyerere's figure at the university commencement, this meant that more than a half million of Tanganyika's workers would be turning their entire income over annually for the education of the nation's children and youth.

The goals of the previous 1961–64 plan were extended. Where there had been 32 new secondary classes, there would be 48 more high-school classes created by 1969. Instead of the 5,250 students entering high school in 1964, there would be 7,070 in 1969. The number continuing after high school would be doubled, from 680 to 1,280. Instead of 320 students being trained as teachers, there would be 1,500 by 1969.

As part of the educational speed-up, the plan called for the reduction of the primary school period from eight years to seven. Traditionally, the school session for the first primary school grades was only a half day. It was now decided to make Standards III and IV full-day courses and add to Standard IV many of the courses taught in Standard V. Children in Standards V, VI, and VII were to be taught according to a program that would bring them to the same level as that previously reached by Standard VIII.

A total of $15 million was budgeted for development of the University College for the next five years. A science faculty was added and new degree courses in arts and social science were organized for 1965. Another $4.5 million would go to developing technical colleges in Dar es Salaam and Moshi and for eight craft training centers in various parts of the country.

Julius Nyerere stoutly defended the massive expenditures. "We are not expanding because we wish to create a new privileged class which has had the opportunity to develop itself at the expense of the community," he told a conference of teachers in Dar es Salaam in December 1964. "We are expanding because we need the products of our schools to participate in, and guide, the enthusiasm and energy of the people devoted to building our country and overcoming national poverty."

Young Tanganyikans henceforth being graduated from Form VI, or junior college, would come face to face with this policy. According to the Five-Year Plan, all students obtaining their higher school certificate after Form VI were to teach for six months in the national adult education program before proceeding to the university or entering regular employment.

On January 16, 1965, the government's determination in the field of education was expressed in an order under the Education Ordinance, making it compulsory for boys and girls to attend public school and complete the seven-year primary course.

In a country of ten million with an average annual income of $58, disease has followed poverty. The words with which Tanganyika's health program was introduced in the Five-Year Plan are stark: "There is good reason to believe that between a quarter and a half of children born in Tanganyika fail to reach adult life. Half the people of the country are children under 16 and the large majority of these are in infancy or early childhood. Those who survive the hazards of infancy and childhood continue to be subject not only to the threat of epidemic disease, but also to chronic infection, parasitic disease and malnutrition." Thus one to two million of the nation's children were doomed to death.

Nor were the planners overly hopeful that much could be done about it. As had earlier been stated in the Three-Year Plan, it was conceded that, however pressing the people's medical needs, the limited funds of the country must be invested first in economic and educational development so that greater resources eventually would be produced for financing of social services.

Nevertheless, the country had a rich store of medical history. The missionary explorers, many of them doctors, brought the first fruits of modern medicine to a country racked by malaria, cholera, smallpox and plague. Dr. Livingstone had founded a small hospital at Ukaguru, on the slave route to Lake Tanganyika, which the Church Missionary Society reopened in 1873. Another explorer, Dr. Ebenezer Southon of the London Missionary Society, had built a clinic at Ujiji which he operated until his death at Urambo in 1882. The missionaries accounted, too, for the first African to practice medicine in the interior. A liberated slave whose name has been lost, the man was sent by an early mission to study in Malta, and when he returned in 1888, landing on the east coast at Sadani, he walked overland through 700 miles of jungle and bush. He wrote of his epic journey: "One morning I arrived at a place through which a slave caravan had passed. About twenty people had been abandoned there, and near them were several vultures waiting to devour them when they died." When he reached Lake Tanganyika, the venturesome medic founded a clinic at Karema.

The German East Africa Company's colonial administration, which began functioning in Dar es Salaam in 1891, included a small medical section. It was headed by Dr. Alexander Becker, who not only started the first hospitals at Tanga and in the capital, but launched Africa's first mass vaccination campaign. Results of this campaign were studied by Dr. Robert Koch, who in his pioneering work with the microscope had discovered the microorganisms causing tuberculosis, cholera and other diseases. Dr. Koch originally came to Dar es Salaam in 1897 to study rinderpest which was causing famine in Masailand. Dr. Koch also went to Usambara to observe a strange new disease which he was able to diagnose as subtertian malaria.

A member of Dr. Becker's infant medical service was Dr. Hans Schelle, whose removal of an 81-pound tumor from an elephantiasis sufferer in Tukuyu had attracted wide professional notice. Tumors of such size, sited usually in the male scrotum, were not uncommon. Nor was it unusual to see a sufferer bearing his burden in a special harness slung from his shoulder, or even in a wheelbarrow. Still, the victims were reluctant to submit to surgery for their burden was regarded among tribal women as evidence of great virility.

When British medical officers succeeded the Germans, they concentrated on fighting the all-pervasive malaria. A bacteriologist, James Mackey, found that eight out of every ten inhabitants in Dar es Salaam were infected with malaria, though fortunately the mortality rate was not high. He found, on the other hand, that the type of tuberculosis widely afflicting Tanganyikans was highly destructive, causing death in 41 per cent of those infected.

The staff malariologist, Dr. D. F. Clyde, later conducted a dramatically effective campaign against malaria among the 3,000 inhabitants of Mto wa Mbu, near Arusha. A tiny amount of the drug chloroquine was mixed with the salt used by the villagers, all of whom were malarial. No other salt except that which had been medicated was available. In two months malaria in the village was virtually eradicated.

Convincing evidence that the new British medical department was concerned about public health came in the late 1920s when a massive campaign against yaws (frambesia) was launched. Half the population seemed afflicted with the disease, which caused ugly, raspberry-like tubercles to break out on the skin. When it was discovered that an injection of bismuth salts could cure the condition, tribespeople for the first time queued up for clinical treatment. In 1929 alone, more than a half million people were cured of yaws by injections.

Smallpox broke out sporadically in the country, but because medical staff and supplies were limited, so were vaccinations. Health officers were astounded to find, however, that some tribespeople were already familiar with vaccination. Dr. Edward deSouza, reporting on an outbreak of smallpox at Mohoro in 1959, told of a woman who came to the infected town with a healthy infant. She went to the home of one of the first smallpox victims and scratched a bit of the purulent discharge into the skin of her child. Dr. deSouza later checked the case and found the infant had gone through a very mild case of the disease without ill effects.

Syphilis was difficult to control and until the advent of the new drugs the incidence was disastrously high. In Bukoba, in 1929, it was estimated that 80 to 90 per cent of the inhabitants were infected. Among tribes near Lake Tanganyika, the incidence was high because victims believed they would be cured if they passed the disease on to someone else.

Much of the work of the slowly growing medical service was to combat such superstitions. In this task health officers in the field called upon the new community development workers for help. An education section was added to the health division and a nation-wide poster campaign was started. Most effective was a series of posters urging villagers to build latrines.

Africanization of Tanganyika's medical services was slow. The first African medical officer appointed was Dr. Joseph R. Mutahangavwa of the Haya tribe, who at thirty-five was graduated from Makerere College in 1940 as a doctor of medicine. In 1942 Dr. Mutahangavwa performed Tanganyika's first all-African major operation at Ocean Road Hospital, Dar es Salaam. It was successful. After eleven years with the health division, Dr. Mutahangavwa retired to private practice at Murongo, on the Uganda border. Another Makerere graduate joined the service in 1944 and rose to the highest career post in the division. Dr. Charles Vincent Mtawali joined as an assistant medical officer, became principal medical officer in 1961 after special studies in Birmingham and Liverpool, and two years later became permanent secretary of the Ministry of Health.

In 1961 when Tanganyika became self-governing, the country had only twelve other African doctors. For a population of nearly ten million the territory had 520 doctors, or barely one to 20,000. The world standard at the time was one to 1,000. The bulwark of Tanganyika's health service were the 243 African medical assistants, who served the rural villages.

The Three-Year Plan did not do much to promote medical services. Only 4 per cent of the $70-million program was earmarked for health. Plans called for increase of hospital accommodations so that there would be one hospital bed for every 1,000 of population. But this was a goal that had been fixed as early as 1949 and, by 1964, was still to be attained. Many other health objectives in the years 1961 to 1964 also were not achieved because of the demands made upon the medical service by the effects of the famine of 1961.

The brightest achievement of the period was not even in the plan: the beginning of a School of Medicine in Dar es Salaam for the training of "medical practitioners." The training of full-fledged doctors of

medicine was to continue at Makerere College (where more Tanganyikans were being graduated each year), but the new school would
help provide sorely-needed assistant medical officers for the health
division. The school opened in April 1963 with a class of fifteen—the
only candidates who could qualify for entrance. By the end of the first
year five of these found themselves insufficiently prepared for keeping
up with the courses and dropped out. Setbacks like this underline the
grievous shortcomings in education that must be overcome by the
young nation.

In 1963 a broad study of Tanganyika's health needs was made by a
team of British medical experts led by Professor R. M. Titmuss, and
sponsored by the African Medical and Research Foundation. Although some of the group's recommendations, particularly on the pro-
vision of hospital beds, were regarded as too ambitious, a medical
development committee set up by the Ministry of Health incorporated
many of the team's findings into the program that was published as
part of the Five-Year Plan. The plan's medical program for 1964–69
emphasized preventive medicine and the extension of health services
into rural areas, with curative services to remain virtually at a stand-
still. In the face of increasing demands for curative services it was a
courageous policy but one which best served the country. Over-all,
the plan appropriated 20 per cent more for health projects than had
been spent under the Three-Year Plan.

Rather than attempt to provide, as the Titmuss Report had recommended, a minimum of 200 hospital beds for each of the country's
districts (increased now to 61), the plan called for a full-scale hospital
in each of seventeen regions, and for 83 rural health centers and 300
rural dispensaries. The health centers were to be controlled directly
by the Ministry of Health and would supervise the work of the rural
dispensaries, which would be the responsibility of local authorities.

The health planners now took their most revolutionary step. It was
decided that in each of the 61 districts of Tanganyika a standing health
committee would be created, to serve, as Health Minister Derek Bryceson put it, as "action groups" for the plans of the Ministry. Members
of the committees making up this national health network would be
the local health official, the area commissioner, medical and education
officers in the district, and other people drawn from various fields.
They were to meet monthly and follow procedures laid out in a Min-

istry handbook. Each meeting would review what had been done and what there was yet to be done under five action headings: epidemic control, general sanitation, nutrition, health education, and clinical and health facilities. A monthly report from each district would go to a regional health committee, which was responsible directly to the Ministry of Health. Each health committee would be subordinate to its respective regional or district development committee. As with the development committees, the motive behind those for health was to mobilize the will of the people to improve both themselves and their community.

In the field of health there was a desperately long way to go, but as the many projects in training, services and education began to take root in mid-1965, and the people assumed their new responsibilities in the national program, there was considerable promise that the health of the country would, though gradually, be vastly improved.

CHAPTER TWELVE

THE WOMEN AND CHILDREN

The typical woman of colonial-day Tanganyika was a demure, quiet figure who carried a bundle balanced on her head and a baby on her back. In keeping with tribal tradition, her inferior role demanded that she walk six or eight paces behind a spouse who carried a light-weight walking stick. As a mother, she was responsible for the nursing and upbringing of the children. As a wife, she took her place in the fields to help cultivate the crops. She washed the clothes and made the mud walls of the family hut. She cooked and cradled, bathed and built in a weary succession of tasks unchanged through the generations. She did not wander far from the hut and her voice was not heard in the village council.

Her humble station had been determined partly by the fact that she was regarded as a household possession, bought as part of a marriage transaction. For it was still the custom, not only in the rural villages but in the growing towns, to pay a "bride price" of so many head of cattle or so many hundreds of shillings for a woman. Also, in the many tribes which practiced polygamy she might merely be one of two or three wives. She was illiterate and she was made to feel her inferiority.

Within the decade preceding 1965, the women of Tanganyika spectacularly altered their role. They had become a potent political force. There were seven women members of the National Assembly. Three were junior members of the Nyerere cabinet. The women's section of TANU was a powerful arm of the party. (Some even credited the women's vote with having obliterated the United Tanganyika Party when it challenged TANU at the polls.)

The Tanganyikan woman still worked in the fields and took care of the home, but in 1965 she had a voice in national and local affairs. She sat on committees, went to the university (one of the first twelve law graduates in 1964 was a woman) and took executive positions in the cooperatives and in private business. The lowliest village women went to literacy classes, then on to further studies. Women made up the vanguard of the national drive for a better life.

What had transformed Tanganyika's passive second sex of a decade ago into an active, articulate force in the new society? A revolution had indeed taken place, and, as Julius Nyerere pointed out, revolutions do not just happen. There have to be reasons.

The spirit of the national struggle for freedom—*uhuru*—undoubtedly had the most to do with the advancement of women. Young TANU leaders, coming to the villages to speak of political freedom, infected the women particularly because for the first time something reached out directly to them from the world outside. The promise of national identity meant little to them, but to be told that they could now be involved in something larger than the narrow routine of the hut and the *shamba* was irresistible. They signed up eagerly as TANU members. They learned the party songs and sang them with tuneful fervor. They formed committees and sponsored fund-raising projects. Most important, they joined the United Women of Tanganyika and made it the party's militant feminine force.

The UWT was created deliberately to harness the interest and energy of the country's newly liberated women. While it was being formed other groups, including the Tanganyika Council of Women, were also attempting to organize those who wanted to play a more effective role in building the nation. It was in 1962 that President Nyerere suggested to the Ministry of Cooperative and Community Development that it set up a single agency—the UWT—to consolidate the diverse efforts of the nation's women.

Under CD auspices, 200 women leaders, representing the various groups, met at Anartouglo Community Center in Dar es Salaam late that year and formed the UWT. Bibi Titi Mohamed, who had done so much to recruit women's support of TANU, was elected first president, and a delegate from the north, Mrs. Kanasia Mutenga of Moshi, was elected vice-president.

Bibi Titi, an elected member of the National Assembly for Rufiji and parliamentary secretary to the Ministry of Cooperative and Community Development, set forth the UWT platform: "As the one and only national women's organization, we women are determined to help, not only in the fight against the three enemies—poverty, ignorance and disease—but to raise the social, economic and educational status, and to make the role of women a more dynamic one, thus enabling us to fulfill more effectively our own needs, those of our families and those of our country. The UWT's special contribution will be to encourage women to take an active part in promoting family welfare through full participation in the fields of health, education and social development." She urged the women leaders to promote UWT branches in every community, which would work closely with district and village development committees.

A small working committee, spurred by their exuberant new president, established headquarters in the old TANU building in Dar es Salaam, and in a matter of weeks they had set up a national structure that reached into every district. At headquarters, as well as at regional and district levels, five functional sections were established: education, economics, health, youth, and fund-raising. In many towns and villages the UWT branch soon overshadowed the TANU affiliate it was pledged to support. Within months the organization was heavily involved in adult education, in cooperative agricultural projects and in public health instruction.

Maria Nyerere, the President's wife, was in charge of the UWT's national poultry-raising program. To set the pace, she sponsored a five-acre poultry farm outside Dar es Salaam and organized a women's cooperative to run the project. UWT members sold cooperative shares in the farm at seven dollars a share. The farm was also to serve as a marketing outlet for individual breeders. Noting that between 1961 and 1963 Tanganyika had imported 2.5 million eggs from Kenya,

Mrs. Nyerere called on the UWT to urge every family to have a small holding in the poultry enterprise.

In Dodoma district, the Ikowa branch of the UWT operated a twenty-acre farm, and raised a crop of maize and rice using a tractor borrowed from agricultural authorities. Tanga district reported that the UWT was operating one of the new cattle and coconut farms, with 203 head of cattle and 13,000 coconut trees on a 690-acre plot. In Bumbuli, also in the Tanga region, UWT members operating a vegetable farm realized $750 with which they planned to build a maize flour mill.

In Dar es Salaam the UWT started the first of a network of nursery schools. The first, built at Magomeni township in the capital, was near the community center so that mothers could attend classes there while their children were at the nursery. As in other nurseries throughout the world, these sought to teach children social habits that would prepare them for primary school.

Politically, too, the UWT was active. Because of the organization's large membership, its views were regarded with respect in the National Assembly. In 1963, its leaders, Bibi Titi and Lucy Lameck particularly, sponsored in the Assembly the hotly debated Affiliation Ordinance. Among other things, the bill required that all children—including those of mixed marriages and those born out of wedlock—had to be supported by the father. A group of male MPs banded together to fight the measure, but the women sponsors convincingly routed the opposition and the bill became law. The distaff MPs spoke effectively on all manner of legislation. There was no questioning the fact that women now had a voice in national affairs.

The solidarity of the women's political role was dramatically demonstrated when the army staged its mutiny in January 1964. The word went out from UWT headquarters in Dar es Salaam that something must be done. Women delegates hurried to the capital from all parts of the country. Placards were prepared and a drum corps organized. On the morning of February 3, women assembled by the thousands outside headquarters, bearing banners from Morogoro, Kisarawe, Bagamoyo and a hundred other towns.

The capital had never seen anything like it. For three and a half hours a procession of more than a mile of women marched from their headquarters in the south part of town, along Independence Avenue through the business district and around the waterfront to the government office area. The drums beat. The songs of TANU were sung in powerful chorus. Placards flashed in the sun: "Down with Violence Mutiny and Treason!"

As had the earlier march of the labor unions, the great UWT procession halted outside the State House and waited for the President. When Nyerere appeared at the door a mighty shout arose, mingled with the weird half-whistle with which tribal women acclaimed their warriors Bibi Titi stepped forward. In ringing Swahili she greeted the President in the name of all the women of Tanganyika. An affirming chorus broke from the ranks behind her.

Concluding her prepared statement, the UWT president said: "Our loyalty, our devotion and allegiance go to you, the loving father of our young nation." Expressed in these words, the group's stirring demonstration of support very probably had much to do with the atmosphere of stability that soon resumed throughout the country.

The effectiveness of the UWT was due to a considerable extent to the preparatory work done in the field by women officers of the Ministry of Community Development and National Culture. CD assistants helped to recruit and train leaders of the UWT branches, organized their literacy classes and arranged for child care and health instruction. Most of the new field officers added to the CD staff were women and more and more were being trained. In 1964 there were 60 CD assistants under training at the new Rungemba center in Iringa, and classes were being registered for courses in homecraft instruction at the new Musoma training school.

Two trained officers were in charge of the CD division's work with women. Marthe Bulengo, wife of a Tanganyikan physician, served as CD liaison officer with the UWT, coordinating the work of the two organizations with that of the various government departments. Bassilla Renju, a former Moshi teacher and Oxford graduate, was senior CD officer in charge of women's projects and training.

Both subscribed ardently to the proposition that cultural, social and economic progress of the country depended on the widening of its women's spheres of influence. The two officers saw the village homecraft and mothercraft instruction as vital to national progress. "The focal point must be the home, the family, and here is where the

MARCH OF THE UWT: The loyalty and solidarity of the emergent women of Tanganyika were shown after the army mutiny in January 1964, when thousands of members of the United Women of Tanganyika joined in a stirring testimonial to the leadership of President Julius Nyerere. On February 3 they marched from UWT headquarters in downtown Dar es Salaam to the State House. Carrying placards and with banners flying, they went to assure the President that the women of the nation stood solidly behind him. At the head of the mile-long procession (third woman from the left), was Bibi Titi, fiery president of the UWT.

UNITED LEADERSHIP: Following the surprise announcement of the union of the Tanganyika and Zanzibar republics on April 23, 1964, leaders of the new United Republic met at the National Assembly in Dar es Salaam, where the union was formally ratified. Julius Nyerere, right, was named President of the United Republic. Abeid Karume, former president of the Republic of Zanzibar (at Nyerere's immediate right), was named First Vice-President of the union, and Rashidi Kawawa, in robes at left, was named Second Vice-President. Two leaders of the Zanzibar Revolutionary Council stand in the rear: Abdulla Kassim Hanga (fourth from left), who became Minister of State in the president's office, and Abdulrahma Babu (third from right), who was named Minister of Commerce.

women's special role and their most important contribution must take place," Mrs. Bulengo emphasized. The 990 women's groups supervised by CD personnel in 1963 had increased to 1,440 in 1964. A total of 66,096 women were being trained in these classes. These were in addition to the more than 300,000 in literacy classes.

To give impetus to the CD division's work with women, President Nyerere appointed three of the country's women MPs as parliamentary secretaries to the Ministry of Community Development and National Culture. Besides Bibi Titi, Nyerere appointed Miss Lucy Lameck (who was a nominated member of the National Assembly) as a junior member of his cabinet to work with the Ministry, particularly in the field of cooperatives. In the reshuffle of cabinet posts in 1964, when the cooperative work was shifted to the Ministry of Commerce and Cooperatives, Lucy Lameck went with that ministry. Mwami Theresa Ntare, MP for Kasulu, was appointed parliamentary secretary to replace her in the reorganized Ministry of Community Development and National Culture.

Where Bibi Titi had worked her way to national prominence equipped only with her self-education and a fierce resolve to show that women were vital to national progress, Lucy Lameck was a sophisticated product of England and America's best schools who had dedicated her career to helping the women of Tanganyika. A trained nurse in Moshi before joining TANU to help organize the women's section, Miss Lameck had also taken a two-year diploma course at Ruskin College, Oxford, and then studied political science at Western Michigan University.

Speaking to a student seminar in Dar es Salaam, Miss Lameck explained her commitment: "Those of us who have had the privilege of a first-class university education with the resultant increase in personal prosperity must not forget we are the few amongst the many and as such have what I can only describe as a terrifying responsibility to our brothers and sisters. We must strive night and day to help those less fortunate to improve their lot, whether by giving money, or better still, by giving our time and our hearts."

Lucy Lameck, in her post as parliamentary secretary, campaigned energetically to promote community development and cooperatives. She worked long into the night at her ministry desk, pleaded eloquently with the National Assembly to put everything possible into develop-nent projects, and went out into the country on exhausting tours. In ne three-week period she swept through the eastern region of the ountry, visiting the Morogoro, Mikese, Kingolwira and Kilosa dis- ricts. She then pushed on through the central region to Dodoma, Mpwapwa, Singida and Iramba. At Msasnga village in Dodoma she helped the women carry bricks for a school, and joined them in singing TANU songs. At Mpwapwa she climbed Behero Mountain to inspect a well built by the villagers as part of their self-help program.

Miss Lameck made it a special point on these tours to discuss local projects and problems with the CD field workers. She spoke with feeling of the CD assistants. "They are the agents," she said, "of a peaceful, silent revolution that will transform our national life." In expressing their affection for her, CD workers employed the well- known American expression, "We love Lucy."

The third woman parliamentary secretary, Mwami Ntare, brought to the ministry an impressive background of leadership. The only woman chief of one of Tabora's biggest tribes, she had the hereditary right to wear a leopard skin. Educated at the Tabora Girls School, she entered the field of politics in colonial days when she was nominated to the Legislative Council. After independence she won a seat in the National Assembly in both the 1958 and 1960 elections.

Besides these three African parliamentary secretaries, there were four other women members of the National Assembly—two Europeans and two Asians—or a total of seven women MPs.

Notable among these was Marion, the Lady Chesham, who had founded the pioneering Tanganyika Community Development Trust Fund. There was no more ardent spokesman for self-help as the key to Tanganyika's development than she who had championed the pro- gram since being elected to Parliament in the country's first national elections.

Lord and Lady Chesham had been in Tanganyika only a year when the outbreak of World War II in 1939 prompted them to return to England to serve in any way they could. They plunged into war work. Lord Chesham served in the R.A.F. main control room 60 feet under- ground. It was a duty that taxed the lungs—and Lord Chesham's had already been damaged by gas during World War I. Lady Chesham served as senior commander in the Auxiliary Territorial Services in Bucks County. When American troops began to arrive in England, she was appointed liaison officer for the Bucks County services with the U.S. Eighth Air Force. Transferring later to the Red Cross, she helped launch the Clubmobile service for troops and selected the 600 Club mobile Girls who made up the first Red Cross unit to cross the Channel after the invasion.

After the war the couple returned to make their permanent home in Iringa. Lady Chesham helped to manage their estate at Rungemba. She became active in community affairs and was elected chairman of the Iringa branch of the Tanganyika Council of Women. Among the Hehe she was affectionately known as *Mtage,* or Stranger Friend from Far Away. When later they began to call her their *Ndugu Zangu* (Our Sister), she knew she had been accepted as a member of the family, and no longer as a visitor from a foreign land.

It was after Lord Chesham died in 1952 (an event which plunged the Hehe community into nine days of mourning) that she turned to politics as an outlet for her boundless energies. Her fondest memory of her first political victory was the election night in 1958 when the votes were coming in.

As the ballots were being counted it seemed a nip and tuck race until the Iringa returns came in. As vote after vote went for Lady Chesham, the young colonial officer checking the ballots shouted, "Look out! The Hehe are coming!" The tribe had voted solidly for Lady Chesham and their support gave her a three-to-one victory over her UTP rival.

Lady Chesham had been unofficially supported by TANU since 1958 and, after the 1960 election when she was returned unopposed, she joined the party and was named to the executive committee of the TANU Parliamentary Party. This key place in deciding TANU policy on national legislation brought her closer to Julius Nyerere. Their friendship had begun during the 1958 election and the TANU leader often visited at Rungemba with his wife to escape the burdens of life in the capital.

Observing some of the pioneering self-help work being done around Iringa (sponsored at that time by the Social Development Department), Lady Chesham became deeply interested in the work. She went to Horace Mason, then Commissioner of Social Services, and asked how she might assist the program. "Money," said Horace Mason. "Money is desperately needed. Something to prime the pump." Thousands of self-help projects, he said, lacked only the little investment necessary for materials.

Lady Chesham went promptly to Prime Minister Kawawa and offered to found a fund-raising organization to aid community development. She repeated her belief that the self-help approach could be the key to national progress. Rashidi Kawawa was enthusiastic. He accepted the chairmanship of the newborn Tanganyika Community Development Trust Fund and gave Lady Chesham (who went to work as its executive secretary) his blessing plus a personal donation of $600. Job Lusinde was named honorary treasurer of the fund and Chief Adam Sapi Mkwawa of the Hehe, Solomon Eliufoo and Cleopa Msuya were named members of the fund committee.

Lady Chesham set off on a whirlwind fund-raising tour of the United States. She addressed groups in New York, Washington, Philadelphia and Minneapolis and set up an American Committee for Tanganyika with headquarters in New York.

She returned to Dar es Salaam with enough money to finance scores of self-help projects throughout the country, and with promises of thousands of dollars more. Often only $50 was needed to purchase cement for a village well or $100 for materials for a bridge. A health center was started for $716 and a village market for $359. Besides paying for materials, the small cash grant was often in itself enough to provide the psychological encouragement needed to put plans into motion. Within a year the country was dotted with projects that the fund financed, all with prior approval of the CD division.

Having become a Tanganyikan citizen in 1961, Lady Chesham was now investing all her generous energy in the struggle to improve this country of her choice. She was one of Tanganyika's women who surely could be described as a national leader.

The other European MP was Barbro Johansson, a Swedish educator who had come to direct a mission school for girls of the Haya tribe in Bukoba, on Lake Victoria's western shore. Miss Johansson's great competence as a teacher, and her friendly services to the tribe, had established her reputation throughout the lake region. When the second half of the Legco elections were held in early 1959 she was persuaded to stand for the seat from Mwanza. Supported by TANU and unopposed in the campaign, she took her place that year in the first elected legislature of the country. Her impressive fluency in both the Haya and Swahili languages, and her espousal of socialist beliefs, made her a popular spokesman for TANU policies in Legco, and later for the government in the National Assembly. As Lady Chesham had done, Barbro Johansson joined the party and also became a Tanganyikan citizen.

Moving to Mwanza after the elections, Miss Johansson became the government's best interpreter of its plans and policies among the vast Sukuma tribe. When the Five-Year Plan was broached in 1964 she was its top salesman, conducting a series of seminars throughout her constituency and meeting constantly with regional and district committees.

Besides her legislative tasks, Miss Johansson was also a counselor, head nurse and ambassador for the region. In 1964 she became involved in one happy episode of an international character. That year the Bonn government voted a special fund to reimburse African veterans who had served with General von Lettow's guerrilla force in East Africa during World War I. The German Embassy at Dar es Salaam requested Barbro to locate any such veterans around Mwanza. She sent word out among the Sukuma, urging any who had served with the Germans to report at her Mwanza office on a certain day. A few, she thought, might turn up. Three or four days before the assigned date, people began to pour into town: the lame, the halt and, literally, the blind. They camped by the score in the clearing opposite her office. Barbro set up a canteen service to feed them.

A German businessman, Erich Clausen, arrived in town on the appointed day with pay-out funds from the German Embassy. Astounded when Barbro reported there were 300 claimants waiting, Clausen suggested that their credentials be checked. Barbro joined him in questioning the veterans. Some, it turned out, had old German marks which they had kept since 1918. Some had bits of uniform or equipment. Some showed battle wounds (one, standing before Barbro's desk, dropped his trousers to show her a great gash across his left buttock). Some spoke a little German or recalled officers' names. Based on such "proof," all these were accepted. For the remainder who had no demonstrable proof, Barbro and Clausen devised a plan. Using a broom handle as a dummy rifle, Clausen had the remaining claimants go through a manual of arms test. He barked German commands at them: "Left shoulder, arms!" "Present arms!" "Rest!" To his amazement, all passed the test. Of the 300 gathered Sukuma, there was not a single bogus claimant. Each of them was given 100 shillings (about fourteen dollars), compliments of the West German government. Barbro remembered the incident as "one of the last vestiges of the German Empire."

When she was not promoting the Five-Year Plan, Barbro Johansson was busy in 1964 and 1965 raising funds. In addition to aiding dozens of community development projects in her constituency, her efforts helped to build the new TANU college at Mwanza and the CD training school in Musoma.

Another of the MPs, Mrs. Sophia Mustafa, was a housewife who had also served on the Arusha Town Council. Largely because of her TANU support, she won the Asian member seat in the 1958 Legco elections over five Asian men who opposed her for the northern constituency seat. Mrs. Mustafa won 2,248 votes while her closest rival was given only 864. In the 1960 election, she ran unopposed for one of the eleven seats in the National Assembly reserved for Asians. Mrs. Mustafa, a champion of nonracialism, was sometimes criticized by friends in the Indian community because she insisted on putting national interests ahead of communal loyalties.

The seventh woman MP was Mrs. Celia Paes, a nominated member from Dar es Salaam.

A Goan, Mrs. Paes had earned a Bachelor of Science degree in microbiology at St. Xavier College in Bombay. She was elected the first president of the Asian Women's Association in 1940 and in 1949 was elected president of the Tanganyika Council of Women.

While the first women MPs were being elected, the country's women were busy getting into another new field by forming the Women Police of Tanganyika. The service began in 1958 with eight women recruits joining the national police force after six months of intensive training. For the first two or three years of its formation, only a handful of women were in the service, and these dealt only with cases involving women and children. In 1963 it was decided to expand the Women Police, with a woman police superintendent from Liverpool assigned to build up a modern unit. By the end of the next year there were 91 women constables and inspectors, and an African officer, Assistant Superintendent Edna Malanda, took over command from her British predecessor.

One of the young policewomen, Constable Esther Ryoba, emerged as a heroine of the January 1964 army mutiny. She was on duty at the Central Police Station in Dar es Salaam when a band of soldiers surrounded the station and demanded that she turn over the keys to the armory. She refused to do so or to reveal where they were. She also refused to tell where European police officers could be located at the time. For four hours the mutineers ransacked the station and several times turned on the young constable. She was searched so thoroughly that most of her uniform was torn to shreds. But the invaders did not find the keys (hidden in her armpit), and finally released her. Had the soldiers been able to get into the store of arms, as they had on Zanzibar, the mutiny might have taken a more violent turn. On May 1, 1964, Constable Esther Ryoba was awarded the Police Commission's Certificate for Bravery.

The less spectacular, but no less real heroines of the emerging nation were, however, the vast army of village women who were responding to the call of their government and community leaders and were joining in literacy or educational classes, expanding their farming activities, and helping in every way possible to achieve national goals.

The youth of Tanganyika rallied, too, to the nation's cause. First efforts to mobilize the nation's youth were made in 1956 when the TANU Youth League was organized as an auxiliary. Each TANU branch was urged to organize its own youth unit. Rashidi Kawawa was elected first chairman of the TYL and Joseph Nyerere its first vice-chairman.

In the turbulent political times prior to independence, TYL branches held meetings every Sunday, where they heard rousing talks of freedom and sang party songs. Joseph Nyerere encouraged the composition of political songs and promoted group singing as an effective stimulant for party spirit. He also recruited TYL leaders as teachers for adult classes. It was in a TYL class that Bibi Titi Mohamed began to master English.

There were two age groups in the TYL, one for boys from seven to eighteen, the other for young men from eighteen to forty. Those in the older group had to become regular TANU members but were urged to stay on in the Youth League. The membership charges were nominal: twenty cents as entrance fee, five cents as monthly dues. In addition to this income, the TYL received appropriations from TANU.

At TANU's early political rallies TYL members assumed the duties of aides, ushers and guards. They also served as clerks, drivers and messengers for TANU branch offices. Some, unfortunately, began to misuse their role as patrolmen, making house raids and arrests, all in the name of what they conceived to be the law. This was countered by Minister of Home Affairs George Kahama, who called a conference of 58 TYL delegates in Dar es Salaam to clarify the role of TYL. He explained that TYL was part of TANU, but TANU was not the government. "We don't want private armies or private police," he said, "because they only lead to trouble." TANU's regional leaders and district police, as well, were instructed to restrain the militant youth in their areas.

But in general the country had cause to be proud of its young men. When in August 1963 flood waters of Lake Nyasa wiped out the whole village of Mwaya, 300 members of the TYL at Mboya volunteered to build a new settlement for the victims at Tenende. TYL members from Dodoma and Kigwe operated a 76-acre communal farm at Ikowa. In Dodoma itself, the TYL operated the bar at the community center, using the profits to pay teachers for adult education work. Many of the 300,000 attending literacy classes were being taught by young TYL leaders. In Lindi district alone, the TYL had organized 74 adult classes. In Handeni district the TYL recruited 1,200 boys to build three new wards at the village dispensary in Mgera.

In Mtwara district in the south the TYL offered its services to the campaign being conducted by regional medical officers against hookworm, which was rampant because of primitive sanitation conditions. Virtually every inhabitant of the district had been infected by the debilitating disease. In April 1964, the TYL began a house-to-house drive to build family privies. At the rate of nearly 700 a month, by October they could claim more than 4,000 homes with a new toilet facility.

Members of the Mtwara TYL also were active in commerce. At Nanyama they operated nine *pombe* bars, butcher shops and several stalls in the public market. At Ruvuma the regional commissioner opened bank accounts for five TYL income sources: the Brickmaking Cooperative, the Native Dancers Club, the Special Constable Choir, the Jazz Band and the Youth League Bar. At nearby Masasi the TYL operated a hostel and travelers' rest.

One of the best demonstrations of youth's support of government

plans was given by the TYL in Songea district in the Southern Province. In 1963 the TYL started a communal settlement at Litowa, to
grow tobacco. The farm showed such promise that a $20,000 grant
was given to the group by the Oxford University Food and Famine
Relief Organization. The OXFAM gift went toward a new tractor,
pumping equipment for irrigation and a few head of Ankole cattle.
The following year young farmers of the Songea TYL founded seven
other communal settlements, and it was planned eventually to put
60,000 acres of land under tobacco cultivation. Agricultural officials
hailed the TYL program as reviving the important tobacco industry
in the area.

As the government had encouraged participation of Tanganyika's
women in nation-building by sponsoring the UWT, so it now took
steps to harness the energy of youth to promote the national program.
In 1963 a National Service Section was created to be part of the Ministry of Defense, a portfolio held by Vice-President Kawawa. David S.
Nkulila, an assistant commissioner of police, was named to head the
proposed youth service.

The new service followed generally the proposals of Lady Chesham,
who had drawn up a youth program in 1959 based on the Civilian
Conservation Corps in the United States and youth organizations in
West Germany. It was to include basic military training but primarily
would be a national labor force, with voluntary recruitment for two-
year duty. David Nkulila was assisted in organizing the National Service by a team of Israeli youth experts. A base camp was established at
Kurasini, south of Dar es Salaam, and work squadrons began to go
out on various projects before the end of the year.

One force went to Nachingwea (one of the hapless Groundnut
Scheme sites), and opened up 250 acres to the cultivation of—ironically—groundnuts. Another group at Tabora started a cattle-breeding
ranch. A force of 200 left the new training camp at Ruvu to go to
Handeni, near Tanga, to begin clearing some of the 40,000 acres on
which communal settlements were being founded to grow sisal. Late
in 1964 a work squadron was dispatched to Newala in the south to
build camps for refugees coming over the border from Mozambique.

At Kinondoni, on the outskirts of Dar es Salaam, the National Service established a permanent youth work camp. There a force of 300
was maintained to assist the carpenters and bricklayers in building a

huge complex of modern homes for the National Housing Corporation. Families evicted from downtown Dar es Salaam as part of the slum clearance program were going into the new homes.

By 1965 basic training camps for the National Service were being built in every region in the country and young men were volunteering by the thousands. From the regional commissioner at Mwanza came the report that there were so many volunteers a waiting list had to be set up.

Vice-President Kawawa, visiting the camp at Nachingwea, called on the whole world to note the spirit of Tanganyika's youth. "Work such as this," he said proudly, "is unknown anywhere else in the world and is worth all the praise we can give. Their act in volunteering to help their country increase its production is worth international repute."

As Tanganyika ended the first year of its Five-Year Plan it could point with pardonable pride to the unsparing support its women and youth were giving to the over-all national effort. Anyone who was there in that eventful first year of the plan would agree that a revolution of all the people was taking place. Among these observers would be many who were not of Tanganyika, but who nevertheless had some personal part in the exciting changes taking place. The foreigners in Tanganyika were, in fact, taking a vital part in the way the nation was developing. Their contributions could drastically affect the country's future.

CHAPTER THIRTEEN

THE FOREIGNERS

When Nyerere announced his policy of nonalignment, he realized that Tanganyika would be in the very thick of what he called "the Second Scramble for Africa." "Just as in the First Scramble for Africa," he said, "when one tribe was divided against another to make the division of Africa easier, in the Second Scramble one nation is going to be divided against another to make it easier to control Africa. Don't for a minute think we are going to be left alone."

Tanganyika was not left alone. Emissaries of East and West bargained, wheedled and threatened; to survive the pressures required a diplomacy compounded of compromise and evasion. In mid-1965 Tanganyika was still treading warily amongst the adversaries and accepting aid from various directions. The primary goal remained national development, regardless of the source of aid.

For this reason foreign aid brought complications. As explained by one young official of Oscar Kambona's new Ministry of External Affairs, "In giving aid diplomats of the donor countries themselves expect no commitments in return, but as soon as we accept aid from a rival power they suspect us in this case of making commitments. Actually, donations from both sides have been most generous in this respect, with no references being made to any ideological debts that might be incurred by the gift. Not," he added wryly, "that a certain indebtedness has not been inferred."

Tanganyika's spokesmen made it clear that noncommitment did not mean negative neutralism. "We are ready to commit our country to support everything we believe to be right and just in international affairs," said one Ministry of External Affairs official. "We intend to judge each case on its merits. We are not going to reject some measure just because the West brands it as a 'Communist-inspired plot' or blindly criticize some other action because it was described as 'an imperialist maneuver.' We hope to be friendly with all nations but these bonds will not entitle our friends to choose our enemies."

Nonetheless, Tanganyika's diplomatic intentions did little to dissipate the atmosphere of rivalry and intrigue that surrounded foreign aid negotiations in the first years of independence. Initially, when England, the United States, West Germany and Sweden poured millions into the country, it seemed that nonalignment meant at least a tacit orientation to the West. But after Rashidi Kawawa's fruitful tour of Russia, Eastern Europe and China in 1964, nonalignment took on new proportions. When Russian, Yugoslav, Czech, and Chinese delegations began to appear in Dar es Salaam and move easily through government offices, it seemed that the pendulum had swung far to the East. Officially, it was insisted that this was merely nonalignment fully in practice.

In January 1964, the ousting of the Sultan of Zanzibar and takeover of the island by the Afro-Shirazi Party (of nationalists) alarmed Western emissaries in Dar es Salaam with prospects of a ruling party dominated by pro-Communist Young Turks. When the Zanzibar Revolutionary Council immediately invited Russian, East German, Chinese and Yugoslav diplomatic missions to the island, Western fears increased. For the East Germans it was their first success in establishing an embassy in a non-Communist country. An eighteen-man mission was soon functioning and their Deputy Foreign Minister hurried to Zanzibar for a ten-day visit. He offered housing aid, civil advisers, a radio transmitter for propaganda broadcasts in Swahili and a fleet of fishing boats. The Russians were taken on to equip and advise the island's Liberation Army and to reorganize Zanzibar's port system.

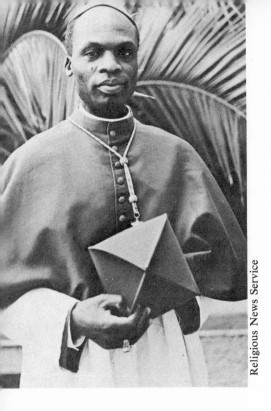

RED BIRETTA: Ordained to the priesthood in 1943 after studies at Africa's Katigondo Seminary and at Rome's De Propaganda Fide University, Rugambwa was appointed Bishop of Rutabo in 1953. On March 28, 1960, Pope John XXIII created him the first Negro Cardinal in Church history.

CD DEMONSTRATION: In the best tradition of the self-help spirit, these girl trainees at the community development training center at Tengeru, outside Arusha in northern Tanganyika, pitch in to help build some of the classrooms at the rapidly expanding center. The CD buildings were once a small part of the agricultural school at Tengeru, now boast a fine campus looking out to the slopes of Mount Meru. Both the young men and women trainees, as part of their training course, learn how to make mud and cement bricks for home-building, as well as the rudiments of improved structure.

From Peking came a shipload of buses. The Czechs sent a four-man trade delegation.

The Afro-Shirazi Party's president, Sheikh Abeid Karume, who for twenty-two years had been a seaman on British vessels, was president of the new government. But militants of the Revolutionary Council appeared to be taking charge. Western newspaper correspondents described Karume as a virtual prisoner of the group, and reported that the ringleaders were Abdulrahma Babu, Kassim Hanga and Hassan Moyo. Babu, operating as Zanzibar's foreign minister, was the acknowledged strong man of the council.

Near-anarchy prevailed on Zanzibar in early 1964. Most of the civil servants, being British, had been sent packing, as were a team of Americans manning a space tracking station on the island. The press claimed that the Asian population was being terrorized and that hundreds of Arabs, regarded as sympathizers of the deposed Sultan, had been deported. There had been no functioning court since the revolution, only the council's drumhead system. As each week brought some new pro-Communist gesture, the Western press began to label the spice-rich little island, hardly twenty miles off mainland Tanganyika, as "The Cuba of Africa."

Then the unexpected happened. On April 23, after President Nyerere made a flying visit to President Karume, a government statement revealed that Tanganyika and Zanzibar had decided to join in a United Republic that would make them one sovereign state. Two days later, Tanganyika's National Assembly and the Zanzibar Revolutionary Council, meeting in separate emergency sessions, unanimously ratified the union agreement. Julius Nyerere would be president of the United Republic, Abeid Karume first vice-president and Rashidi Kawawa second vice-president. Tanzania was born.

Foreign reactions varied. A U.S. State Department spokesman hailed it as "an excellent example of how Africans work out solutions to African problems." The *Financial Times* of London sourly described it as "a union that exists only on paper." Some claimed a victory for the West, some a dangerous concession to the East.

Julius Nyerere heatedly denounced all such conjecture. "The union has been determined by our two governments in the interest of Africa and African unity," he stated. "There is no other reason. Unity in our continent does not have to come via Moscow or Washington. It is an insult to Africa to read cold war politics into every move towards African unity. We did not propose this union in order to support any of the 'isms' of the world. We proposed it in order to support and strengthen Africa, and our particular part of Africa."

Then he announced his new cabinet. Most of his own ministers remained but six Zanzibarians were also included. Among these were the three revolutionary firebrands: Babu, Hanga and Moyo. While Western observers were dismayed by these appointments, they were mollified somewhat when Nyerere took a bold step in the other direction. He announced that all embassies on Zanzibar must be reduced to consular status. This meant little to countries which already had embassies in Dar es Salaam, but it was a severe blow to East Germany and its burgeoning embassy on the island.

However, the problem of dealing with the two Germanys was not solved by this June 30 decision. It remained a thorny issue. At the time of the creation of Tanzania, Oscar Kambona was in Bonn, discussing the problem with the federal government. He was told unequivocally that if an East German ambassador were allowed to stay in Zanzibar, West Germany would withdraw its mission in Dar es Salaam. President Nyerere's dictum in June presumably took care of this, although the East German Embassy continued to operate in Zanzibar as though it retained full diplomatic status.

Meanwhile both German governments were generous with aid. In Tanganyika, West Germany pledged support of the proposed $3 million hospital in Moshi and granted a $2.5-million loan for public housing. Another $600,000 went for the new College of Business Education in Dar es Salaam. A group of 40 German Air Force officers was still in the capital training Tanganyikan pilots. A team of West German veterinarians arrived to advise on cattle breeding. Volunteer service workers poured in from Bonn. East Germany matched this aid to Tanganyika with gifts to Zanzibar. The German Democratic Republic sent funds and technicians for a $1.5-million housing project at Mnazi Moja on the island. Shipments of school supplies came from the Young Pioneers of the Republic for pupils of Zanzibar. The Federation of Revolutionary Trade Unions, on behalf of East Germany, sent a shipment of tractors to the workers of Zanzibar. On September 5, 1964, three months after the East German Embassy presumably had become a consulate, the East German Ambassador formally opened on Zanzibar the German Democratic Republic's Friendship House. Two weeks later the Ambassador, Mr. Gunther Fritsh, saw a five-man Zanzibarian delegation off to Berlin to attend the fifteenth anniversary of the German Democratic Republic.

In January 1965, after months during which West Germany demanded that something be done about the status of Mr. Fritsh, Oscar Kambona went to Bonn to discuss the delicate situation. He carried a message from President Nyerere to Dr. Erhard, the West German Chancellor. Mr. Kambona returned with a report that the discussions had been most cordial. But all cordiality abruptly ceased the next month when it was announced in Dar es Salaam that East Germany was being allowed to open a consulate-general in the capital. A notice appearing in the February 19 issue of the *Government Gazette* was meant to placate West Germany. It said: "The decision to accept the establishment of a consulate-general is not intended to give and does not imply diplomatic recognition of the German Democratic Republic."

West Germany was not placated. A stiff note from Bonn announced termination of all military aid to Tanzania in reprisal for allowing establishment of the consulate-general. The next day West German air and naval instructors serving in Tanzania under the 1964 agreement were recalled by Bonn. On February 28 President Nyerere informed the West German Ambassador that Tanzania now rejected all assistance from Bonn. The government newspaper, *The Nationalist,* estimated the total West German aid program at $33.6 million. It was a bold decision for Julius Nyerere, but a necessary demonstration of nonalignment. It demonstrated that his friends were not to be allowed to choose his enemies.

President Nyerere also had to deal with aid from the United States and Communist China, both vital to Tanzania's development plans. To negotiate with one without offending the other required the ultimate in nonalignment diplomacy. By mid-1965 a precarious balance was still being maintained. By that time the United States had contributed an estimated $30 million to the development program, including educational, technical and material aid. The Chinese did not get into the race until Rashidi Kawawa's tour in June 1964, but they were moving rapidly. In Peking Vice-President Kawawa was entertained sumptuously by Premier Chou En-lai and assured of an interest-free loan of $45 million. (On his own tour of Africa in late 1963 and early 1964, Chou En-lai had discreetly by-passed Tanganyika and Zanzibar because of the January revolts, so his welcome of Kawawa and his ten-man delegation was exceptionally lavish.)

Almost as soon as Kawawa returned home, Chinese aid began to arrive. When the freighter *Heping* (Peace) arrived in September, it was not merely that the shipment included cases of rifles and automatic weapons, which were unloaded under tight security precautions, which aroused interest. It was also the newspaper report that an eleven-man Chinese team—seven arms experts, four interpreters—would be arriving soon to instruct Tanganyika's novice army in use of the weapons.

This intelligence was duly dispatched to Washington where State Department officials directed U.S. Ambassador William Leonhart to register a protest. Nyerere reacted angrily. Seething over the incident through the night, he called the press to the State House the next morning and warned the West not to interfere and to try to understand what he meant by a policy of nonalignment. He pointed out that hundreds of technicians from the West, including 350 members of the U.S. Peace Corps, had been invited to help his country and the East had not complained. "This country is, in fact, completely Western: in government, in business, in schools," he said. "Now I make a little attempt to be nonaligned and the West asks me if I realize the risk I'm taking. The maximum risk is that the army will revolt. My army revolted in January and it was not trained by Chinese."

He noted that the Chinese experts were to be in the country only six months—a time limit, he said, on which the Chinese themselves had insisted. "The United Republic recently signed a five-year agreement with West Germany for the training of an air wing," he added. "Nobody has questioned me on this. Not a single Communist country has come to me to say 'Why?' I am protesting. I do not expect other people to make decisions for this government. I am completely capable of looking after this country. I do not like this. It must stop. I do not like this pressure."

Two months later the U.S. was accused of conspiracy against the Tanzania government. The charge was made by Oscar Kambona, Minister of External Affairs. On November 10, 1964, he told a press conference that he had documents revealing that certain Western powers were making deliberate moves to bring about disunity in the government of Tanzania and were ready, in collusion with Portugal, to commit acts of subversion and aggression.

The next morning in Dar es Salaam *The Nationalist* published photostatic copies of the documents and did not edit out references naming the United States as the "certain power" allegedly guilty. The documents, in French, were purported to be an exchange of correspondence about plans to instigate trouble between Mozambique and Tanzania and arrange the overthrow of the Nyerere government. U.S. Embassy officials immediately replied that the very wording of the messages was obviously specious and the documents bogus. Ambassador Leonhart stated that while he had not seen the actual documents, the newspaper reproductions indicated they were clumsy forgeries. His brief statement about the documents concluded: "Their allegations concerning the United States are wholly without foundation." The Embassy later requested a study of the papers by a documents expert from Washington.

Addressing a public rally held that week to protest the alleged plot, President Nyerere said the documents would be turned over as requested. "If they are found not to be genuine," he said, "I would be the first to thank God." His people were not so reasonable. In nearly every town in the country, anti-American protest parades were held. Oscar Kambona led demonstrations in Arusha and Moshi. On November 15 a procession of 10,000 marched on the U.S. Embassy in Dar es Salaam chanting and singing. They carried placards reading: "Nyerere Si! Yankee No!" The marchers included the Speaker of Parliament, Chief Adam Sapi Mkwawa, Bibi Titi Mohamed, Minister of Industry Jeremiah Kasambala, Dr. Wilbert Klerruu, TANU's publicity director, and a number of MPs.

Kambona cabled an official report of his charges to the Organization for African Unity headquarters in Addis Ababa. The OAU's Committee of Nine, sitting in Dar es Salaam on refugee problems, passed a resolution condemning the plot. Students of University College staged their own protest march in Dar es Salaam. From the Chinese Committee for Afro-Asian Solidarity came a message to President Nyerere describing exposure of the plot as "an important victory."

A week later a documents analyst arrived from Washington. He pronounced the correspondence forged and submitted several points of evidence as proof of it. The Embassy drew up a lengthy report for President Nyerere. On December 9, 1964, the anniversary of Tanganyika's independence, the President told a public rally somewhat obliquely that the matter of the plot was officially being buried. "I gave the documents to the Americans and now they have written a long letter saying that the documents were forged. I have also written to them. It is our hope that this exchange of letters will be the end of everything connected with the matter."

Later in the month Oscar Kambona was in Washington and paid a friendly call on G. Mennen Williams, Assistant Secretary of State for African Affairs. Asked about the charges of a plot against his government, Kambona replied, "According to my President, in a public statement in Dar es Salaam, this was a closed matter."

For the harassed U.S. Ambassador in Dar es Salaam the respite was brief. In mid-January 1965, he was informed by President Nyerere that his two highest-ranking aides were being ousted from the country on charges of subversive activity. Each of them, Robert C. F. Gordon, Counselor of the U.S. Embassy in the capital, and Frank Carlucci, U.S. Consul in Zanzibar, was declared persona non grata and given twenty-four hours to leave the United Republic.

Mr. Leonhart had no public comment on the matter except an official denial of the charges, and the Tanzanian government declined to explain or document the claims against the two diplomats. But presumably a great deal went on behind the scenes. The U.S. State Department described the charges against Gordon and Carlucci as "absolutely without foundation, absurd and totally inexplicable" and recalled Ambassador Leonhart temporarily to Washington as an expression of official displeasure. In Dar es Salaam, a *Nationalist* editorial derided the recall.

Does the United States seriously think that this action would put pressure to bear on our government to rescind its decision? We believe that the earlier Americans stop thinking that they can throw their weight around and can buy the good will of poor, young and developing countries with money, the better for them. Surely, when their policies in Africa are being condemned by all truly independent African states it should register to the policy makers in Washington that there must be something fundamentally wrong with their way of reasoning and general policies.

On February 14 the U.S. State Department asked Counselor Herbert Katua of the Tanzanian Embassy in Washington to leave the country "within a reasonable time," admittedly in retaliation for the expulsion of Gordon and Carlucci. Whereupon President Nyerere recalled Tanzania's ambassador to the United States, Sheikh Othman Shariff. In doing so he explained that the expulsion of Gordon and Carlucci was "not an affair concerning relations between governments" but was "between the Tanzania government and two American individuals who happened to be servants of the American government." The expulsion from the U.S. of Counselor Katua, with no suggestion that he had been behaving in a manner inconsistent with his diplomatic status, changed the matter, he said, "from a problem of personalities into a matter affecting relations between two states." The President elaborated on this at the annual congress of TANU by noting, "Our differences with the U.S. have turned from an issue of individuals to that of relations between two governments. However, our policy towards the U.S. remains the same." The latter comment could hardly have been reassuring to U.S. Ambassador Leonhart, by now returned to Dar es Salaam.

Meanwhile, in the Embassy of the People's Republic of China in Dar es Salaam, Ambassador Ho Ying was achieving diplomatic successes. A chubby man full of cheerful bustle, Mr. Ho had just signed protocols elaborating on China's June 1964 loan agreement. These provided for the $7-million Mao Tse-tung cotton mill, a 5,000-acre experimental farm and a farm-implements factory. Extensive press coverage, including photos of farming equipment being handed over, had accompanied the signing. There had been a round of dinner parties for the visiting Chinese Economic Mission. Another team of nine Chinese broadcasting experts and engineers had newly arrived to build two high-power transmitters for Tanzania at a cost of $980,000. On top of all this, President Nyerere was about to take off in mid-February for a fortnight's visit to Peking.

When Nyerere did arrive in Peking on February 15, fresh from his diplomatic scuffles with Washington and Bonn, he spoke to Peking as he had spoken to the United States and West Germany. "We offer the hand of friendship to China," he told a public rally in his first speech, "just as we offer it to America, Russia, Britain, and others. We shall see for ourselves what China's intentions are toward us. We shall not be told by others." He said that Tanzania was ready to expand its trade with China. "But we will buy from you and sell to you as we buy and sell with our traditional trading partners." When Nyerere left Peking eleven days later, he had signed a five-year treaty of friendship but had kept his policies intact.

Four months later Chou En-lai made his long-postponed trip to East Africa, arriving in Dar es Salaam on June 4, 1965. If the visit was to show the world that Tanzania had moved closer into the orbit of Communist influence, the hope was again deflated. The Chinese Premier was borne triumphantly from the airport and cheering thousands lined the way but that proved the extent of his triumph. That night at a state banquet in Diamond Jubilee Hall he spoke about revolutionary prospects. "An exceedingly favorable situation for revolution prevails today," he said, "not only in Africa but also in Asia and Latin America. The national liberation movement in Africa, converging with that in Asia and Latin America, has become a mighty torrent pounding with great momentum at the foundation of the rule of imperialism, colonialism and neocolonialism."

He identified the United States at once as the archvillain. "U.S. imperialism in particular not only supports old colonialism but is ambitiously making a bid for world hegemony. But in the face of the revolutionary storm sweeping Africa, Asia and Latin America, it becomes a cornered dog and is increasingly revealing its true nature, which is even more ruthless than old colonialism and Hitlerite fascism."

He congratulated Tanzania for resisting this imperialism. "Recently you have uncovered one subversive plot after another of the imperialists and expelled the U.S. diplomats involved. These dauntless acts of yours serve as a forceful warning to the imperialists; the people of Tanzania have stood up and are not to be bullied."

Julius Nyerere sat calmly through the speech. When he spoke, he spoke mildly, but again stated a clear-cut declaration of nonalignment. He first thanked Chou En-lai for the $45-million loan agreement and paid tribute to China's revolutionary spirit. Then he restated his principles: "We have to guard the sovereignty and integrity of our United Republic against any who wish to take advantage of our current need in order to get control over us. From no quarter shall we accept direction and at no time shall we lower our guard against subversion.

Neither our principles nor our freedom to determine our own future is for sale." Tanzania thus demonstrated that the diplomacy of nonalignment could be carried out with character and courage, even when dealing with the biggest cold war powers.

With neighboring states and with other emergent countries of Africa, diplomacy was another matter. Tanzania could, and did whenever necessary, deal boldly. The Republic of Ghana represents an example of this. In a feud with Tanzania that lasted more than a year, the West African state eventually conceded diplomatic defeat. The difference began when heads of state met at Addis Ababa in May 1963, to found the Organization for African Unity. Ghana's President Kwame Nkrumah protested loudly when Dar es Salaam was designated as headquarters for the OAU's Liberation Committee, arguing that it should meet at Leopoldville in the Congo. When he was overruled and Oscar Kambona was chosen as committee chairman, Nkrumah refused to help finance the committee and attacked its work in his Accra newspaper. Too, he lobbied through diplomatic channels against Tanzania's plans to join with Kenya and Uganda in an East African Federation.

Julius Nyerere and Oscar Kambona tried to ignore Nkrumah's displeasure, but when Ghana's ambassador in Dar es Salaam publicly ridiculed the government for calling in British troops to quell the January 1964 mutiny, the ambassador was ordered to leave the country and both Kambona and Vice-President Kawawa in public statements censured Ghana for spreading disunity rather than the unity espoused by the OAU. But it was left to President Nyerere to deliver the coup de grace. He waited until the OAU Conference in Cairo in July 1964.

When called upon to speak, Nyerere first hailed the progress of the OAU in its first year and welcomed new members. Then he took up the matter of Kwame Nkrumah. He told the conference the Ghana president had charged that by being in Dar es Salaam the Liberation Committee was exposed to espionage, intrigue and frustration, and that the training of freedom fighters against imperialism had been entrusted to an imperialist agent.

"If the Great Osagyefo's reference to an imperialist agent refers to my country or any of its leaders," said Nyerere evenly, "those who know the country, its leaders and its people, and all those who have any respect for the truth, know that such a statement is a lie. Some people are willing to use their very great talents to wreck any chance of unity in our continent so long as some stupid historian could record that they wanted African unity, but nobody else really did. You can fool some of the people some of the time, but quite frankly this attempt to fool all the people all of the time does not show very much respect or concern for Africa."

He argued for an approach to continental unity through the formation of federations such as that planned in East Africa and declared that the United Republic of Tanganyika and Zanzibar was committed to the achievement of a united Africa under a single continental government. Before concluding, Nyerere, typically, said a good word for the enemy. Referring to proposals for a common market in Africa he said, "I want to add my voice to those who have already made this plea, and I am glad to say that this plea was made by the President of Ghana, that we should consider very seriously the possibility of allocating certain industries on a continental basis, or at least on a regional basis."

Nyerere sat down to a thunderous ovation. Many of the delegates apparently had long been waiting for someone to censure Nkrumah. Nkrumah himself accepted the scolding. A few weeks later when Ghana's foreign minister visited Dar es Salaam he brought to President Nyerere a warm note from the President of Ghana congratulating Tanzania for its work for the OAU and hoping for close cooperation between their states in the tasks ahead. In January 1965, a new ambassador for Ghana arrived in Dar es Salaam. Welcoming him, President Nyerere said: "We in Tanzania certainly do not forget the inspiration we received from the success of your freedom struggle in 1957, when the sovereign state of Ghana first came into existence."

Together with other states in East Africa and with OAU members, Tanzania in 1964 and 1965 was deeply involved in efforts to bring peace to the bloodstained Congo. In September 1964, Oscar Kambona went to Addis Ababa for the emergency session of African foreign ministers called by the OAU to discuss the Congo situation. At that meeting the special committee headed by Premier Jomo Kenyatta of Kenya was appointed to work on a Congo settlement.

This ad hoc committee was in session in Nairobi on November 24 when the controversial "invasion" of Stanleyville took place. In Western eyes this was a rescue mission. Belgian paratroopers were dropped into the Congo from American planes to save European hostages held by savage rebels. The slaughter of 80 of the hostages, including an American medical missionary, horrified the West. The OAU committee, and leaders throughout Africa, were equally horrified for in their eyes the Stanleyville raid was a betrayal of the sovereignty of a new African state. Pronouncements of rage were heard in capitals all over the continent.

In Dar es Salaam Julius Nyerere denounced the paratroop operation. "In an action reminiscent of Pearl Harbor," he said, "foreign troops were flown into the Congo at the very moment negotiations were taking place to secure the safety of all who lived in the Stanleyville area. This unashamed foreign interference has been taken in defiance of the whole of Africa."

Another march on the U.S. Embassy in the capital took place to protest the Stanleyville operation. Three hundred university students, many of them wearing their saffron-colored undergraduate robes, ran rather than walked down Independence Avenue to the Embassy. The banners they carried proclaimed: "No Vietnam in Africa" and "Sons of Africa Unite against American Neo-Colonialism." Ambassador Leonhart accepted the protest of a delegation of the students and defended the operation as a humanitarian action.

The following month Oscar Kambona appeared in New York before a special session of the United Nations Security Council on the Congo situation. "The paratroop operation will go down in history as the meanest, most unwarranted and most provocative interference by the Western world in the affairs and peace of the African continent," he told the UN. "This military intervention was a clear affront to the OAU and shamefully detracts from the United Nations' efforts in the Congo during the past four years. My delegation deems this intervention all the more reprehensible for the excuse that it was undertaken, not to bring peace to the Congo, but to save a few lives so that tenfold more should die."

To learn for himself something of the rebel side of the Congo story, Julius Nyerere went to Mbala in Uganda on January 13, 1965, with Premier Kenyatta of Kenya. At the invitation of Premier Milton Obote of Uganda, they went to meet Christopher Gbenye, leader of the Congo rebels. Nyerere returned to Dar es Salaam not at all convinced that Gbenye was either a Communist or a murderer.

"I say quite frankly I was highly impressed by Mr. Gbenye," the President told newsmen at the airport. "He is as responsible as any African leader I have ever met; he is committed to the same objectives of African dignity, unity and the Organization of African Unity as anyone. He did not look or sound like a hypocrite or self-seeker." He indicated that Kenyatta and Obote had been similarly impressed.

Meanwhile the OAU Liberation Committee (or Committee of Nine as it became known) was meeting regularly in Dar es Salaam, under Oscar Kambona's leadership, on problems of African refugees from colonial areas and on plans to liberate these areas. The committee revealed that there were over 250,000 refugees in East Africa alone; 100,000 in Uganda, largely from the southern Sudan; 80,000 in Burundi from the Congo and Rwanda; and 77,000 in Tanzania (mostly from Rwanda but being increased steadily by thousands escaping from Mozambique).

At a 1965 meeting of the Committee of Nine, Chairman Kambona emphasized that first attention must be paid to the explosive situations in Mozambique and Rhodesia where he said there had been an intensification of government intimidation and terrorism. The committee's work with the nationalist military forces from colonial areas was understandably little publicized, but five American missionaries inadvertently turned the spotlight on the Mozambique freedom fighters in November 1964, when they stumbled into a training camp area. Near the old groundnut site on Kongwa, a wrong turning took them into the heart of the secret camp, where hundreds of recruits were drilling. The five were arrested and convoyed to Dar es Salaam as spy suspects. Ambassador Leonhart eventually was able to arrange their release.

In 1965 Tanzania was still negotiating for the creation of an East African Federation but much of the first enthusiasm for the merger of states was waning. The three governments already were cooperating in a common services arrangement under which joint rail, airways, postal, and harbor facilities were operated. The East African shilling was still common currency and services affairs were decided by a Central Legislative Assembly.

An incident in June 1965 threatened to jettison cordial tri-state relations. That month Kenya police stopped a convoy of eleven heavy trucks operated by Uganda soldiers, who said they had just driven up from Tanzania and were taking a short cut through Kenya. Seventy-five tons of Chinese weapons were found aboard the trucks. When Premier Kenyatta heard of the seizure he angrily denounced the convoy as a violation of Kenya's territorial integrity. He impounded the arms cargo until Premier Obote arrived from Uganda and personally apologized for the incident. At the time hopes for a federation never were dimmer.

An effort to revive the waning vision of a political federation was made in August 1965, when Nyerere, Kenyatta and Obote met in Nairobi to reaffirm agreements on some common objectives. The state leaders agreed there would be no raising of tariff walls between the three countries and no withdrawal from the University of East Africa. More important, it was agreed to appoint a study commission to review economic ties and make recommendations regarding political unity. This move, at least, kept the concept of federation alive.

But relations with Tanzania's neighbor to the west, newly independent Zambia, could not have been more cordial. An impressive pledge of this friendship was the ambitious joint plan to build a $200-million cross-country railway that would link the capitals of Dar es Salaam and Lusaka. President Kenneth Kaunda of Zambia viewed the line as a vital outlet for his country's vast copper resources and an access route for imports to his landlocked republic. Politically, the railroad was even more urgent, for Zambia's existing outlet was the line which ran through Rhodesia and Mozambique, where European-dominated governments could overnight throttle Zambia's trade. For Tanzania it would mean opening up the Southern Highlands area of the country and also greatly enhance Dar es Salaam as an international port of call.

With Malawi, the neighboring state to the southwest (formerly known as Nyasaland), matters were a bit more difficult. When its premier, Dr. Kumuzu Banda, in 1964 suddenly dropped six ministers from his cabinet, three fled to Tanzania and were granted political asylum. Irascible Dr. Banda announced he wanted them back "alive or any other way." When they chose to stay in Dar es Salaam, Banda accused the Nyerere government of plotting with them to invade and destroy Malawi. He charged that mail between the two countries was being censored and that people crossing the border were being screened. He also accused Tanzanian police of arresting eight leaders of the Malawi Brotherhood in Dar es Salaam because they supported him. Another unrelated charge claimed that the Chinese Embassy in Dar es Salaam had tried to bribe Banda into recognizing the People's Republic of China with the offer of a $50-million loan. Both the Chinese Embassy and the Tanzanian government denied all charges. The government statement noted that there were 10,000 Malawians living happily in Tanzania, many of them in important civil service posts.

There were thousands of others who had for generations lived happily in Tanzania but who were now wondering what the future held for them after independence. Some exulted in the new freedom, feeling deeply and confidently that as equal partners their lives would be enriched by it. Others had their doubts, claiming they sensed a new discrimination. These—the confident, the defiant ones and the doubters—were Tanzania's long-resident, peace-loving minority: the Asians. In the mid-1960s they represented one of the republic's most sensitive domestic problems.

CHAPTER FOURTEEN

THE ASIANS

Sundays in Dar es Salaam a holiday ritual symbolized the social dilemma which faced the people of Tanzania. This ritual was the pilgrimage of the capital's Asian community to Oyster Bay, a lovely palm-lined stretch of tropical beach north of the city. In the late afternoon as the heat of the sun subsided, cars came swarming out of the dingy downtown sections, like lemmings scenting the sea, to converge in the bay area. By sunset the cars were there in the thousands, a majority of them expensive European and American models. The passengers stayed for the cooling first hours of the evening, then returned to their broiling tenements in the city.

The Oyster Bay section was traditionally the residential reserve of Dar es Salaam's well-placed Europeans: the diplomats, the business managers and the civil service elite. The roads of Oyster Bay were smoothly surfaced and lined with shade trees. Each home had its landscaped garden. A well-kept park called The Green graced the center of the area.

By 1965, Oyster Bay's population was changing from European to African. None of the beach homes, it was safe to predict, would be

217

taken over by Asians, who would remain Sunday visitors. Independence meant that Africans eventually would succeed to all the positions and places once held exclusively by the Europeans. The process of Africanization saw the Asians—the Hindu Indians, Moslems, Goans and Sikhs—losing ground both in government and in private trade.

But most of the Asians had been in East Africa for generations and knew no other home, no other place where they would be welcome. They were strangers to their ancestral land, and while Tanzania invited them to full citizenship, they wondered if in the long run they would be accepted as equal partners. They did not feel that they truly belonged. It was like their Sunday migration to Oyster Bay. They had the means to go there, but they went only as transients.

In 1965 there were 100,000 Asians in Tanzania, some of them the descendants of Indian mariners who ventured to the East African coast centuries before the first Christians arrived. Marco Polo wrote of Indian ships at Zanzibar and an Indian sailor joined Vasco da Gama on the East African coast in 1498 in order to pilot his ship across the Indian Ocean. When Sultan Seyyid Said moved his court from Muscat to Zanzibar in 1840, he brought many Indian traders with him: Moslems from Bombay, and a number of Hindus from the west coast of India. By 1866 there were 6,000 Indians in his East African empire, many of whom had made fortunes. One was the Sultan's collector of customs, Jairam Shivji, who died that year leaving $2 million.

When independence came, the majority of the Indians were Hindu, many of them belonging to the ancient Bhattia trading caste. There were about 25,000 Moslems, for whom the Aga Khan was religious leader. The majority of the 20,000 Sikhs of East Africa were in Kenya but the several thousand in Tanzania constituted most of the artisan class: the mechanics, carpenters, masons and railwaymen. The 10,000 Roman Catholic Goans in Tanzania and the rest of East Africa filled clerical posts and preferred to be linked with the Portuguese rather than the Indians.

Today, Zanzibar is overwhelmingly Moslem (97 per cent) with a sprinkling of Hindus and Christians, while Tanganyika is a mixture of Moslems, Christians, Hindus, and animists. Catholicism alone has 1.7 million adherents or 18 per cent of Tanganyika's population. This was the fruit of intensive missionary activity during the colonial period, culminating in the naming in 1960 of Laurean Rugambwa, born into a pagan family in 1912, as the first Negro Cardinal. In addition, President Nyerere was a convert to Catholicism. While Tabora and Iringa became Roman Catholic strongholds, the Episcopal missionaries were particularly successful in the large urban communities, the Lutherans in Bukoba and Lushoto. In several inland districts, Christianity became the predominant religion.

Politically, the Asians were active—within limits. Under the 1945 constitution three of the fourteen nonofficial members of the Legislative Council represented the Asian community. This representation was improved in 1955 when the 30 nominated members of Legco represented equally the African, Asian and European communities. After independence the Asians were allotted nine seats in the National Assembly, the Europeans eleven and the Africans 50. When the first elected Legco met in March 1959, the Speaker was the Hon. A. Y. A. Karimjee, a Moslem Indian who had been Mayor of Dar es Salaam for four years. The Karimjees were a distinguished family that had lived in East Africa for five generations.

The Asian Association, active principally in Dar es Salaam and a focus for Asian political activity, stood solidly for a nonracial, secular state. When the UN Mission visited Tanganyika in 1954 the association urged new elections with representation for each of the racial divisions—African, Asian and European—but to avoid communal voting it was urged that each voter should be entitled to vote for a candidate of each race to represent his constituency. The association also urged universal adult suffrage.

In the first elections in 1958 the Asian Association denounced the new United Tanganyika Party for supporting policies which would entrench racial differences, and for violating democratic principles. An association announcement said: "As stated in the past, belief in nonracialism and nationhood is a matter of conviction with us, and not of expediency. We take this opportunity of reiterating these principles and are prepared to join hands with others in taking practical steps to achieve the nationhood of Tanganyika, without presumptions, without reservations and without fear." At that time the association supported TANU to the extent that it opposed the parity system of representation as giving exclusive political privilege to the racial minorities.

In the 1958 election the association's president, Mahumed N. Ratansey, was a successful candidate for the Asian seat in the Western

HOUSING, SUKUMA STYLE: In the spirit of ujamaa, or tribal cooperation, a neighbor joins a Sukuma family near Lake Victoria in building their mud and wattle hut. The woman of the family heats some mealie-meal, the maize porridge that is the basis of all meals.

UNITED REPUBLIC ACCLAIMED: President Julius Nyerere and his foreign minister, Oscar Kambona, at right, join Zanzibari representatives in acclaiming the union of the Republics of Tanganyika and Zanzibar on April 23, 1964. Scene outside Karimjee Hall in Dar es Salaam took place after Tanganyika's National Assembly on April 25 ratified the agreement which created the United Republic.

Province. Another winner in that election, one who was to reach a high position in government, was Amir H. Jamal, a Moslem native of Mwanza. Elected from the Eastern Province, Jamal was an economics graduate of the University of Calcutta who had early declared for TANU. In his election campaigning he strongly urged all Asians living in Tanganyika to identify themselves with the African majority. Al Noon Kassum, another Asian soon to gain prominence, won a Legco seat in the early 1959 elections. A young Dar es Salaam attorney, he was educated at Muncaster School in England's Middlesex and called to the bar at Lincoln's Inn, London.

Amir Jamal was the first Asian to be appointed a cabinet member when he became Minister for Urban and Local Government and Works in July 1959, under Governor Turnbull. When Julius Nyerere formed his first government as Chief Minister in 1960 he had appointed Jamal his Minister for Communications, Power and Works. At that time Al Noor Kassum was named a member of the executive committee of the TANU Parliamentary Party and became chief whip for the party. In May 1961, Kassum was appointed Parliamentary Secretary to the Minister of Education. Jamal was appointed a member of each succeeding Nyerere or Kawawa cabinet until 1965 when he was named chairman of the reorganized National Development Corporation.

The Indian community had gradually taken over all small business in Tanganyika. Each village had at least one *duka* run by a Hindu or Moslem trader. When the Germans evacuated during World War I, the Asians had the means to buy their property, so they acquired most of the real estate in Dar es Salaam, and many of the German sisal plantations. By 1924, Asians owned more than a quarter of a million acres of land in the territory. When World War II broke out in 1939, it was estimated that Asians controlled more than $10 million in property, including 80 per cent of the sisal and cotton industries, 90 per cent of all town property, 55 per cent of the import and export trade and 80 per cent of transport services.

The Asian community maintained its own school system until the Ministry of Education announced its integration policy in 1964. In 1938 there were 55 Asian-financed schools operating under an Advisory Board of Education that included six Moslem and four Hindu members. In 1939 the Moslems built the first high school in Dar es

Salaam and allowed up to one third of the students to be non-Moslem. Another was built in Tanga. By 1963 there were 25,000 young Asians in school, 8,000 of them continuing on to secondary education. At the time there were 514 Asians from Tanganyika studying abroad.

The Asians in Tanganyika's civil service were the first to suffer ill effects from independence. Of 8,000 of them, most were employed under "local conditions" contracts which did not qualify them for the generous compensation awarded to British civil servants under "overseas" contract. In 1962 the Tanganyika Overseas Recruited Asian Civil Service Association sent two members, P. K. G. Nayar and M. C. Zachaviah, to protest to the UN Trusteeship Council in New York that Asian officials were being discriminated against in the allowance of compensation when their posts were Africanized. Nothing came of this appeal nor was anything gained when association members protested to Colonial Secretary Iain MacLeod during his visit to Dar es Salaam in the same year.

Another visitor in the capital in 1962, the British MP Francis Noel-Baker, was quoted as saying that the attitude taken by Indian civil servants "invited" persecution. The visiting Laborite also undiplomatically noted that many of the well-placed Asians were descendants of slave traders and imported laborers. This brought a quick retort from Mr. C. D. Shah, president of the Asian Association, who claimed that many Indians came to the territory as merchants and as contracted civil officials. He added that Asians were not "nervous" about the prospect of independence, as Noel-Baker had also commented, but were eagerly anticipating *uhuru*.

Asians had been criticized both officially and privately for organizing communal trade unions. When a British survey team made a study in 1960 of the civil services operating the territory's railways and harbors, one of its principal recommendations was for the integration of the separate African, European and Asian unions. "Present racial organization of unions is completely contrary to the fundamental principles of trade unionism," said H. A. Whitson, study chairman, in submitting the team's report.

The schoolteachers were the first to follow this advice. In January 1962, the Asian Teachers Union merged with the African Teachers Union to form the National Union of Teachers. The Railway Asian Union, on the contrary, talked that year of joining with other Asian unions in a joint national strike. N. K. Karmal, president of the RAU, charged that the colonial administration had betrayed the Asian civil servants. "We know we are doomed," he told a meeting of Asian unions in March 1962. "We shall not remain more than three or four years." Africanization of the civil service was not that precipitous, but the prediction was accurate in regard to the Asian unions. The 1962 legislation making the Tanganyika Federation of Labor the "designated union" for all labor organizations began the process of eliminating the Asian unions, a process completed in 1964 with the creation of the official National Union of Tanganyika Workers.

In other areas, the Asians faced wholesale adjustments. Government spokesmen were candid about this. Minister of Industry Kasambala, opening the Kondoa Cooperative Union in 1963, told the Indian community it made no sense for them to operate "a large number of small unproductive shops which inevitably sold the same line of goods." He urged Asian traders who had business experience in running such shops to join the cooperatives as salaried managers. Later, in the National Assembly debate on the Five-Year Plan, he announced that the goal set for COSATA, the merchandising cooperative, was to take over at least 30 per cent of the nation's retail trade, traditionally in the hands of Asians. The new Tanganyika National Transport Cooperative Society Ltd. announced in 1965 that by 1970 it would control 80 per cent of national transport—before independence, Asian firms controlled 80 per cent of the transport trade.

Unquestionably, the Asians were at a disadvantage. By and large, they were generally disliked by the Africans. The feeling arose not from any social or religious circumstance, but, rather, from a historical one. The disadvantaged African, particularly the urban dweller, had only recently been shaken out of the security of the old tribal life and was relatively slower in adapting to modern ways. He was attracted by European power and culture, but was still less qualified than the Asian. He tended to regard the Asian as a foreign competitor who had little to offer in return for his presence. Yet in trade and in public service the Asian occupied the job just ahead of the African. The African resented less the higher wage level of the European than the far lower average income of the Asian. Also, there was something humiliating about his dependence on the Asian trader, particularly since the Africans held political power.

The Asian, for his part, was being called upon to surrender ancient principles of caste and affiliation. Because his inbred sense of frugality and his industry were affronted by the African's carefree spirit, the Asian had turned to his own people, who had become more and more closely knit as a community. But this was now something to resist in the adjustments the Asians had to make.

The enlightened leaders in the Asian community appealed to fellow Asians to make these adjustments; the most eloquent was Amir Jamal, the young Moslem cabinet minister. Addressing a rally marking the tenth anniversary of the birth of TANU, Amir Jamal went to the heart of the dilemma when he said:

Independence was achieved peacefully, but the fruits of past policies and habits remain with us. The supreme question which now hangs over all of us in the republic is: will the Asian community identify itself effectively in time with the social and economic revolution which is now taking place in the same way as it did with the political revolution?

The first thing which strikes any new visitor to our country is the fact that the division between those with comparatively comfortable standards of living and those with low living standards is also a division between races. In so many countries the differing rural and urban circumstances pose special problems. Where, in addition, we have the situation where the Asian community is mostly urban and in the relatively higher income group, while being such a tiny minority in the country, only the blind can fail to see the dangers facing the society as a whole.

There are so many reminders of this state of affairs every day. I experience within myself a most discomforting feeling when I see a concentration of ostentatious cars full of non-African and particularly Asian faces along the sea front, or cinema houses full of mostly non-Africans. And when at times I see a total absence of these faces at mass meetings organized for various political programs or when I observe that no Asian has volunteered for the National Service, I feel myself missing a heartbeat or two.

I am not suggesting that the non-African, and particularly the Asian community, has not tried to make adjustments. I am not saying that there has not been a feeling of frustration at times on the part of those making these adjustments. But let us be absolutely clear in our minds. Not all the cheques and cash payments made by way of contribution to various funds and causes put together will bring racial harmony in this country. Only a fundamental change of heart will meet the need of the situation.

The need is to begin in the home, in the shops, in the factories and offices, in the schools, in the settlements. One truly hearty handshake and smile across the racial barrier is worth incomparably more than a contribution to a particular fund.

The basis of the struggle for independence was the feeling of humiliation of being ruled by a foreigner. In political terms the Asian community identified itself with this humiliation. But there is the continuing humiliation of poverty, ignorance and disease, which the obtaining of independence has only served to emphasize throughout the country.

The challenge now is whether the non-African, and Asians in particular, will demonstrate effectively that they share this humiliation as well.

There is not a great deal of time left to harness all the good that no doubt exists in all sections of the society. The freshness and the resolute determination of the majority of the people, the inherent discipline and loyalty of the Asian, the maturity and global understanding of the European, all these could be welded together so that, when we come to celebrate the birth of TANU at the end of another decade, we can say with satisfaction and pride that we have built a sure foundation for future generations to progress in peace and prosperity.

There is a song which I am unable to forget easily and which the Asian community in the republic in particular may want to think about. It was sung by the American Negroes last year while on their historic march to Washington almost one hundred years after Lincoln proclaimed the end of tyranny of the Negroes. The song's words are: "The only thing we did wrong was to stay segregated one day too long."

In the months following Jamal's appeal, criticism of the Asian community's failure to respond was increasingly heard, particularly from some of the more militant government commissioners. The issue came to the surface late in 1964 when TANU's plan to organize ward development committees in urban communities was put into effect. Vice-President Kawawa explained, at a community meeting in Arnautoglu Hall, Dar es Salaam, that city blocks were being divided into TANU wards and cells, each cell of ten houses to be led by a chairman. This house-to-house organization, he said, would ensure more cooperation among the people in the building of a united nation. He appealed to the individual householder to help by ferreting out possible criminals and those who seemed to have no work to do. Reports should go to the cell chairman, who, in cases where he deemed it advisable, would make his report to the police.

On December 7 the area commissioner for Dar es Salaam, Mustafa Songambele, announced that he was forming five ward development committees in the Asian sections of the city. He explained that this was being done because Asians were regarded as citizens of the republic and should therefore take part. "If the Asians consider this move as unfit for them," he added, "they will be thinking contrary to government policy to treat all its citizens equally. It is the government's desire to extend its policy to all its citizens with regard to peace and development." He announced that a meeting of Asians would be held in the Avalon Cinema on December 14.

Both Mr. Songambele and Selemani Kitundu, coast regional commissioner, were speakers at the meeting. The area commissioner called upon the assembled Asians to stop the practice of segregating themselves into closed communities. "Unless you abolish this practice," Mr. Songambele said, "it will be difficult for the government to understand your needs and for the rest of the people of Tanzania to accept you as real Tanzanians."

Said Mr. Kitundu: "Some Asians have been adopting a policy of sitting on the fence and being contented with whatever was taking place if it did not affect them. This is unwise because it arouses a sense of resentment in the minds of your counterparts, the Africans. You are a people sitting on dynamite."

Three days later the *Tanganyika Standard* published an angry letter from an Asian student, M. R. Jain, at University College, describing the statements as an insult to the Asian community:

I regret that not a single Asian came forward to reply and point out that the speakers concerned were trying to bury the past and forget everything that Asians have contributed to bring TANU into existence, to fight for *uhuru* for Tanganyika, to back Mwalimu Nyerere on his demands for independence, and fight imperialism and colonialism. The speakers may not know or may not wish to read history but these are the hard facts which cannot be altered. . . . I assure Mr. Kitundu and Mr. Songambele that Asians do consider themselves one with the indigenous people. It is only the irresponsible speeches of some leaders which encourage them not to do so. Why are they called Asians, Africans, Arabs or Europeans if they have accepted Tanzanian citizenship? Why not call them one entity? If they are citizens of this country they are and should be regarded as one and one only whether they be black, brown, yellow or red in color.

An official government statement was published two days later reaffirming a policy of equality:

The declared principle of this government has always been that of equality of mankind. The very first creed of TANU says, "All human beings are my brothers." Because of this principle the government opened the door soon after independence to all people of all races to be citizens of Tanzania, and to be full members of the party, if they wished. But it soon became apparent that many Asian citizens, either because of inherent fear or because of lack of understanding did not get fully involved in the activities of this country. It was, and still is, the duty of government to try and correct this anomaly, which might otherwise spoil the good reputation we have hitherto created of being the best country in the world in which equality of mankind is not only professed but also fully practiced.

At this juncture, one element of the Asian community did get into action. On the day the government statement was published, an article in the same issue of the *Standard* described how a force of 300 young Asians from five Dar es Salaam schools had volunteered to spend their summer vacation as laborers at the Kinondoni housing project in the capital. Ministry of Education spokesmen hailed the student contribution and government officials noted that Asian youth had set for their elders a splendid example of what was meant by national solidarity.

The praise was small comfort to a minority expected to yield government positions and turn over businesses they had long looked upon as their commercial inheritance. But such adjustments were the prospect. There were two other capacities, Minister of Industry Kasambala advised the Asians, in which they could serve: as administrators of co-operatives, or as pioneers in small industry. The new Tanzania could thus remain a land of opportunity for its Asian minority, who could stay and become an integral part of the future republic—but under certain conditions.

CHAPTER FIFTEEN

THE FUTURE

An old African saying claims, "There is no past, no future, only the present." But in the emerging Africa the past is best forgotten, the present a time primarily for building, and the future an obsession. The whole force of national effort is focused unreservedly on the future.

This epitomizes Tanzania's social revolution. The nation as a whole has declared for the future. Stirred by the vision of Julius Nyerere and by the zeal of his TANU disciples, the people pledged themselves to the future goals embodied in the Five-Year Plan. Liberated through their leaders from the burden of colonialism, Tanzanians had agreed to join the struggle for a greater liberation from generations of backwardness and self-neglect. National zeal was the first great breakthrough of the plan which instilled in the people the conviction that a better life was possible for everyone. In 1965 one had only to go to Mwanza, to Songea or Morogoro to see how thoroughly this had been accepted. Throughout the country there was the same mood for change. The mold of old patterns—the way of life in the mud huts and of work in the mean *shambas*—was everywhere being broken and re-formed.

228

In the first year of the Five-Year Plan, popular acceptance of self-help was confirmed by construction of thousands of new schools, dispensaries, roads and bridges, wells, communal storehouses, and irrigation projects. These not only meant an improvement in standards of living, but spurred the all-important drive toward increased production. By the end of 1965 the people had demonstrated that, nature and other forces cooperating, they could attain national goals with the "improvement approach."

Similarly, the opening year's success in recruiting and organizing the teams of farmers to work the communal settlements indicated that goals of the "transformation approach" were well on the way to achievement. The first of the million farmers eventually to be settled were cultivating thousands of new acres opened up by irrigation. And with mechanized methods of agriculture they already were proving that unprecedented increases in production could be expected.

The country's cooperatives were setting a phenomenal pace. In mid-1965 a spokesman for the Ministry of Commerce and Cooperatives predicted that the cooperatives would achieve by the end of the first year almost all of the goals set for them in the whole Five-Year Plan.

Financially, enough of the promised foreign aid materialized to put into motion virtually all public works, program expansions and staff training projected in the 1964–65 period. The $20-million loan granted by the United Kingdom late in 1964 for local costs enabled the government to meet the more critical of the first year's cash demands. The major disappointment was withdrawal of West German aid, which was a grievous financial loss. It became obvious that a major objective for 1966 would be to gather millions more in non-aligned foreign aid.

The willingness of other countries to proffer such aid was certain to be predicated upon the question of Tanzania's national stability, which could stand up well under inspection. To question the political stability of Tanzania was to question the leadership of Julius Nyerere. Even more than the other leaders of Africa—Nkrumah, Touré, Kaunda and Kenyatta—Nyerere was the acclaimed master of his people. His image as the nation's father and guardian shepherd overshadowed everyone. In less than a decade he had led his people to national independence and now he was guiding them to freedom from illiteracy, poverty and disease.

PRIDE OF THE COOPER-ATIVES: The Victoria Federation of Cooperative Unions (Mwanza), was created in 1953 and within a decade represented more than 150,000 cotton farmers of the lake province. These central headquarters were built in 1959, near the spot reached by Speke in 1857.

ON THE MOVE: Sukuma tribesmen of the Mwanza region, near Lake Victoria, bear loose bales of cotton from their farms to the highway for transportation to the ginning mill. Cotton is grown on individual farms but is marketed cooperatively. These farmers are members of one of the 360 primary societies of the giant Victoria Federation of Cooperative Unions.

Spectacular evidence of Nyerere's continuing popularity came in the September 1965 national elections when he was returned triumphantly to the presidency. He won 2,519,866 of the 2,612,225 votes cast—an almost unanimous victory. But the election resulted in a wholesale reshuffling of both Parliament and the cabinet. Of 50 TANU men and women who had been members of the National Assembly, only four were returned to the new Assembly which, under the interim union constitution, had been enlarged to 204 seats. Many MPs had decided, having completed a decade of pioneering work for the party, to make their seats available to others. Ten of the veteran MPs, however, did not win nomination when two candidates were chosen by TANU members for each constituency. A further nine of the former MPs won party nomination but were defeated at the polls.

President Nyerere hailed the election of new representatives of the people as confirmation of his argument that under a one-party system the spirit of democracy was well served. Speaking at his inauguration ceremony he said:

"Our elections have clearly demonstrated that the people are provided with the power to remove their leaders if they don't want them. That has been done; it is important. People must feel they can remove their leaders, that they can remove the government in the same way. They could have voted out all the ministers. It is essential people have this right."

Another salutary aspect of the election was the fact that it had been nonracial. With constitutional elimination of seats reserved for European and Asian MPs, there had been much speculation that an all-African Parliament and government would emerge. Most of the former European and Asian MPs, including Lady Chesham, did not stand for election. But two who did—Derek Bryceson and Amir Jamal —were not only elected but were reappointed by President Nyerere to higher office in his cabinet. Jamal became Minister of Finance (replacing Paul Bomani, named Minister for Economic Affairs and Development Planning), and Bryceson was appointed Minister of Agriculture, Forests, and Wildlife.

Another major cabinet change was the transfer of Oscar Kambona from Minister of External Affairs to the new portfolio of Minister of Regional Administration. In his new post Kambona would not only direct internal administration of the republic but would carry on his key role as TANU secretary-general. Nyerere retained for himself the Foreign Relations portfolio.

A month after the elections President Nyerere nominated six of the ten MPs which the revised constitution empowered him to name. Among them was a European: Marion, the Lady Chesham. Her nomination was a thoughtful tribute to this lady from America for the inspiration and leadership she had given to the community development which now was so vital to the future of her adopted country.

For Julius Nyerere the Five-Year Plan contained a certain amount of political risk. Its failure could be his failure and the signal for incipient rivals to emerge. In 1965 there seemed only two sources for such rivals: the trade unions and the army. Both had already tentatively and unsuccessfully challenged Nyerere's and TANU's leadership. Both still seemed unlikely claimants for political power.

The army in 1965 was a well-screened force of only 1,300. Renamed the Tanzania People's Defense Forces, it was commanded by Brigadier Sarakikya, whose loyalty during the 1964 mutiny had not been questioned. Battalions were stationed at Dar es Salaam, Tabora and Nachingwea and the army also had incorporated the former Liberation Army of Zanzibar as an integrated battalion. (The Chinese small-arms instructors left in 1965, and a team of Canadian officers arrived to set up an over-all system of military training.)

Apparently to exert a check on political activities within the army, President Nyerere in 1965 appointed coast regional commissioner Selemani Kitundu as political commissar for the defense forces with the rank of colonel. In addition, an army reserve called the United Republic Volunteer Corps was organized among members of the TANU Youth League. John A. Nzunda, deputy secretary-general of the party, was named as director. Precautionary measures such as these made political activity in the army somewhat less likely.

The situation in the trade unions was also reassuring. Even those who questioned the wisdom or ethics of the government take-over of the labor movement could not fail to be impressed by the 1965 report by Minister of Labor Kamaliza on the first-year accomplishments of the National Union of Tanganyika Workers. Labor strife, the Minister reported, had been almost eliminated. During 1962, the year prior to NUTA's supplanting the Tanganyika Federation of

Labor, there had been 417,500 man-days of work lost because of industrial disputes. In 1964, only 5,855 had been lost.

In the same period, said Kamaliza, the average wage of Tanzania's 400,000-odd workers had increased 44 per cent: from $17.08 to $24.64 a month. And NUTA agents had negotiated most of the increases. The Minister said that government policy was to disallow wage increases for workers receiving more than $140 a month until the wages of every worker receiving less than $56 a month had doubled.

Workers were reminded by Mr. Kamaliza that NUTA would not negotiate indiscriminately for wage increases which, he said, must be related to the country's limited resources as well as to the needs of the wage earner. He spelled it out further: "The prime purpose of our wages policy must be to provide wages which are related to improvements in productivity and efficiency whilst encouraging our rapid economic development." Mr. Kamaliza reminded employers, on the other hand, that workers could not be expected to accept wage restraints indefinitely. Profits therefore were to be restricted. Companies making excessive profits would be expected not only to pay better wages but to invest surplus profits in national development projects. He announced that a development levy would be imposed on companies which did not conform to this policy.

The government expected the employer to accept two principles, said the Minister of Labor: "to exercise his managerial functions in a spirit of genuine partnership with his workers" and to cooperate with the Workers Investment Corporation "which seeks to work and expand in cooperation with private businessmen who can supply much of the business expertise which is so rare yet in this country." He in turn called upon wage earners to demonstrate a sense of responsibility.

Mr. Kamaliza realized that he was demanding something of a revolution in labor relations but, he said, that was exactly what NUTA stood for: "In Tanzania we have helped to give birth to a new concept of African trade unionism in which the interests of the individual and of the worker are indissolubly merged as citizens. NUTA is in the vanguard of our march to increased self-respect, greater human dignity and material well-being. That march has just begun and, if it is to reach its objectives, it must be made in the company of all other sections of our nation."

It was impossible to determine to what degree these laudable motives were accepted by the rank and file of Tanzania's labor force. But certainly during 1965 there was no public dissent, as would have been heard in the old TFL days. An undisclosed number of former union leaders were still in detention in what was called a process of "cooptation," but the more effective unionists were promoted to official posts not only in NUTA but in other government and semigovernment organizations. Thus if the workers were to emerge as a political force opposing TANU, they must look for new leadership within their own lower ranks. And in 1965 there was no indication that they were doing so. On the contrary, under NUTA's banners the mass of workers were marching hand in hand—as Michael Kamaliza pictured them—as a loyal and vital unit in Tanzania's army of nation-builders.

Meanwhile, Tanzania's Asian community realized more than anyone that the only hope for a future in the republic depended on integration rather than on dissent. Ironically, adoption of the one-party system was the first important step toward identification of the Asians with the majority people. They participated in TANU activities, less as a minority than as an integral part of the whole. The more farsighted Asians, following Amir Jamal's example, were becoming involved in party affairs and urging the rest of their community to follow suit. TANU was encouraging the Asian in politics, Asian youths were enlisting for service programs, and other Asians were working with African neighbors on self-help development projects. The prospects were promising for the Asians at the end of 1965.

While the second phase of the republic's Five-Year Plan appeared secure, external relations were uncertain. In 1965 the winds from abroad had been generally variable. The requirements of the Five-Year Plan and the commitment to nonalignment in the face of competing foreign powers imposed a strenuous task upon Julius Nyerere.

The only slip had been the falling out with West Germany, and the loss of aid from Bonn was to some extent replaced from a new foreign source. After a state visit to the Netherlands in April 1965, Nyerere announced large-scale Dutch investments in fishing and agricultural enterprises in the republic. The same month, Britain announced $2.1-million assistance for the University College and for the proposed new National Assembly building. Nor was there any sign that Nyerere's candid qualifications about Communist China's trade and aid had discouraged Peking from continuing with its $45-million agreement. American assistance, including AID grants for road-building projects and Peace Corps teams, continued to arrive despite the diplomatic coolness that followed the ouster of Messrs. Gordon and Carlucci.

Western observers, both in Africa and abroad, still puzzled over the inclination of Tanzania and other emergent countries in 1965 to regard the motives of the West as suspect, while only occasionally charging China and other Communist countries with neocolonial intentions. Much of the suspicion stemmed from the political manipulations in the Congo, particularly after the American and Belgian rescue of the Stanleyville hostages late in 1964. United Nations delegates who were startled by the vehemence of the African reaction to the Stanleyville operation obviously did not appreciate the sensitivity that had been aroused by persistent propaganda about the perils of neocolonialism. The occupation of a country, even so momentarily as in the Congo paratroop rescue, starkly confirmed African fears. Regarding Stanleyville, a Tanzanian MP bitterly quoted the Austrian statesman Metternich: "You can do anything with bayonets, except sit on them." It was difficult to convince many Africans that there was no ulterior motive behind foreign aid and to assure them that Western powers did not have the slightest wish to occupy African lands.

The doubters did not realize that the danger could lie in the opposite direction. Donor countries like Britain and the United States, weary of abuse and racial virulence, might lose interest in allocating huge sums of taxpayers' money to African states which so critically needed it. Against this possibility, recipient countries knew that the countries of the West feared to withdraw and to have their place taken by Communist donors. All these considerations went into the delicate balancing act which, by necessity, Julius Nyerere had to perform in the interests of nonaligned foreign aid.

In a 1965 state of the union address, Nyerere described another aspect of the dilemma of foreign aid as it applied to the Five-Year Plan. The plan required $150 million a year, he said, and the bulk of it had to be borrowed from abroad. But only a portion of this could go toward paying local costs of the plan—labor and domestic materials—which he said made up nearly half the total cost. Taxes and local investments (such as the savings going into the Workers Investment Corporation) would meet some of the local costs, but Nyerere was now challenging the people to make a further contribution to the success of their national development program.

"If every farmer, every office worker, and every person working on a development project would do an extra hour's work every day without pay, we could raise a great deal of the money we need for local costs," he suggested. "There are five million of us adults in this country. Say that the minimum wage is seven cents an hour and that each of us does an extra hour's work five days a week without pay. The result would be an extra $90 million worth of work done every year. In other words, $90 million would be contributed to our development plan." The proposal was still in its organizational stage at the end of the year, but if this remarkable challenge could capture the imagination and support of the people, it would be further inspiring evidence that here was a nation with a unique capacity to lift itself by its bootstraps.

Involved in the carrying out of the remainder of the Five-Year Plan was realization of the East African Federation. In June 1963 (the month Tanganyika set up the Ministry of Planning to fashion its five-year program), President Nyerere and Premiers Kenyatta of Kenya and Obote of Uganda had met to declare their intention of merging their countries into a federated structure by the end of that year. The federation did not materialize that year, nor in the two years following, yet at various times its creation seemed imminent. In May 1964, MPs of TANU and of the Kenya African National Union met in Nairobi and insisted that federation be entered into without further delay. A majority of MPs from Kenya, in a vote of 59 to 28, set an August 15, 1964, deadline for federation action. But largely because Premier Obote was beginning to have doubts about the political union, the merger was still unrealized.

Meanwhile, economic ties among the three states were strengthened. In 1965 the East African Common Services Organization was operating the railways, postal and telecommunications, airways and harbors systems jointly for the three countries. In addition, EACSO had under its auspices a dozen joint services, including meteorology and a literature bureau and eleven research organizations, primarily in the natural resources and medical fields. In late 1964, the East African National Shipping Line, a fleet of modern cargo ships to serve the three countries, was launched. In January 1965, the three heads of state signed new terms of the Kampala Agreement, which served to adjust balances of trade between their countries and allocate new industries. Sentiment was increasing for joint defense services and cooperation in the handling of foreign affairs, for a central banking system, for joint electrical and water resources development, for cooperation in agricultural marketing and tourism and for regional economic planning.

Undoubtedly agreements would be reached on these and other matters of economic union in due time. But each month since the 1963 agreement to federate has revealed new problems as well as the long preparation required to bring about an acceptable political union. Julius Nyerere, however, continued to be fully committed to the principle of federation, which he visualized as an exemplary step toward African unity as a whole.

President Nyerere said nothing publicly about a proposal, reported to have been broached in Washington, for a giant confederation of southern African states which would have close economic ties but loose political connections. Hub of the confederation would be copper-rich Katanga and Zambia, and other proposed members included Tanzania, Malawi, the Congo, Kenya, Uganda, Somalia, Rhodesia, Bechuanaland, Basutoland and South West Africa, the latter four joining when independent.

Nyerere continued to be the most ardent spokesman for African unification and for the continental government which he predicted would one day encompass all Africa. He told an assembly of students:

African nationalism will not have triumphed until three conditions are fulfilled. First, the whole of Africa must be free from foreign rule. Second, African nationalism must become an instrument of African unity. Third, the freedom of nation-states must be followed by the maximum possible freedom for the individual within the political unit. Until these three desiderata are achieved, the current African revolution will not be complete.

Africa is one. Basically this has been its past, and this will be its future. The present is a period of transition from being one kind of Africa to being another kind of Africa. Although we have a long way to travel and many obstacles to overcome, I believe that African unity will in the future be expressed by the existence of an African government.

I believe, too, that despite temptations and deviations on the way, Africa will ultimately be a continent in which the economic and social conditions allow its inhabitants to live in dignity, and to stand as equals with their fellow human beings elsewhere in the world.

That was the larger vision. In his own Tanzania, Julius Nyerere already had inspired his people with a light of hope that shone into the corners of their dark world of poverty and ignorance. His dream had become theirs and had been put into blueprint. From the drawing boards came the plan that bound the whole nation in a common and consuming effort. They were hurrying toward goals that could give their life new meaning. They were united in the determination to succeed. They would show Africa and the rest of the world the worthiness of the vision.

INDEX

INDEX